Praise for Me

"Vivid writing, entertaining…would make an excellent TV drama."

-Trevor Hodgett
RnR/The Afterword

"A musician's long and winding path to success during a richly evocative time in British and Irish musical history. A great read."

—Jim Clarke
Aiken Promotions, Dublin

"A brilliant human interest documentation of Brendan's interesting life and career and an insight into the world of hard working musicians. I couldn't put it down."

—Bob Hewitt
Producer, Fender®films

"Really engrossing and a tour de force account of the Athens gig with Rory."

—Peter Guttridge,
Novelist, film and book critic
Former Director, Brighton Literature
Festival

Brendan O' Neill played in various blues bands before joining the multimillion selling Rory Gallagher Band in 1981 with whom he toured and recorded for the next ten years in the biggest stadiums in the world. In 1991, Brendan joined the British blues band, Nine Below Zero. He toured internationally with that band sharing the stage with such acclaimed artists as: Eric Clapton, Alvin Lee, Allanah Myles, Sting, ZZ Top, Joe Cocker, The Stranglers, Dr Feelgood and Glen Tilbrook of Squeeze. He now plays with Slim Chance, Mud Morganfield and with Gerry McAvoy in The Band of Friends.

Denise Danks is a journalist, scriptwriter and novelist who has been shortlisted twice for The Crime Writers' Association's Gold Dagger Award.

Meet Mr Sticks

by Brendan O'Neill
with Denise Danks

GT

GlimmerTwin
Publishing
London • Los Angeles

This book first published in 2020 by
GlimmerTwin Publishing
65 Pine Ave. #404
Long Beach, California 90802 USA
GlimmerTwinPublishing@gmail.com

ISBN:
978-1-7328856-5-3 (print)
978-1-7328856-4-6 (ebook)

Cover design by Jennifer O'Neill
Cover photograph by Brian Cooke

Dedicated to the memory of my parents
Elizabeth and Charlie O'Neill and also to
my wife, Maggie, and my children:
Gillian, Connaire, Jennifer and Katherine

Table of Contents

William Rory Gallagher

1948-1995

When Rory Gallagher died of complications relating to a liver transplant on the 14th of June 1995, my wife, Maggie, rang Virgin Radio to tell them the terrible news and would they play a Rory Gallagher song in his memory. They declined.

Clearly, the greatest rock multi-instrumentalist of the past thirty years had been all but forgotten. But, as I write this on the 25th anniversary of his death, his music is being played on radio stations everywhere in remembrance of a great artist, who died far too young. The kids were digging him.

On the 25th and 26th of November 1968, Cream played their last two farewell shows at the Royal Albert Hall, London. Two support bands featured Yes and Rory Gallagher's band, Taste. It was Taste that would pick up the mantle of those great blues-based rock trios, Cream and the Jimi Hendrix Experience. John Lennon loved the band, which he regarded as a 'bright spot' among the copycat guitar acts of 1969. Hendrix rated Rory as the best guitarist around, Bob Dylan was a fan and Rory influenced Brian May, Slash and Johnny Marr to name but a few.

When Rory went solo he went big. His live performances were legendary and he toured incessantly, making a point of playing in places that were 'difficult' politically and that other mainstream bands would avoid: Belfast during the Troubles, Communist Poland and Yugoslavia, Greece, edgy after the fall of the Junta. His third album 'Live in Europe' captured that energy.

When Mick Taylor left the Rolling Stones, Rory was the obvious choice as a replacement. He spent some time with the band in 1975 but, ever his own man, he decided to follow his own path.

He recorded 14 albums with many more compilations and collaborations. He recorded with his heroes: Muddy Waters and Jerry Lee Lewis. He sold over 30 million albums worldwide.

Those who knew and loved him remember him generously giving of his time to others. His fans remember him as a hero, approachable, down to earth, one of them.

And, man, I got to play in his band.

EARLY YEARS

My name is ...

My name is Brendan Mary O'Neill.

I was born a full six pounds two ounces on December 8th, 1951, at home in Etna Drive on the Glenard Estate in the Ardoyne district of Belfast, Northern Ireland. I was the first of my parents' six children and the first of the O'Neill family's many grandchildren.

In the Roman Catholic calendar, December 8th is The Feast of the Immaculate Conception. My mother, Elizabeth, a deeply religious woman, took my birth on such a significant date as a sign. Surely, I was destined for Holy Orders, for sainthood even, God willing. To be certain that the Mother of God took note of her gratitude, my mother gave me Her name.

My father, Charlie, saw all too clearly the implications for me growing up in a tough area with the name 'Mary'. He argued my case as best he could but my pious mother, and my even more pious Grandmother Lagan, were immovable and together they had the beating of him.

I was duly baptised according to their wishes and what my father feared came to pass. I've been ribbed about my name from the time I can remember, even by my own family. My O'Neill uncles, who came by regularly when the pubs had shut, would chime in when it was time for me to go to sleep, "Yes, time for bed. There's a good *boy*.

At least it wasn't my first name and I am in good company. John Wayne was born Marion Robertson Morrison and Johnny Cash must have had someone in mind when he wrote 'My Name is Sue'.

So, how do you do?

We were working class. My father drove a lorry and my mother was a flax mill worker. My mother's family, the Lagans, and my father's, the O'Neills, were large, hard working, Irish Catholic families. There the similarities between them end. My mother's family was loving, teetotal and inclusive while the O'Neills were aggressive, boozy and fractious.

The Lagans were abstemious: no alcohol, no tobacco, no nothing. Grandfather Lagan, whom I never knew, was a member of the Pioneer Total Abstinence Association of the Sacred Heart, an Irish organisation of Roman Catholic teetotallers. I remember a photograph of him wearing a little round badge on his lapel that meant he was a teetotaller and people were not to offer him alcohol.

Your first Holy Communion is a significant rite of passage in any young Catholic's life. You receive the actual Body and Blood of Christ in the form of a little penny-sized wafer. I remember getting a complete new outfit for the occasion. The settee in our front room was moved away from the bay window for me to have my picture taken. My younger sisters were dressed like little brides and the boys like grooms in suits and ties. The whole affair was very dapper.

The service though was long and
tedious and the wafer dissolved so
quickly - poor Jesus was spread very thin
- it hardly seemed worth it. Things
perked up afterwards when we visited
family and friends and they all gave me a
little bit of money. I received twenty
one shillings for my initiation into the
flock *and* a new suit - there's money in
religion, I can tell you.

The closest my Dad ever got to
profiting from it was by making cribs for
Christmas. He crafted them from moulds
and plaster of Paris and left them to set
before painting every detail on every
character. They sold well and,
eventually, the neighbours would actually
commission him to make cribs for them.

Whenever my father was working and
he came across copper cable, he would
bring it home, burn the outer layers and
sell the copper for beer money. It stank
to high heaven but it was one of his
little idiosyncrasies so no-one
complained.

The men in my father's family grew
up around the docks and were most
definitely men of the flesh. They were
men's men's men's men. They drank, they
smoked, they fought, they danced, and
they had that twinkle in their eye, if
you know what I mean.

Once, my father spent six weeks
away from home because the family had had
a row. He'd argued over something with
his father and they fell out. They were
reconciled, eventually. That was the
O'Neills - a big blow up, some trying
things said in the heat of the moment,
and then, after a wee while cooling off,
back down the pub.

Despite my given name, in me the O'Neills are ascendant. I keep time for the Devil's tunes. I've been known to have a smoke. I like my Irish whiskey. I can handle myself in a fight. In fact, I inherited the infamous O' Neill shillelagh though I have never had to use it.

Family legend has it that the mighty shillelagh is two hundred years old and belonged to a grandfather, generations gone. It was given to my ancestor by a landlady in Derry, a married, Protestant woman, with whom he lodged when he was working there. They had a romantic liaison and she gave him this giant, blackthorn stick, with its knobbly end, as a love token. Nevertheless, his descendants would be breaking Protestant heads with it in the infamous, sectarian, street riots of the 1930s.

There wasn't much to shout about being from Ardoyne in the 1950s but one local hero went the whole way. Freddie Gilroy lived a few houses away from my Granny and Grandad O'Neill. He was the first Irishman to defend his British Bantamweight title three times and win the Lonsdale belt. He was Commonwealth and European champion and he won a bronze medal at the 1956 Melbourne Olympics. Freddie narrowly missed a world championship in 1960, losing on points.

My dad drove a delivery lorry for various companies but when we lived in Ardoyne, he worked for a firm called QT Barry, which was situated off York St. He delivered potatoes for the firm all over the North of Ireland. Every so often he would make a trip south to 'export' spuds, or as Grandmother Lagan would call them 'purdies', to Ireland.

One summer, when I was about eight or so, I went with my Dad on one of these trips, possibly, to give my Mum some peace and quiet. By then our family had grown to include my sisters, Bernadette, Teresa, Elizabeth and my brother, Emmanuel.

We set off early at about seven in the morning. Mum gave Dad his packed lunch with his flask of tea and I got mine, which included a chocolate log, wrapped up in brown greaseproof paper, for us to share. I couldn't reach the step of his flat-backed lorry and had to be lifted up into the cab.

When we got to QT Barry's, he reversed into the warehouse next to the other lorries and we got out. It reeked of dry, fusty earth, sackcloth and tubers stacked wall to wall. Men milled around in their caps, baggy jackets and trousers with shiny fronts. It was all action and the lorry was quickly loaded. With the tarpaulin and ropes in place and the documentation in order, we were off, driving through Belfast from the high vantage point of the cab. The one hundred mile journey to Dublin would take five hours. There were no motorways back then and we had to drive through every little town en route. The road surfaces then were not that great. It wasn't called the Rocky Road to Dublin for nothing.

9

We were barely an hour into the journey and I'd almost finished all of the chocolate log. When I told my Dad that I felt sick, he thought it was the motion of the lorry that was the cause. He realised his error when an hour or so later, he fancied some of that log himself. He took my misdemeanour pretty calmly, which was a relief, as you will find out.

It was a two hour drive to the border back then and we had to stop and clear Customs. Once that was done, we were in the 'Free State' as my Dad and all Catholics in the North would call it. We chatted all the way to Dublin, the mood was light and, for me, it was a great adventure. We arrived at about lunchtime.

Dublin seemed so much bigger and grander than Belfast as we drove out towards the docks. We eventually pulled into a narrow, cobbled lane, flanked by busy warehouses. Their windows were open with pulleys and chains hanging from them to hoist goods up to and down from the upper levels. The men got to work unloading and the whole operation took no time at all. My Dad had a cup of tea with them and there was a lot of banter back and forth about my father's 'new helper'. It felt pretty good.

I never repeated that trip again with my father but later on I was to make that crossing many times with the bands I played with, including Rory Gallagher.

I remember one time being picked up from work at Short Brothers and Harland aircraft factory on Queen's Island in Belfast, driving straight to Dublin for a gig and being back again in time for work in the morning. Once, I was found asleep at eleven thirty in the morning in one of the mock-up planes at the factory's apprentice school where I worked. Music was everything to me then, as it is now.

It was music, after all, that brought my parents together in their unlikely union. They met at a local singing club and sang together in a group. Both had beautiful voices. Growing up, our house was filled with their music. There was always singing, especially after a good O'Neill night out. The house radio was always on, tuned to play the pop music of the day.

My father played the accordion and he absolutely loved accordions of every size, shape and sound, button key, piano keyed, you name it. He played mostly a large piano keyed instrument and practised in his bedroom in the evenings and weekends. His heavy right foot kept time, of sorts, to the point that it seemed the ceiling would cave in.

He wanted us all to learn to play the thing but none of us kids got the hang of it. In fact, I never played an instrument of any kind as a kid.

"None of youse is taking after me," my father would complain.

Come July 12th, my Daddy, naturally, wanted to see the Protestant accordion bands marching in the parades. I remember walking with him from our house in Etna Drive, the lowest of the three main streets that cut across Glenard estate. Just the two of us went. It wasn't the done thing for our Catholic community to go and watch but the pull of music was too strong for us.

We walked alone from the area behind where we lived, a wasteland called The Bone, to the Old Park Road, which was lined with crowds waiting to see the marching bands. It took a good couple of hours for the bands to pass by and I had the best view being on my father's broad shoulders. I was so tired on the return journey, I usually fell asleep up there.

These were the good times with my father but the bad times were truly terrible. My mother was a very loving woman, kind but firm. She would give me a slap on the legs, for sure, if I crossed the line. My father had a harder edge. I learned that at an early age.

When my mother reported misbehaviour on my part to my father when he came home, he would call me to stand in the middle of the room in front of him.

He was a very imposing man and, in this mood, his presence was overwhelming. He would stand there and order me to show him where I came up to him on his body. I would have to measure along my head and point to where. Then, he would say, "No, you're not big enough yet." In other words, not big enough to take him on. I was never too small, though, for him to give me a beating.

My father had a lightning quick temper. I was under no illusion who was the man of the house and it wasn't me. Sure, my Dad was popular and well-loved, a sociable man, known around as a big character, but his moods could turn ugly very fast at home. My mother summed it up perfectly, "The trouble with your Daddy is that when he comes home, he leaves his fiddle by the door."

Nerves

If being called Mary wasn't bad enough, I also have a stammer. It was very obvious even before I went to primary school. I was a nervous child. When confronted with any stressful situation such as school or a figure of authority, I froze, consumed with panic that I might stutter and I didn't want to. It was terrible. The more the stress and panic set in, the more my mind and body succumbed to the chaos raging through me. My hands and feet would contort and my breathing would virtually stop as the calamity perpetuated itself.

My mother's younger brother, my uncle Peter, also stammered and my mother was desperate for me not to suffer what he did because of it. She took me to see all sorts of doctors and specialists, all the men in white coats, to no avail. There was not the same will or energy to confront the problem then as it is now. I got so stressed by the testing they did that I stammered even more.

My education was greatly affected by it. Rather than risk having to speak up in front of a class of forty children to read aloud or answer a question, I would migrate to the relative shelter at the back of the class where the less inclined to learn hung out.

Growing up and going to school with a speech impediment was an emotional minefield. You cohabited your formative years with boys and, sometimes, even schoolteachers, who either didn't understand it, laughed at it, or didn't have the patience to give you that chance to be heard. Most teachers then didn't have the understanding or compassion needed. No one at school ever spoke to me directly about it. After two or three false starts at hearing me reading aloud, they moved on to the next kid. After all, they had a whole class to teach.

It was, and still is, very frustrating. Ideas you have in your head and want to express can't be expressed. The words don't form into anything articulate. Ultimately, it led me to despondency, depression and withdrawal. I never told anyone how I felt about it. I wanted to be left alone, invisible. The less attention I got, the better.

My father blamed himself. We talked about it later in life. He felt that his intimidating character, his rages and authoritarian approach had affected me. My mother knew that the situations he created made my stammer worse. Her family life when she was young was not so confrontational. My father didn't know any better. He was just being himself. He may have exacerbated it but he wasn't the cause. Any stressful situation caused it. My stammer was, we discovered, probably hereditary.

Fortunately, it has lessened considerably over the years. I don't stammer much, if at all, now. Oddly, I don't stammer when I sing. I understand that no-one does. Nowadays, they teach kids with stammers to sing so that they can learn to control their breathing.

Something you have to learn very early on, however, is that people find stammers funny. It's incredible to me. Ironically, people laughing at you gives you time. Time to get control of your breathing is the one thing that will snap you out of a stammer.

There was a cafe called Concetta's in Belfast that me and the boys used to go to after gigs. There would be a whole bunch of us including our two guitar players, Gerry McAvoy and Jim 'Fergie' Ferguson, and Jim Clarke, a DJ, who called himself 'Lord Jim'. I'd known him since Scouts.

Fergie found out that there were three of us stammerers in the place one night so he engineered it so we would all be sitting at the same table just so he could hear us all trying to converse. Too cruel. To be fair to Fergie, though, even I found that amusing.

Another time, Gerry, Fergie, Clarkie and I were in a hotel after a Rory show in Dublin. Clarkie had met, or heard of, this guy, Finbar Nolan, who was said to be the seventh son of a seventh son. (Rory had written a song about the seventh son of a seventh son, and I think that's why the bloke had turned up.)

Some believe that such a man has healing powers. So, Jim Clarke suggested we should meet him so he could 'cure' me. I'm at a loss as to why he thought it would work. Clarkie is actually far too intelligent to believe in such superstitious whimsy. I can understand *why* he wanted to do it. It was simply his concern for me. He was a friend, and remains so, but people's concerns and people's cruelty can both blight your life equally.

Anyway, we didn't meet the seventh son of a seventh son. Too many drinks were consumed and the conversation moved on.

Much later on in life when Gerry and I left Rory and joined another band, we were on the road and out to dinner when someone, who shall remain nameless, thought it would be a good idea to slap my face to stop me stammering. The shock worked. I did stop but I wasn't impressed.

"If you ever do that to me again, it'll be the last thing you ever do, believe me," I told him.

I can express myself pretty well now. I love language and I love reading. However, the terrible truth is I never completed reading a book until I was thirty years of age. The book that popped my literary cherry was 'The Hitchhiker's Guide to the Galaxy' by Douglas Adams.

Boyhood

One summer morning - I was about six - I opened the back door to our yard to go and play in the stream that went through a small field at the back of our house. I was confronted by three traditional, horse-drawn, Romany caravans parked in the field and one gypsy lad having a dump.

I ran straight back inside to 'grass' them up. No-one wanted these gypsy families around because everyone thought, rightly or wrongly, that they were trouble. My Daddy got together with a few neighbours and had a word with them. The gypsies stayed a couple of days and were gone. That was how things were done,

I may have been a very nervous boy but I was always full of energy and mischief. My mother often had to change my clothes three times a day because I had fallen into the water trying to jump over that stream.

If we weren't over there in the field, us kids played in the street, close to the house. I remember an old boy at number seven. He had an old 'penny' ride - basically an old horse and cart with benches longways on each side. He used to take us - me and my sisters, Bernadette and Teresa, and our neighbours' kids - the length of Etna Drive and back for a penny. Just to put it into perspective, you could buy a Lucky Bag of sweets in those days for threepence. Our next door neighbour used to sell candy apples in the summer from her front door for twopence each. This is what we spent our little bit of pocket money on.

We played innocent old fashioned games such as quoits, hopscotch, which along with skipping, were the only games we played with the girls. We played football and handball against the Whelan's gable wall, which invariably got us into trouble. Old man Whelan would come out and we'd clear off, sharpish. We tried to set up cricket stumps, which wasn't successful. We played 'kick the bucket' - a tin can was placed in the middle of the street and a sentry posted. We had to creep up and kick the bucket without him noticing. We had no idea what 'kick the bucket' really meant.

We played 'pirry and whip', and 'hoop and cleak'. We made cleaks out of coat hangers, which we bent into a type of scoop. We then took the spokes out of a wheel to make it lighter and the trick was to guide it at speed on the 'cribby' - the footpath. My daddy had a special cleak made for me out of wrought iron. It was the best cleak on the block - a Harry Potter's wand of a cleak.

We played 'cowboys and indians', of course. We'd cut two ends of a stick, groove it and sling a cord on it for a bow. The arrows were bamboo cane that we got from the hardware store. The arrowheads were made out of our neighbours' metal netting fence. By the end of the summer, the fence would have a great gaping hole in it.

When we played war games, we were Japs and Germans, who, you will recall, never actually fought each other. No-one ever was the British, because, you know, they weren't the good guys.

Like everyone else on our street, my mother would hang our washed clothes on the hedge at the front of our house in the summer. We only had a dark yard at the back with a wall and a door to the field. In the summer, the front of those terraced houses were like a patchwork quilt.

On one such day, my Dad decided to water the front garden, not a lengthy job, you understand, but coincidentally, one of the young women from next door had the same idea. My Dad loved a bit of mischief and thought it would be a great idea to assist our neighbour in the watering process. She got soaked.

She didn't think it was a very neighbourly gesture and made her feelings plain. When the women told you off, they used your full name. No swearing, mind.

"Charlie O'Neill,' she said, aiming her hose at him. He got drenched and, before you could say 'two pints of Guinness', there was a full scale water fight but not before the washing had been brought in, of course. The whole street got involved and, of course, the O'Neills, never lay down.

My mother hid while I ran about with the other kids. There were hoses and buckets of water everywhere. Someone even chucked a full bucket of water through somebody's front window. People chased each other up and down the street and laughed and laughed till everyone was exhausted with the fun of it all.

November the 5th isn't celebrated in Northern Ireland. There was no Guy Fawkes as in the rest of the UK but we did have our fireworks fix with sparklers and bangers on Halloween. As I remember it, in Belfast, Mum, like her neighbours, would bake flat apple cakes and within the cake, wrapped in tinfoil would be a threepenny or sixpenny bit. That was the treat that we had to find. No-one went around the neighbourhood demanding treats and there were no tricks.

There would be family games. My Dad would suspend apples from the ceiling and again in those apples there was a threepenny or sixpenny bit stuck in them. You had to try and bite the coin out of the fruit with your hands tied behind your back. I was OK at it but Dad, having the biggest mouth, always won.

When I was a kid, Saturdays were special. Dad worked Saturday morning and I was allowed to lie in until ten instead of seven as on a weekday. The Brian Matthews Show on the radio started at ten. It had all the rock on roll and was unmissable. Elvis was on it. Cliff was on it. Mum listened to it all and loved it. Through her, I learned to love it too.

After lunch, Mum and her younger sister, my aunt Sally, went shopping with me with my sister in a pram. This was quite an affair. Man, how those women liked to get involved. It was in that lull between the Fifties and when the Troubles started in the late Sixties. They would walk freely to the Shankill Road in the Protestant area. It was a great High Street, full of clothes shops and general hardware and furniture stores. It was always busy with a good crowd of Protestant and Catholics - Belfast people - out and about.

Other Saturdays, we would go into 'town' which meant Belfast city centre - Royal Avenue and North Street- also great shopping streets. The draper's shop, being full of cloth, was very boring from a young lad's point of view. The magic only began when an order was placed. They had a contraption on the ceiling where a note was placed in a canister and went flying across by means of a series of pulleys and wires. It was fantastic.

I recall going to a furniture store called Gilpins on one of these outings. It sold radiograms. The story goes that I lay on the floor and refused to leave unless one of the aforementioned was purchased. It went on tick, of course. Spoilt? Maybe, but I know my Mum really wanted it anyway.

Home around five thirty and just one errand for me to do before tea; walk down Etna Drive to the moneylender to make my parents' weekly repayments.

The moneylender's house seemed so rich and posh compared to ours. It was in our road so it had to be the same but it just felt different. The moneylender always gave me a couple of coppers for my trouble, which certainly added to my sense of self importance at having been trusted with the errand. I never lost the attitude instilled in me then. You do a job. You get paid. Never truer than in the music business.

There were no pubs on the Glenard estate because it was a Catholic enclave that had been commandeered by the Church some time past as a place of safety for Catholics. Trickily, it was also slap bang in the middle of a Protestant area that had been built for mill workers.

Saturday evening, the men - my Daddy, Grandad O'Neill, my Uncles O'Neill - would go off to The Wheatfield pub at the junction of the Crumlin Road and Flax Street, where the mills were. It was the closest pub to where we lived. The men played darts, drank stout and come ten when the pubs shut, they came home with a 'take away', i.e. more stout. Only then would the women join them.

There were only two places the family could party. Ours or my grandfather O'Neill's house in Highbury Gardens around the corner. At ours, my mum would have soup ready, pearl barley and vegetables, slow cooked with a great big bone for flavour. I would have been in bed since seven, of course. Then some boozy uncle would suggest that I join them for the sing song.

"Where's wee Brendan?" would be the refrain.

My mother's protests would fall on deaf ears. So, sitting on my Dad's lap, a quick rendition of 'Twinkle, Twinkle Little Star' and 'Three Blind Mice' and then it was back to bed for me.

I loved the atmosphere of those nights, the smell of homemade soup and stout and the men and women singing the popular music of the day. As I lay in bed, I would hear Hank Williams' songs, the Mills Brothers, Al Jolsen, all the great show tunes. My Dad would be on the accordion with that incessant right foot.

My Mum and Dad's party piece was 'Moonlight and Roses'. I have them on tape singing 'In Your Easter Bonnet' and 'On Moonlight Bay' so beautifully together.

Babylon

The first day I went to The Holy Cross School for Boys, Butler Street, it was a beautiful, warm, sunny morning. The school didn't have enough built classrooms then so the classes overflowed into Nissen huts in the playground. All the windows were open in the hut that was to be my classroom.

I was so nervous that I asked to be excused to go to the toilet almost immediately. The concrete toilets were next to the hut but I turned left instead of right. This confusion as to where I should be going is a life-long trait and earned me the band nickname 'Sense of Direction'. Anyway, I bashed my little head on an open window and duly crapped myself. It was not a good start.

A girl called Avril Brown walked me to school. She was a couple of years older than me, the daughter of one of my Aunt Sally's friends. I wonder sometimes where Avril is now. She really looked after me. I have a sense of those times of always being in the company of women. They were always in our front room during the day, chatting, knitting, and drinking tea.

I would arrive home from Holy Cross at about three thirty but we didn't have our evening meal - our tea - until my Dad got home from work at about five thirty to six. So, to put some fuel in my little tank for all that running around, Mum would give me a sandwich. It varied depending on what was in the cupboard but sometimes it was simply a sandwich of brown sugar. Occasionally, I'd have a little, white, twopenny bag of dolse - dried salty seaweed - which I loved.

Unfortunately, the brown sugar had a detrimental effect on my little gnashers. I had to go to Mr Wolfe's dental surgery on the first floor of what must have been a lovely Victorian home on the Crumlin Road opposite Holy Cross Chapel.

The reception was at the top of the stairs. Turn left up three more steps to the landing and straight ahead was the Wolfe's den. A big, leather chair sat in the middle of the room. It seemed ever such a climb to get up and sit on it.

The gleaming, chrome instruments went into my unwilling mouth as a great big face loomed behind them and peered in. I needed just one filling. There was none of this make another appointment in two weeks' time. Mr Wolfe got straight to work. The black, oval-shaped mask descended over my mouth and nose and I heard the words, "Breathe deeply," followed by the strange, surgical smell of gas.

Like a silent, creeping, Vapour Monster, it seeped in, up my nostrils, behind my eyeballs and into my tiny brain until I tipped over into a wonderful, dreamy free fall. As luck would have it, Elvis appeared suspended in a pink cloud, swivelling his hips as he danced. He was singing but I couldn't hear him. Though I couldn't tell what song he was singing, I knew he was performing it just for me. Elvis left the building and that would be my one and only hallucinogenic trip.

I was a bit of a marble shark. All the boys in the last two year groups loved to play with those little, coloured glass balls. Luckily for us, an old building next to Holy Cross had been demolished and the area levelled off leaving a ready made arena for the games. At lunch time, that waste ground was full of eager players hunting glory.

A competitor would set his marbles out in a row opposite a designated line where opposing players would stand and shoot their marbles at them. If you wanted to lay out six marbles, the shooting line would be six paces from them, if five, then five paces and so on. Any number of players could shoot and the shooting marble was held between thumb and forefinger and flicked. Miss and you lost your marble to the person who laid theirs out. If you hit, you captured his and it was your turn to set up.

It was so popular that capitalism, red in tooth and claw, inevitably took hold and a market in marbles grew. Kids bartered 'beauts'. A single 'beaut' could command up to six in exchange such was its colouring and effectiveness.

One lunchtime I was on a roll and I returned to class with the pockets of my grey shorts bulging, full to the brim with booty. The fact that I was as thin as a stick insect meant I cut a comical, and obvious, figure. As the marbles tumbled out behind me, a teacher spotted me and confiscated all my bounty. A general note was sent out to everyone about the marble tournaments and how they were disrupting school life.

It was taken very seriously. My Dad had my pockets sewn up for good measure. He did the same thing years later to stop me walking with my hands in them.

My Dad read The News of the World newspaper 'religiously' every Sunday. It was tucked under his arm wherever he went until he had finished it. The paper would then be left around for any inquisitive mind to investigate.

While perusing it myself, aged about ten, I discovered something quite miraculous. Down the right hand side of one of the pages was a cartoon strip featuring a series of naked females. The strip always ended with a joke but I wasn't interested in that. This was the closest I had ever been to seeing a naked woman. When the paper were chucked out, I retrieved it and cut out the cartoon strip. For what other reason, readers, than to show to my school mates. This was my first class ticket into the inner circle of popularity.

The next day in class during break time, we gathered in a steamy huddle, sniggering at my deviously acquired supersoft porn. We were so engrossed that we failed to notice a large, dark, presence overshadow us. A teacher, whose name escapes me, in a tweed jacket trimmed with leather buttons and elbow pads, and enormous, grey flannels, had crept up behind us. We jumped out of our skins when his big, booming, voice demanded, "Who owns this filth?"

There is a saying, 'victory has many owners, defeat but one', and it was never truer than on that day. Talk about rats deserting a sinking ship. I was on my own and on my way to see Mr Morris, the headmaster. What I had done was considered so wicked that the priest was sent for.

Who else would it be but Father Brendan, the priest that had married my parents. The priest who had baptised me and whose name had saved me from having the first name of Mary. The crying, begging and pleading for him not to tell my parents seemed to work. I heard nothing. Four or five months later, something my father said in passing made me realise that I had been betrayed.

My parents had wisely chosen to ignore the incident and there were no repercussions at home. The genie, however, was well and truly out of the bottle. My interest in the beautiful, female form continued unabated. No threat to date, spiritual or physical, has been strong enough to alter that. As for my faith in men of the cloth, that is another matter.

No Harm Done

My first pet was a bitch called Peter named after my Uncle Peter not the saint. She was a kind of cross collie, cross-crossed. Together with my best friend, Paul McKibbin, we were, of course, Peter, Paul and Mary.

Peter and I went everywhere together. She was never on a lead. When we kids were out playing, one or two of our family pets would just be around. When Peter was on heat, she had to be shut inside the house. I can still hear my parents yelling out, "Shut the front door!" but despite their warnings, the inevitable happened. One day, Peter gave us the slip.

We couldn't find her anywhere, until later in the day when a neighbour came to tell us that she had been spotted in Alliance Avenue, on the edge of the Protestant district. When we got there, she was still there but she was welded to the hindquarters of another dog. Every time the dog tried to drag himself away, Peter would whine and yelp. It broke my heart to see and hear her with everyone running around with buckets of water to throw over them to dampen their ardour. They eventually separated but the dirty deed was done. Peter had about six puppies as a result.

Paul was a year younger than me and lived further along Etna Drive. He was my best mate for a couple of years at primary school. We were always together after school. We would go catch tadpoles, frogs and tiddlers at the mysterious Mill Dam where us children were forbidden to go.

The Mill Dam was a large oval pond where the flax workers used to soak the flax. It was a derelict, fenced piece of still water, overgrown with weeds and reeds and teaming with tempting wildlife. People used to say that once a boy had lost his footing there and drowned.

My O'Neill competitiveness developed early and Paul often came off worse when we disagreed. My Aunt Sarah was looking after us one afternoon when my mum was working and she got us to help her with the washing by wringing the wet clothes. Paul and I had different ideas about which was the correct way to feed the clothes into the mangle - a mechanical device with two rubber rollers pressed together that wet clothes were passed between. As a crank wound the clothes through, the water was pressed out and the clothes were 'wrung'. As Paul fed the wet clothes in, instead of just guiding the clothes out, I tugged them impatiently and poor Paul's fingers got caught and pressed flat between the rubber rollers.

Another time, my Daddy had been chopping sticks for kindling in our back yard and hadn't put the hatchet away. Paul and I came across it and thought we'd do some chopping ourselves. We sat on the step opposite each other, both holding the handle of the axe. A tug of war escalated quickly for who was to have the first go. As Paul made a pull, I decided to let go and the hatchet hit his head hard. Luckily, the blade wasn't sharp enough to scalp him but he got a nasty bruise on his forehead.

My Daddy didn't find out but my Mum gave me a massive telling off. I didn't see much of Paul after that.

Gerard Gillespie was a thin, sandy-haired boy, a couple of years older than me. When I was five and he was seven, he lived two doors below us at number five. I didn't play out in the street with him because he had his own group of friends. Every time we came across each other, he thought it his civic duty to give me a thump and I would run home to tell my Mum.

One wet Sunday morning at about ten o'clock after Children's Mass, I was out playing and GG gave me my regulation wallop. When I ran home to tell of my misfortune, it was my Dad and not my Mum who was at home to hear it. She was at Mass with her sisters. I can only think that he must have gone to an earlier one or, more probably, not at all.

His reaction was uncompromising.

"Get back out and hit him!"

"But I can't, Daddy," I said.

"Go out and hit him."

I didn't move.

"If you don't go out and hit him, I'll hit you."

He took me by the scruff of my neck out the front door and back to the piece of waste ground where my ginger nemesis stood with his friends. GG was completely terrified at seeing my father, but that wasn't my problem. He and I stood staring at each other.

The paternal instructions were the same.

"Hit him, or I'll hit you."

I had no choice. I lunged at GG with the full force of my tiny frame. Before long, a crowd of neighbours, kids and adults, had gathered to see what the heck was going on. GG and I punched, kicked, gouged lumps out of each other and rolled around on the ground.

It was not so much The Rumble in the Jungle more of A Thud in the Mud but it was life and death and it went on for what seemed like an eternity. Finally, I pushed his freckled face into a dirty puddle and began to drown him. That's when I felt myself being lifted up into the sky and away.

My Daddy placed me back on terra firma and told me with utter confidence, "He'll never hit you again."

He was right. I never had any trouble again. I don't know what happened to GG. He never went to my secondary school. I think they moved away.

All that running around the streets and the wild places where we lived in those days had its consequences. My knees were permanently bruised and scabby. My hands and face were forever needing medical attention. I didn't walk downstairs from our bedroom. I jumped from the small landing, caught hold of the banister rails opposite before dropping to the floor eight feet below.

Once, I fell on my face and my two front teeth went through my lower lip, blood everywhere. It was bad but not that serious. The most serious was an accident I had while playing by the forbidden Mill Dam. I fell and cut my left wrist. I still have a tiny scar to remind me, as if I could ever forget what happened there and its aftermath.

It was a small nick about a quarter of an inch long. It was innocuous enough but even so, that night my mother washed it and put antiseptic and a plaster on it. The routine was the same with most cuts.

After a day or two, a little scab developed covering the wound but the skin around it was red. Mum was very concerned. I cannot remember whether or not we went to the doctor's but the cut was bathed again, more cream was applied and some type of poultice was created to cover it. The next day, a red line was threading from that angry-looking scab up my arm to just beyond my wrist.

Nevertheless, I went to school as usual and my mother went to the flax mill to work. The evening my cut was seen to again. More cleaning was done and another poultice applied in the hope it would draw out what was an obvious infection in my arm.

The following day was a Friday and by the time my mammy inspected it again that evening, the poisonous red line had almost reached my shoulder. She got into a terrible state about it and was anxiously washing my wrist with warm water in a basin on a small table in the front room when my daddy came home from work.

He was late and, being Friday, he had nipped into The Wheatfield for a couple of pints, en route. When he saw that red line snaking up my arm and the panic in my Mum's eyes, he acted impulsively. He went to the kitchen, boiled a kettle of water, returned to the front room and poured the scalding water in the basin. Before we knew it, he had grasped my wrist and plunged it into the basin.

I screamed in agony, and my mother, with shock. Exactly how long my father held my hand there I don't know but it felt like a very, very, long time. The intense pain of the burning water certainly made me forget about the pain in my arm. I don't remember much else about that evening. The next morning, however, my hand and wrist were completely bandaged.

There was a terrible atmosphere in the house when I went downstairs. It was one I had not really experienced before. My mother was there with my two younger sisters, Bernadette and Teresa. My father had gone to work. Even though it was a Saturday, there was no music. The mood was dark and heavy and quiet.

My mother undid the bandage to reveal a swollen palmful of horrible blisters. She was physically shaken by the sight of it but, miraculously, the poisonous red line had disappeared. She boiled and sterilised a pair of scissors and began to cut the blisters to release the liquid from them.

I don't recall any more being said about the incident but it was the first time I was aware of real tension between my parents. Like the red line on my arm, from then on there was a nasty dark thread that tracked through our family life while I was growing up.

Come Sunday and my hand on the mend, my mum asked me to go to one of our two local shops for something for Sunday dinner. She knew that I ran everywhere. Sometimes, she'd say to me "Run as fast as you can, I'll time you."

This time, she said, "Walk. Don't run."

No sooner had I turned the corner of Etna Drive than I ignored her warning and started to run. I couldn't help myself and the inevitable happened. I tripped and fell.

OUT OF THE FRYING PAN

Drums

I was twenty years old before I touched a drop of alcohol. My mother was teetotal as was my father when he and she first met. He told me that he saw the negativity it caused. I came to agree with him.

When I was very young, drinking was always associated with good times and parties but, as time went on, it changed. Unfortunately, for my father and for us, everyone around him at work and in his family drank prodigiously and, while in their company, he made up for lost time.

My mother became increasingly concerned about the influence my Dad's family was having on him and she made it clear that she wanted to move. They found a place by Carlisle Circus, where the Crumlin Road and the Antrim Road met, in Fairview Street, which linked the Crumlin Road with the old Lodge Road. It was a grand, Victorian area right next to the Church-funded Mater Hospital run by nuns, the Crumlin Road Jail and the Courthouse. It was, and remains, a largely Protestant area.

My Grandfather O'Neill pleaded with my dad not to move. His arguments were: strength in numbers; stick together; too risky for the children; but my mother was adamant that she wanted out and she got her wish.

When moving day arrived in late July, the neighbours came out and waved us goodbye. Dad and some of his brothers made the two mile journey a couple of times before the remainder of our belongings together with us older kids - I was between eight and nine years old - were put on the back of Dad's lorry and left the only world I had ever known. It was both sad and exciting at one and the same time. The lure of an uncertain future was beckoning.

The fact that we now lived outside the Ardoyne did make me feel differently about it but I still had close connections. After all, I was still an altar boy at Holy Cross Chapel and would attend primary school there for a couple of years after we moved. The big change was that I took the 49 bus to school. It terminated at the Ardoyne depot at 08.55 every morning. I felt very grown up.

Forty-five Fairview Street was a small townhouse, untouched since the time it was built in the late 1800s. It had a staircase leading up to the attic, the third level. There was a small vestibule with three rooms on the ground floor and three rooms on the second floor, which was split-level. The big attic would eventually become the girls' bedroom. The kitchen-come-living room had an ancient, black open range against the wall with a huge, black mantle above. Our place in Glenard may have been much smaller but at least it had a bathroom. This place had no bathroom, just an outside toilet.

The yellowing decor throughout was like an old, sepia photograph. The previous owner had been an ancient, Jewish lady and nailed to each door frame of every room was a sealed metal tube about three inches long. Inside these were rolled up scrolls of Jewish prayers written in Hebrew. A neighbour told us that the lady would pray before entering each room.

My dad had a job on his hands modernizing and decorating the place. I became his little helper, finding things and handing him tools as he worked. It was the summer holidays so I had plenty of time to adjust and explore before going back to school. It was here that I made my first ever Protestant acquaintance: Billy McFall.

I did miss my old friends in Glenard, though, and the outdoors. There were just six Catholic families living on Fairview Street. Two of those families had boys a couple of years older than me: the Morrisseys and the Williams.

In Ardoyne, so many essential products had to be brought in: freshly baked bread, coal, milk and even lemonade. The bread server's van was really long and the breadman would bring out the warm bread from deep inside the wagon with a long-handled scoop. The coalman carried his great, big black sacks through the house to the yard. Milk and buttermilk arrived every day and the lemonade man brought white, brown and sarsaparilla in crates. We had one of each, every week. When we returned our bottles, we got the deposit back, of course.

Simple things like these deliveries made the Ardoyne an insular area, very unlike our new home in Fairview Street, where needing to go to the shops for our supplies meant going and getting them. Our world immediately expanded.

What we hadn't realized before moving to our new residence was that on July 12th, when the Orange Order marched to Finaghy and the Field, Fairview Street was one of the assembly points for the Protestant bands and the Lodges.

The flute, accordion and pipe bands with all of those wonderful drummers began warming up in a generally relaxed mood from between eight and nine in the morning. Their large cloth murals leaned against our walls while men convened in black suits and bowler hats with their all important sashes emblazoned with Lodge insignia. They smoked as they chatted, waiting for the call to march. It wasn't frightening at all. It was fun.

I'm not sure if the pubs were open at that early hour but some of the men certainly needed to use the lavatory and people in the street gladly gave them access. My parents complied with the tradition of offering relief. When these men of King William passed through the front room to the outside toilet, they could not help but see the large picture of the bleeding Sacred Heart on the chimney breast. You could see the doubt and confusion in their eyes.

The 1960s was a much mellower time in The Six Counties and what harm was there in a man using your toilet if he needed to? As my mother used to say, "Wherever you may be, let your wind go free, church or chapel, let it rattle!".

Some of my new friends were members of the Catholic Boy Scouts of Ireland. The Scout Hall was behind St Patrick's Church on Lower North Street and a fifteen minute walk from our house. I was too young to accompany them but when I was eleven, my parents gave me permission to attend.

Joining the Scouts was the best thing I could have done in my life at this time. I met boys who made a lasting impression on me. Some would become lifelong friends and lead me to opportunities that would shape my future.

The main room of the hall was rectangular and was used for the meetings of the three troupes that made up St Patrick's: the Eighth, Tenth, and Twelfth. I joined the Tenth and we met on Monday nights. There were two adjoining rooms where the Twelfth troupe had meetings in one and the other was where St Patrick's CBSI's pipe band equipment was stored.

Imagine it, being involved with something that had its own pipe band. This was where and when I first learned to play the drums. Band practice was every Friday night and I never missed it. We just practised. The only time we ever went out of the room was on some Church march, once or twice a year, when we might go south to a church festival in Drogheda. On one of these excursions, I was the lead off drummer, which was a pretty big deal, I can tell you.

We played table tennis on Thursdays and went camping every weekend possible to the Belfast hills. We were taught to be concerned about our environment. If we dug a sod for the fire, we had to roll it up, water it and replace it when we left. We cooked for ourselves, learned to make knots and even furniture. The camp we made was often left there for future use when we returned, if someone hadn't demolished it in the meantime.

The social life of those few rooms in St Patrick's Scout Hall was all consuming. I met great lads including: Brendan Star, Tim Duffy, the leaders of our troupe, and brothers Tom and Paul Gibbons, Kevin Rafferty and Jim Clarke, a good friend to this day. These boys became my new family and a badly needed escape.

It was around the time of the move to secondary school that I got a couple of severe hidings from my father. His temper was ferocious and when he lost it, he could lose all sense of reality. The results were often extreme and out of proportion to the 'crime' itself. It was how I imagined a shark attack might be. The eyes would roll and the brute would emerge and come at you.

One beating I got was for being late home. I was eleven years old, in the first year of secondary school and still in short pants. I was half an hour late. I'd broken the rules. My mother wasn't there and my father was sitting waiting for me. He asked where I had been, my answer wasn't good enough, so he took off his belt and let me have it.

The second time was when I had been outside pretending to be the leader of a marching band, throwing my brush shaft - a broom handle - baton up in the air. My enthusiasm carried me inside the house and into the living room, where I hurled my 'baton' into the air and smashed to pieces the chandelier that had been my parents' wedding present.

Unfortunately, my father was upstairs on the landing decorating. He hadn't heard so I had to go and tell him what I'd done. The consequences for me were devastating. He grabbed me and threw me over the bannisters down the stairs. I picked myself up as fast as I could and, stupidly, ran into the living room where he cornered me. He took the brush shaft and beat my back with it. The 'baton' broke in three places.

My mother's reactions to both these incidents was horror. My father was always full of remorse afterwards. He actually cried after the 'baton' incident but my attitude towards him completely changed after that. He'd lost my trust. I came to fear him and avoid his company. I would do anything to be out of that house. I'd literally go anywhere, to a friend's or the Scouts when I could. I would involve myself in almost anything rather than be at home. Other things were happening to me, I was growing up and my father's behaviour just accelerated my need for independence.

My mother began to openly disagree with him. They argued more. His drinking got worse. One drink was too many and ten was not enough. I don't know why. It created a heavy atmosphere at home. Sometimes he would come home from work at the normal time and I would go to the pub on the corner and get him a couple of bottles of Guinness porter. I would help him off with his heavy work boots. He'd be worn out. We'd have dinner and all was fine.

Other times, he wouldn't come home for dinner but went to his local, the King's Head on the Old Lodge Road. Occasionally, Mum would send me to the pub to tell him his dinner was ready. It was a seven or eight minute walk and every step filled me with dread.

When the door of that pub opened, I felt sick with trepidation. The place was filled with hard-handed working men, who hadn't gone home either. They were drinking stout and whiskey. The air was thick with smoke and loud with banter and laughter. No-one was ready to leave. I'd tell my father what my mother had said and he'd answer that he'd be "back in ten minutes". I'd leg it home and get to bed, out of his way when he eventually did come home. It was all so different to the times gone by at the O'Neill parties in Glenard with their singing and soup.

Secondary Modern

I vaguely remember taking my 11+ but I didn't pass. So, instead of taking the 49 bus, it was now the 55, which went all the way to Ligoniel and dropped me off at St Gabriel's Secondary Modern Catholic School for Boys where I would spend six years in a futile quest for an education.

It was a modern building up the road from the main shopping area at the top of the Crumlin Road, past the bus depot, past Everton Protestant School for Girls and Boys - now that was something, seeing girls in their uniforms.

St Gabriel's sat back off the main road on the right hand side and was the last landmark before Ligoniel. We needed to be there earlier than primary school to be in time for the morning assembly, roll call and prayers in the school hall, which served as a dinner hall, retreat room and all things musical happened there.

The catchment area of St Gabriel's was much wider and my first two friends there were from the Falls Rd. They were the two Dannys: Danny McGonicle and Danny O'Neill. We were three half-pints together. Dressed in our oversized burgundy blazers and short grey flannel trousers, we were very obviously first years. We sat together in the first three desks in the front row of the classroom. Jim Clarke also went to our school and was my link between the worlds of St Gabriel's and St Patrick's.

When we were a wee bit older, the two Danny's and I fell out about something. I really don't remember what, but it was a serious dispute because we decided that the only way to resolve it was for me to fight them both after school.

Allegiances were changing. While I was being drawn to the more creative influences outside of school life, they were taking off somewhere else. When we met - for the second important pugilistic encounter of my early life - they brought along a third boy whose name was Meekan, aka 'Meeky'.

Meeky had a bad reputation and looked suitably menacing. His suggestion to me was simple. Why fight two when I could fight just the one i.e. him? It would be more even, he argued. I told him that my honour was at stake here and I had no beef with him. I wanted to go along with things as planned. It wouldn't be the first time that my instincts served me well.

There wasn't much to it really. The Dannys and I pushed and shoved each other, rolled around on the ground for a while, called each other a load of ugly names until we finally agreed never to socialise with each other again. I caught the bus home, pretty satisfied with myself.

It wasn't until a few months later that I realised my good fortune on insisting on fighting the two Desperate Dans instead of Meeky. He stabbed a boy from the newly-built Protestant School for Boys, causing mayhem on a school bus route.

At lunchtime the following day, as tensions rose, boys from each school confronted each other and engaged in a mini riot resulting in both schools being closed for the afternoon. For the first time, I became conscious of the sectarian problems between Protestants and Catholics in Northern Ireland.

That apart, what a set of oddballs me and my school friends at St Gabriel's were.

There was Francis 'Spud' Murphy, who had the biggest gulder of a laugh. He became the lead singer in our first band: Pride. He's a lawyer now, I believe. Davey Rosatto was an Italian boy, so quick witted and funny. Hilary 'Stinker' Ward was about six foot two when he was just 14 and was a really wonderful human being. Malachy Donnelly was pristine. His mum must have given him a spray over with Mr Sheen before he left for school. John Price was really posh and arrogant - he was our know-all. Arthur Kahl, was easy going and gentle, a sweet-natured, mixed-race kid. One time turning into the corridor, we found poor Arthur, upside down, being held by his ankles by two bullies shaking him down for his dinner money.

Arthur became a bass player and still is. I remember we used to practice round his and listen to music. It was his dad, who lost it and broke Gerry McAvoy's guitar in a fit of temper at our 'noise' or, in our minds, our pursuit of musical creativity and stardom.

Some of the teachers were memorable characters.

Mr 'Stocky' Stockman was our form teacher and taught Irish language. All I can remember are the first three lines of the 'Our Father', my name in Gaelic and the word for 'and' which is 'augus'. Stocky was good natured except when doling out corporal punishment. He had a strange way of flicking his hair back before whacking you across the palm of your hand with his thick leather strap. Eventually, that wonderful man got a Doctorate and became a Professor of Languages at the St Malachy Grammar School.

We called our headmaster 'The Bat' because of his dark and spectral presence. Mr 'Jeeves' Moore looked like a butler and was always immaculately turned out. He taught English and Music - mostly hymns. I remember he taught us Brahms Lullaby, which we all sang and I thought was lovely. I remembered it well enough to sing it to my own children before they went to sleep.

Mr 'Pocket Billiards' Higgins kept his hands in his pockets the better to fumble with whatever was therein or thereabouts. His catchphrase was to call everyone who annoyed him a 'goat' in his country accent.

We were streamed, of course, and put into classes according to our ability. We had three A classes - A1, A2, A3 - and one B, C, D, and F. Much to my surprise I found myself in A2. How could they possibly consider me to be bright enough to be in an 'A' class?

The school was well laid out, easy to get around but it was daunting. There were about seven hundred and fifty boys there going all the way up to sixth form - years 12 and 13 in new money. There was a playground to the right of the main building next to the Science wing and one in the centre, which was squared by a gymnasium and corridors. It had a tuck shop where we spent the morning break. There was a woodwork and metalwork department - I was pretty good at both those skills.

There were a number of football pitches at the back. Even though I was athletic and pretty fit, I wasn't much good at sports. I got picked once for the Gaelic football team but the first time I played, it poured with rain and, being knee deep in mud, it was an effort to lift your leg never mind kick a ball. Anyway, I kicked it the wrong way and was never picked again.

A few years later, the band, Ten Years After, played on one of the flat roofs of the school building. They were fantastic but little did I know what my future held. I could only wish. Years later, Nine Below Zero, a blues band that I was a member of for almost 25 years, toured the UK and the USA with Alvin Lee of Ten Years After. Gerry and I served as the rhythm section for both bands. Guitarist Gary Moore, who would eventually join Thin Lizzy - another person with whom I had the pleasure of performing later in life - and a really popular and influential local band, Just Five, also played at our school.

Altar Boy

I didn't know my Grandfather Lagan. He died, aged 54, when my mum was in her early teens. His family came from the market areas of Belfast. This was before the Partition of Ireland in the 1920s. He was a cabinet maker, as was his father before him.

As I've said, the family moved to Glenard during the troubles of the Thirties and were able to settle when the Church bought up the estate. My grandfather opened a window cleaning business but, through that, he contracted the pneumonia that killed him from being wet and always in the cold. As a widow, Granny Lagan always wore black in the traditional Irish way and she held the household together remarkably well considering that she had been left with 12 children to look after.

My grandfather was about six foot two and my granny was five foot two, 'the long and short of it' people used to say. Unusually, my grandfather used the front garden in Estoril Park as an allotment. Mum used to tell us about having to retrieve horse manure from the street and being highly embarrassed at being seen out there with their buckets.

I thought the world of my Granny Lagan. I would go to her house at lunchtime from St Gabriel's. She baked soda bread in the oven and then it was browned off in the fire on two large griddles that would pivot to and from the flames. I ate it spread with a knob of butter spread on it. It tasted wonderful.

I'd be on my own with her because the girls' school was quite a way away up by the Church. It was to please her and my mum that I agreed to become an altar boy.

Joining was one thing, learning and reciting the Latin call and responses with my stammer was another. This is one of the reasons why I have such affection for my late Uncle Peter. He had been an altar boy too. To get me started, he advised me to stand in front of the mirror in my bedroom and concentrate on what my reflection was saying and not what I was. It was a diversionary tactic and it worked.

Once on the altar with the other boys, it was easy - strength in numbers - but without his help and patience, I'm not sure I could ever have done it. I really enjoyed it, actually. We used to get a couple of quid for serving at weddings. If you served seven o' clock mass, the priest used to give us a pot of coffee. That was the first time that I'd ever tried coffee and I really got a taste for it.

With things going so well, my mother and Granny Lagan could now see a future in the priesthood for me. They did not suspect that I had pressing corporeal rather than spiritual matters on my teenage mind.

Protestants call their place of worship a church. Catholics in Northern Ireland call theirs a chapel. Size doesn't come into it although Catholic chapels tended to be smaller than churches. The Holy Cross Church 'Ardoyne Chapel' is different. It's a huge house of God by any reckoning with a large central altar and two smaller ones on either side. There's a central aisle leading to the former and two narrow ones leading to the latter two. In my day, the ornate wooden confessional boxes were grouped on either side in twos and threes. They weren't all always occupied. It depends how bad the sinning was, I suppose.

Confession was a weekly affair for most Catholics after which you received 'penance' for your sins. It is customary to state how long it has been since your last visit. "Bless me, Father, for I have sinned. It has been one, two, three months, ever such a long time, since my last confession."

One Saturday morning when I was 14, I was waiting my turn to enter a cubicle. It wasn't that busy and my turn had come around soon enough. I went through the black curtain on my side of the cubicle and knelt. After the usual formalities, I unburdened my conscience to the shadowy unknown presence behind the lattice mesh that divided us.

I could see him nodding. It was the usual adolescent stuff. However, when I confessed my persistent masturbatory habits, he stopped nodding. There was a deathly silence in the darkness. Finally, he told me that my sins were so heinous that he could not offer me Absolution. I was instructed instead to return home and refrain from such practices forthwith. I was to return the following week and let him know how I had got on.

Mortified is not a strong enough word to describe how I felt. I left the cubicle with a heavy heart and knelt to say the few Hail Marys that he had given me as penance for my other, more trivial, sins. I sat in the Chapel for a while thinking about what had just happened and what it had meant. I was torn but, after much soul searching, the answer became clear to me. I decided that there was only one thing I could do. I would never go to confession ever again.

Sorted, as they say nowadays.

My brother, Martin, was born late in November in 1962, which makes him a Sagittarius like me but 11 years younger. It was a home birth and I remember the day well. I was old enough to realise my Mum was pregnant, of course, but too young to understand the preparations needed for having a baby at home.

The arrival of newborns can never be an exact science so my parents had some sort of contingency plan for us other children to be looked after and occupied. Bernadette, Teresa, Emmanuel and Elizabeth were with my Aunt Sally while I was at the Scouts, which was more or less my permanent home.

When I got home at about four there was an eerie silence in the house. I was about to call out when I heard movement upstairs and my Granny O'Neill came downstairs to see who had come in. It was a surprise to me to see her as she wasn't a regular visitor, but she had come to assist the midwife and take care of my mum after the event. It was all over. We had a new baby boy making us six: three boys and three girls. His arrival completed our family. Naturally, my father had already gone to the pub to wet the baby's head.

Time passed and, with Aunt Sally to help with Martin and Elizabeth, Mum needed to go back to work - this time part-time in a couple of cafes, waitressing and cleaning, which meant that for a period of time between coming home from school and teatime, us kids looked after ourselves.

As I was the eldest, I was meant to be in charge. Things never really got out of hand but they did become high spirited. We would argue about trivial things and once Teresa's fingers got caught between the door frame and the door as it was closing. No permanent damage thankfully but I got the blame for it later when my parents got home.

Emmanuel and I would often lock horns. He'd come off worse because I was much older. I wasn't always that kind. I think I took some of my frustration with my father out on him. No excuse but there you have it.

ESCAPE TO MUSIC

First love: The Beatles

The Beatles recorded the Royal Variety Show on November 4th, 1963. It aired on Sunday the 10th. Those televised Sunday night shows were watched by the whole family, the whole nation, in fact, and that night I was transfixed.

The guys, dressed in matching collarless suits,came across as four, mischievous, clean cut, Northern lads. George Harrison was no more than 20 years old and looked it. Paul McCartney was eager and willing to please. John Lennon was cool. He looked unpredictable. My hero, though, was Ringo, a great, solid, back beat drummer, who played with a swing.

Looking back now, it was all so very basic. When the curtains drew back, there was one mike over the drum kit and no monitors through which the singers could hear themselves. They had to rely solely on the PA front-of-house. When they finished the first number, Paul and John both lifted their mike stands to the front of the stage because they hadn't had enough room behind the closed curtains to set up.

No matter. All the parts fitted together like a Swiss watch and I was sold. I'd heard Elvis, Cliff Richard, the Shadows and Tommy Steele et cetera on the radio but the Beatles performing 'She Loves You' and 'Twist and Shout' live in that short set put a whole new perspective on where it was at.

My mother by then had bought me my first little Gigster snare drum from the Scouts for about 30 bob. It became the centre of my homemade drum kit in the loft. I used cardboard boxes for tom toms and my foot on the floor for the bass drum.

The Gigster just had the hoop when it should have had a calfskin head on it for you to hit. The old head was so worn that it wouldn't tension any more. My mother had some old sailcloth and I had to improvise by sewing my own cloth head. It sounded like a sack of shit but it was my sack of shit and I got hours of pleasure out of it.

I hadn't realised it at the time but the Beatles were playing less rock and roll more rock with great melody. For example, if you listen to Chuck Berry's original version of 'Rock and Roll Music' with the great Willie Dixon on bass and Freddy Below on drums, it has more of a rockabilly/swing feel. They don't come any better in that genre. The drumming, however, has a jazz effect. Whereas, Ringo gives The Beatles' version a driving 16th feel, played on the high hat with a real stomp. Even as a kid, I felt that difference.

The physicality and display of drumming, the rhythms and sheer energy are what speak to me about the instrument. When I play it feels like something pouring out of me. You hit the centre of a drum, and when you hit it right, it responds physically. The sound both comes back at you and explodes out towards the audience. It's about velocity. What you feel, they feel.

After The Royal Variety Show, I became obsessed with the Beatles, and Ringo, in particular. I would look out for them on the TV and read any articles about them in magazines in the paper shop. When I was able to convince my mum - the family book keeper - to buy me a small Dansette record player, the album she bought me to go with it was 'Beatles for Sale'. Some say this is their least successful album. I must concede that there are a couple of dodgy tracks on it but, let me tell you, there are also seven or eight brilliant originals on there and their version of 'Rock and Roll Music' remains a classic.

From then on I bought singles such as the Beatles' 'Day Tripper' and 'Ticket to Ride', and the Stones' singles, 'The Last Time' and 'Nineteenth Nervous Breakdown'. I bought them mainly from Harrison's record shop on Divis Street or the old Smithfield Market in the centre of Belfast. Sadly, incendiary bombs set in 1974 by the IRA reduced the latter to ashes.

My fascination with the Beatles left me open to a wee bit of mickey taking. Kevin Rafferty, a friend from Scouts, once gave me a lock of hair in a small, plastic bag. He told me it belonged to Ringo and, because I was such a fan, he would let me have it to keep. What a lovely thing to do, I thought. What a mate.

I'm not sure how long it took for the penny to drop, but it surely did. The whole incident, mercifully, was allowed to fade away.

Around the corner from the Scout Hall on York Street, there was a ballroom and on our way home on Thursday and Friday night, the show bands could be heard playing live versions of Top Forty chart hits. They were the first live bands I had heard apart from the marching bands. I hadn't a clue what the show bands looked like but their sound was exciting.

Show bands come in for a lot of flak because they never played anything original. I understand that criticism but a lot of great players learned their chops in show bands and went on to achieve great things. Both Van Morrison and Rory Gallagher spent time on that circuit, as I did myself.

Once, when we were with Rory in a hotel on the West Coast - we'd played the Lisdoonvarna Festival in County Clare - Van Morrison was at breakfast with Rory outside in the grounds of the hotel.

Van and Rory were chatting over coffee and as we were eating our breakfast inside, we saw Van get up and start jigging around like he was in Riverdance or something, all the while miming at blowing an instrument. We were naturally taken aback by the man's uncharacteristic display of folk artistry. Rory told us later that Van was explaining the dance routine he had to perform while playing the sax in a show band.

Top of the Pops, the vintage British music show, was another must see. It did exactly as the name suggests and had a huge audience. Artists whose songs were in the Top 20 or 'bubbling under' had the opportunity to perform their music on live television to the whole nation. On Thursdays between seven and seven-thirty in the evening, just before Scouts, I was, invariably, sat in front of that screen to see and hear what was new.

On August, 26th, 1964, the Kinks played 'You Really Got Me' on TOTP. The riff was so distorted and dirty, the message so simple and to the point, that there was no misunderstanding: the verse, the chorus, the guitar solo. It was two minutes or so of pure adrenalin rush. When the show was over, I ran the whole way to the Scouts to find out who else had seen them and we raved about it the whole night.

Within the next couple of weeks, the band that had the self-same effect for me was the Buddy Rich Big Band. I fell in love with the energy, the swing and sheer craftsmanship of the performance that I saw on the TV. This time, I couldn't find anyone else who had heard of him, listened to that band or to share my taste and enthusiasm for Buddy.

After the move to Fairview Street, what with music getting to me, the Scouts, school and my paper round, my life was starting to feel quite full. It wasn't long after that the G word raised its beautiful head. At 13, my hormones went pretty crazy. I felt like I was following some sort of periscope that bobbed up on the lookout for girls, twenty four hours a day, seven days a week. It was relentless.

I had a couple of girlfriends around this time. One of them, I remember, was very forward for our age. We would meet a couple of days a week and walk around Alexandra Park off the Antrim Road. Naturally, I looked forward to those investigative meetings very much. Might I say, I did not have sexual relations with that woman but it wasn't for the want of trying. We split up, of course. I found out that she became pregnant at 16. Good luck to her, I say.

St Gabriel's had a Sunday night hop in the assembly hall and I got permission to go. I went on my own and when I arrived, the place was really packed, more than a hundred kids were there. A band called the Misfits were playing. They were a four piece doing covers of Top 40 tunes but, as I watched them, I couldn't take my eyes off the drummer.

The other guys were good but I can tell you no more about them. John Wilson, who later joined Rory Gallagher's fine first band, Taste, in its second line up, was that drummer. He was only three or four years older than me but already an accomplished player. His playing was so full of flair, dynamics and energy, watching him just intensified my desire to play.

(I was too shy to go up to John after the show, but he's a friend of mine now. John always sends me a Christmas text addressed to 'Young Brendan'.)

Years later, when I returned to Belfast to play with my band, Swift, John came to a sound check and actually sat in and played with the band. The bass player of Swift, John McCullough, knew John Wilson's brother, which is why he had come along. This was the first time I was to meet him properly though not the last. The next day he invited me to his house to listen to music and play drums. When I told him that I really wanted a wooden snare drum. He disappeared out of the room, came back with such a drum and gave it to me. I was totally overwhelmed.

Young Lions

My years as an altar boy and priest-in-training came to a close when I decided my time would be better spent delivering newspapers. Disappointed as she was, my mum bowed to the inevitable. The fact that my earnings boosted the family budget softened the blow.

The newspaper shop was next to the roundabout at Carlisle Circus a five- or six-minute walk from home. I delivered the morning papers before school between seven thirty and eight thirty and the evening papers after school between five and six. The shop also sold chocolate and cigarettes and this was when I acquired my first vice.

The fag supplies were kept in the toilet at the back of the shop. Sometimes, a carton would be left open and exposed. I am ashamed to say I did pinch the odd packet of Benson and Hedges, once again to impress my friends at school.

Boy, did it work. Just like when I shared soft porn in the playground, my popularity soared. Unfortunately, I 'got high on my own supply', as they say, and along with my mates, got hooked on the filthy habit early on.

I did this job for about two and a half years, Monday to Friday. Every Sunday morning, the lady who owned the shop and her husband went to the docks to pick up the papers from England, which arrived on the overnight ships. The paper boys would take it in turns to accompany them and load the goods onto the van. We'd then return to the shop and mark the papers up for delivery.

The docks are served by a seven mile waterway - the Belfast lough - a thoroughfare of constantly moving cargo. The survival of Belfast depended on it at that time. Even from Ardoyne, when we were kids, the sound of ships' horns that we could hear in the distance was a haunting, yet comforting, sound.

One Sunday in December 1964, we went down for the papers. The port area was abuzz. Our little van was dwarfed by the huge, imposing ships that lined the wharf, bringing and taking goods to the whole world. As they loomed at the dock edge, everywhere was a blur of activity. Pallets of cargo were being hoisted to and from the ships with great rope, chain and pulley mechanisms. Shouts of instruction and banter could be heard from sturdy men wearing heavy, woollen overcoats and caps, moving about with real purpose on the damp, misty morning.

Along with the Harland and Wolff shipyard, where RMS Titanic was built, there was an aircraft factory alongside Short Bros and Harland, where I would serve an apprenticeship in due course.

We arrived to find the overnight ship due at six thirty was late. So, we went into the cafe to wait for the ship to arrive. It was a cold, damp morning but the cafe was warm and cosy, all decorated for Christmas. It was packed with people waiting for the ship. Condensation ran down the window panes and the smell of bacon and eggs as we walked in was glorious.

For me, the truly magical thing in that place was a great, big colourful machine that stood against one wall. It was a jukebox, the first I had ever seen, and the music it played had the warmest, fattest bass sound I'd ever heard. Two of the songs that stuck with me that morning were 'Downtown' by Petula Clark and 'I Feel Fine' by The Beatles. To this day, when I hear those songs I am drawn back to that wonderful Sunday morning in the cafe.

After school, my mate, Kevin Rafferty, would invite a few friends round his house to listen to music. He lived near the aforementioned Alexandra Park. Bands like The Who, the Small Faces and, of course, the sound of Tamla Motown and Soul were all starting to make a major impact. At Scouts, Jim Clarke and Kevin were both really into all what was going on.

One day, Kevin invited us round and he played the most current Beatles album, 'Rubber Soul'. Another friend of KR's was there, a boy called Jim Ferguson. We were all really into this record. It turned out that 'Ferg' aka 'Fergie' was a guitar player and a Beatles nut. Not only that, he knew the chords to all those tunes. (He also lived next to Alexandra Park and, years later, I found out that he also 'knew' my enthusiastic, young girlfriend.)

Before we left Kevin's that day, we had loosely agreed to form a band. I told Ferg that I'd heard about this guy at school, Gerry McAvoy, who was also a guitar player and that I would find out if he was interested in joining us. I'd seen Gerry from a distance at school. He was in the A1 brainbox stream. I was in A2 so we had a different group of friends. There was no reason for us to come into contact so I had to introduce myself.

Gerry was always really neat and tidy, well turned out and orderly. His Dad would drop him to school every morning in his Ford car, which gave him a certain cachet. Gerry's father was a harmonica player. After a while, we found out that our fathers were acquaintances and drank together in certain clubs around Belfast.

Anyway, within the next few weeks, I bumped into Gerry on the steps of the playground. I asked him if he could play the guitar and whether or not he could use his 'little finger' or not. This was a test question to see whether or not he could play a 12 bar blues. Gerry later admitted that he didn't know what I was talking about but his answer then, of course, was that he most definitely could.

We arranged to meet up at Ferg's after school to work on songs. The name we came up with for the band was 'Pride'. Ferg's memory is better than mine though I'm not convinced about this; he reckons we thought we were young lions - hence 'Pride'.

The Belfast live music scene was healthy and growing. Music in the city was fast becoming a melting pot of styles and beats and people wanted live versions of their favourite songs. There was as much live music as there were DJs playing dance music records. In the same place, one night would be a soul band, the next a blues band, the next, top 40. Most nights there was something to go and see and we were free to do so. The places where we went did not serve alcohol so it wasn't a problem for us kids to get to see who we wanted.

A couple of weeks after seeing the Misfits, I went to the Friday night hop at Ferg's school to see a fantastic soul band called the Interns. Again, they blew me away. They played soul covers that were so much more exciting than the songs the Misfits had covered. It was the first time that I'd heard black music played live.

I had been exposed to two great local bands in short succession and I really wanted to be in one myself. Now, I was but I had one major problem: no drum kit. I had my Gigster and cardboard kit but it really wasn't up to the job I had in mind. So, once again, my dear mum, after a debate with my father, dug deep and bought me a Broadway kit on hire purchase, the good old HP. It had a dark brown wood veneer finish and was a thing of beauty.

By now the idea of getting up at seven every morning was becoming a pain in the backside so I left the paper job and got myself another one working for an off-licence near Alexandra Park close to where Ferg and KR lived. I delivered spirits and mixers to the posh houses on the Antrim Road in the late afternoon from four to six in the evening.

My money went into the house. It was part of the family budget so there was no question of me not getting another job. Doing it brought me my first, though not last, encounter with death.

One winter's day at dusk while cycling back at some speed to the shop after deliveries, as I reached a sharp bend in the road, a car coming the other way lost control and drove straight into me, pushing the bike and myself onto the footpath. I came within inches of being crushed against a brick wall, which separated the road from the garden of a big house. A crowd of people gathered around and an ambulance was called.

I was so very lucky. Nothing was even broken, I was just dazed with concussion, but I spent the night in the Mater Hospital at the top of our road. My parents came, all distraught and worried, but it turned out OK. My lovely, black bicycle with the basket at the front, supplied by the off licence, however, was a write off.

Meanwhile, Fergie recruited Don Donaghy to Pride on bass. While he was with us, Don got a job as an apprentice butcher. The cuts he acquired on his fingers were an occupational hazard that impeded the fluency of his bass playing, somewhat.

Gerry introduced one Francis 'Spud' Murphy as our singer. He had a good voice but he also had a part time job at a fishmongers, which brought its own impediment to our quest for world domination, a truly pungent smell.

No matter, we had the constituent parts of a band. The next thing was to organise a rehearsal and get the young lions their first gig.

Gerry's father had a friend who owned a sweet shop in Ligoniel. He arranged for his friend to let us use the upstairs room of the shop for rehearsals. My dad agreed to drive me and my drum kit there on his lorry. The sight of my little Broadway drum kit on the back of that 40 footer was comical. The future artics for Wembley Arena were just impossible dreams back then.

We young lions discovered soon enough that there's one thing having electric guitars but it's another having the amps to make them audible. We didn't have any.

At our first rehearsal, I took the lead, drowning out everybody else in the room apart from Spud's lovely singing voice. The lads even tried holding their guitars against the wall to amplify the sound but it didn't work. It wasn't a great start but, you know, it was a start.

After that we rehearsed in our loft in Fairview St. One Saturday afternoon, my parents cleared the back room of furniture so we could rehearse there but the neighbours complained. Don's mum then agreed to let us use their basement, if we would agree to dig it out. The subterranean space was filled with rubble and soil from when the house had been built. We dug out a rehearsal room and Don's mum got a basement. Everyone was happy.

By this stage, when we had begun to frequent the clubs, I started to lose interest in the Scouts. I had loved the safety of those few years spent learning to interact with people, the annual two week camps and the freedom and discipline that went hand in hand and made it work. But, it was just the music that was consuming me now.

Clarke's

Cecil and Eileen Clarke's Dance Studio was in Lower North Street where Cecil and Eileen taught ballroom dancing. As music trends changed, Cecil embraced the new crop of young bands that were playing around Belfast. There were four other clubs of this size around town: the Maritime, the Jazz Club, Betty Staffs and the Elizabethan. We chose Clarke's. It was around the corner from the Scouts and on our side of town. My friend, Jim Clarke started his DJ career there. He called himself 'Lord Jim' complete with a top hat, tails and all.

The stage was to the right of a small set of stairs which led down onto the dance floor. The top of those stairs was a great vantage point from which to watch live bands that played on Fridays. This is where I liked to stand and observe them side on. The musicians were older than us but not by much. I saw Gary Moore play there with his band, Platform 3, when he was about 15 and already great. I spoke to him after the show and offered him my services, to which he replied, "We're only doing this for fun. It's just a pastime."

A while later, Pride entered a talent competition at the Floral Hall. Unfortunately, Gary and Platform 3 had entered as well. His band came first. We came third.

In the afternoon of July 30th, 1966, we were all at Clarke's. The club was used for ballroom dancing on Saturday nights so the matinee was ours. Lord Jim was spinning the discs for the first time. He could spot a good song at first listening. Soon, he would be finding more obscure songs to add to our set list.

As I was enjoying the music and watching the crowd, I spotted two apprehensive girls that I hadn't seen in Clarke's before. They both had Mod dress sense and looked great.

I bided my time and then went to ask the one who looked like Ready Steady Go's Cathy McGowan to dance before someone else did. We got chatting and it turned out that they were from the Upper Newtownards Road in East Belfast, somewhere that I had never been because a) it was light years away and b) it was largely a Protestant area.

She said it was the first time that they had come to this part of town and to Clarke's. Her name was Brenda Russell and she was sixteen - almost two years older than me. Undeterred, I asked her if she would like to meet another time and she gave me her home phone number to call and arrange a date.

Telephone conversations filled me with fear because talking into a handset exaggerated my stammer. It also seemed a bit cold and impersonal for such an important task but I was prepared to climb this rocky mountain for love.

A couple of weeks later, I went to the Plaza Ballroom on a lovely Friday evening to see the Pretty Things, the blues-based band of the moment. The opening act was a local band called Just Five. It was the first time that I ever had to queue to get into a gig. The line went all the way around the block.

As the crowd snaked its way towards the entrance, two guys came walking along the road towards the venue. One was tall and thin, the other short and thickset. The tall Mod one wore a trippy, hippy, flowery shirt. His diminutive companion had a mad shock of red hair, which ranged freely down over his shoulders. He wore a big orange coat, white ruffled shirt, cord trousers and animal skin high boots. They just had to be in a band. Turns out they were Billy McCoy and Sam Mahood, guitar player and lead singer, respectively, from Just Five, the support for that night.

Once inside, I made my way to the crash barrier at the front of the stage. We were packed in painfully tight but the excitement and anticipation of the show to come made such discomfort no ordeal whatsoever. There was also a bonus. None of those 15 and 16 year old girls minded being squashed in with us either.

Just Five hit the stage with a purpose. They were a Soul/R&B cross. Sam was a great showman with a gruff voice and charisma to spare. The band was tight and punchy and played through a set of fantastic covers - loads of Otis Redding, Sam and Dave stuff. The crowd were into them and, instantly, Just Five, became my favourite local band.

After they finished their set, the stage was cleared and made ready for the Pretty Things. I was totally unprepared for what came next.

The Pretty Things hit the stage like a hurricane. They were that physical. The drummer, Skip Alan, was bashing the kit like I'd never seen anyone do before. Phil May spat out the lyrics with venom. He poured beer onto the stage and brushed and mopped it with his long hair. It was a performance full of controlled chaos and attitude, hard and angry.

The audience didn't quite know how to react. It wasn't Soul. It wasn't Pop. It was something else. Today, you'd call it Punk/Blues. I'm not even sure if it was all that good but it didn't seem to matter. It was more dangerous and exciting than anything I had witnessed to date. Just Five were more musical, for sure, but not as edgy. The Pretty Things performance required a lack of inhibition that I doubt the young crowd had ever witnessed or even understood.

Against this musical free for all, Pride had been rehearsing. We had worked out some tunes and felt it was time for our first gig. We approached Cecil, a tall lithe man with balding slicked-back hair, a black suit and black patent dancing shoes.

Cecil gave us the nod and his right hand man, Oliver, a similar looking bloke, did the bookings. They let us play the break at a Saturday matinee. Support bands played in the middle of the two sets performed by the main act. When they took their break, we played. The lucky band for whom we played our debut, was Disowned, a competent, Soul/Pop, outfit, who were making a name for themselves around town. We didn't need to bring any amps, which was just as well. We just had to bring guitars, drumsticks and our dapper Mod selves.

Gerry, Ferg, Don, James and myself got there early, full of nervous excitement. Spud had to work at the fishmongers on Saturday mornings so he would come later after work. We had worked out a set list, which included songs such as: 'Watcha Gonna Do About It', 'The Kids are Alright', 'Gimme Some Lovin' and I would have my moment in the limelight singing 'I'll Be Back', an obscure Beatles album track.

At the very last minute, Spud made his entrance. Our chins dropped to our chests. We had assumed that our lead singer would go home to change after work, but he had come straight to the gig. Consequently, he was wearing a green, outdoor, waterproof jacket, a very worn pair of blue jeans and a pair of big, black workmen's boots with fish eyes glinting on the toe caps. He walked towards us with a miasma of malodorous smells emanating from him, oblivious to the impression and stench he gave off. No-one could bring themselves to say anything to him. Anyway, it was too late.

The Disowned announced their last number before the break. The crowd was primed and we were on. We settled ourselves onto the stage, adjusted control knobs, changed mike stand heights, all we needed was my count of four to start. It was a relief to actually start playing and we stumbled through the first few numbers.

We had seen more accomplished bands swap instruments for certain songs and it looked impressive. "Why not?" we thought. Don went behind the drum kit and I went to the front with Spud. Gerry debuted on bass for 'I'll Be Back'. We started but Don couldn't play a back beat so he just followed the melody line of the song, hitting the drums in time to that.

Gerry wrestled with the bass and I felt uncomfortably close to the audience, who had been stunned into silence. We had to abandon that song halfway through, get back to our positions sharpish and try another.

As our performance proceeded, it became obvious that the audience was retreating like an ebbing tide. The gap between them and us was widening by the minute. In the warm, humid conditions of the ballroom, Spud's fishy smell had become unbearable.

When we left the stage, we were quite pleased with ourselves and had the front to ask Cecil for our own show and an increase in wages. Cecil politely declined.

Trouble at Home

Brenda introduced me to her parents a few months later. Mine had yet to meet her. I was spending a lot of time at her house. It was yet another way for me not to be at home with my father. As time went on, I was drawn more and more to the safety and stability of their family life.

Brenda's father, Jim Russell, was Chief Inspector at Short Brothers and Harland Aircraft Factory, the second biggest employer in Belfast, after the shipyards. His signature had to be on every component that left the factory. Jim was a very authoritative, straight-talking family man with a big personality but, temperamentally, totally unlike my father. He was a Catholic and very pro-British. In fact, he volunteered to join the Royal Air Force in the war but was not permitted to because he was in a protected industry. His brother, Jack, however, was totally the opposite, totally Irish, and a nationalist.

I felt very comfortable with Jim. He had a great sense of humour and became a father figure to me. I was also a bit in awe of him because of his position at the factory, He had high expectations of me and I wasn't used to that.

Jim was a big music fan so we had that in common. After shopping on a Saturday afternoon, he would get a couple of gin and tonics and play records in his living room. It was good to see someone have a couple of drinks, have a laugh and be able to turn the switch off. He had self-control and that impressed me. The experience couldn't have come at a better time for me in my teenage years.

Unlike my mother, Brenda's mother, Maureen, did not go out to work but was a busy housewife. Brenda's brother, Brian, who was seven years younger than Brenda, and I became very close friends.

In summary, the Russells were a fairly well off, middle class family and their world was very secure and ordered in comparison to mine. I would go there at every opportunity not just to see Brenda but to experience another way of living and point of view.

Early in 1967, I lost my job at the off-licence. No reason was given but I had my suspicions that they had their suspicions that I was pilfering the stock. So now, after school, us four - Gerry, Fergie, Clarkie and myself - The Four Musketeers as we fondly called ourselves - would strike out for town to hang out or I would meet Brenda from work and invite myself to her house for the evening.

Meanwhile, my home life was becoming more troubled. My dad came home most nights having had a good drink after work, which was always cause for an argument between my mum and him. My bedroom was directly over the living room and kitchen area, whereas the rest of my brothers and sisters were up in the loft room. I lay in bed listening to the low drone and high pitch of bickering. I desperately tried to get to sleep before he came home but to no avail. I grew to expect it but I never got used to it.

One winter night, my father came back at about ten and, almost immediately, an argument started. The next thing I heard was the front door slamming and my mum in hysterics calling my name. I ran downstairs and she told me he'd gone in search of my Aunt Sally's husband, Sammy. The argument was about my dad buying round after round of drinks for everyone in the pub. Money was tight at home and my mother had objected. My father judged that the only person who could, or would, have told my mother was Sammy. Possibly, Sammy had told my aunt, who had then informed my mother.

Sally worked late at the Ormonde Cafe. Sammy often met her there and they walked home together. Dad had headed there. My mum sent me to get a good friend of my dad's from the next road to try to reason with him. His name was Tommy Lauden. I ran there barefoot.

By the time, we both got to the cafe, the damage was done. My mum, my sister, Bernadette, and two policemen were there restraining my Dad. A couple of glass cake containers on the counter were smashed. The police must have been close by because things were under control and no-one had been hurt. Since both Mum and Sally worked at the cafe, the owner didn't press charges. I'm sure some financial remuneration had to be made though. Things were never the same again between my father and Sammy.

On another occasion, my father arrived home in a similar state and was confronted by a barrage of questions and criticism from my mother. He decided to drive back to the pub, the consequences of which were more damage to his marriage and three dented cars that he hit on the way.

Alcohol has the strangest effect on certain people. The flip side of my Dad was that, when sober, he would have travelled the earth to help us all. He never missed a day's work except when he had major surgery on stomach ulcers that almost killed him.

My Dad would also drive the band anywhere. One day, we left our house in his lorry to be dropped off in town. When we turned right out of Fairview St onto the Crumlin Rd, we had to stop at a zebra crossing. Two young 'greasers' in their late teens were crossing from left to right. They wore drainpipe trousers, leather jackets, turned up collars, winklepickers and had shiny, Brylcreemed hair slicked back in DAs - ducks' arses. They also wore an 'attitude', which they signalled to one and all by sauntering slowly across the road in their own good time. It seemed to be taking forever and my father snapped. His quick temper was always waiting to strike, drunk or sober.

The cab door opened, he jumped down. The other lads with me in the cab fell silent but only I knew what was coming. My dad grabbed the two greasers by the scruff of their turned up collars and dragged them to the other side of the road, pushing them up against some black railings. We couldn't hear what he was saying to them but their heads were nodding frantically in agreement.

My Dad got back in the cab without saying a word and we drove off. To be honest, we were all secretly chuffed at what he had done. My father's idea of respect was old school. His sense of justice was immediate and, like his temper, quick and harsh. On occasion though, it was fair enough.

My mother wore many 'hats'. All the usual jobs of running a home, knitting, sewing, cooking, cleaning, accounting and caring for her husband and six children. As well as cleaning the Ormonde cafe on Friday and Saturday nights from midnight to three in the morning after the cafe closed, she also worked full time at The Victoria Cafe in Victoria Square. My sister, Bernadette, and I would often go to help her clean the Ormonde. It was plain to see that it was all getting too much for her but it didn't stop her from buying me a new Premier drum kit when I needed to upgrade.

With our final school exams completed, it was time to look towards the future and gainful employment. The year before, we had sat a series of exams called the Junior Grammar and Junior Tech. These were to assess if you had a practical or academic mind. I did really well in Junior Tech. The subjects included woodwork, metalwork and technical drawing. With this in mind, Jim Russell suggested that I apply for an apprenticeship as an airframe fitter at Short Bros and Harland aircraft factory on Queen's Island.

The factory sat between Harland and Wolf shipbuilding yards and the Naval yards. My parents were very enthusiastic about this so Jim got the application forms and an interview was set up.

Jim and my father had bonded somewhat over music and a pint, though Jim didn't enjoy a pint as much as my father did. My relationship with Brenda meant we were 'steadies' and as time went on and the political landscape changed, my parents were very pleased that I stayed more often with the Russells because it kept me away from flashpoint areas during the Troubles.

I couldn't say for sure but I can only assume that a recommendation from Jim Russell, as the senior inspector, would have held some sway. Jim was a very straight kind of a man so I don't know; all I do know is the interview went well. I was accepted as an apprentice and in September 1968, a new and mind altering stage of my life would begin.

In the meantime, there was summer.

Get the Look

As word got around school about our band, Gerry and I lived up to our reputations as trendsetters. We dressed more and more Mod. I had my hair Stevie Marriott-style with a middle parting. Gerry tried to style his hair too but it didn't work because it's really curly. I once overheard a boy at school say, "That McAvoy has the clothes, but O'Neill has the hair."

(Later in my career, towards the end of my time with Rory, Stevie Marriott, whose style I had mimicked and who I had so much admired as a kid, asked me to be his drummer. I wish I'd taken him up on his offer but that's life.)

I created my own Mod clothes. I took the collar from one old shirt and sewed it on another to make a two-tone shirt. I sewed thick epaulettes to a blazer and viola, a reefer jacket. Another friend, Roddy Hasson, lent me a pair of purple hipsters with a two-inch, white belt. So, with them and the green desert boots that my mum bought me, my hand-crafted, two-tone, blue and white shirt, my reefer jacket and my hair, I was good to go.

One Saturday afternoon at home, I presented myself fit to promenade the city centre with the others. My dad took one look and stated that if I saw him in the street, I was to cross the road and not acknowledge him. He would do likewise. Right enough, I must have looked like a dog's dinner to him but, in my head, I was the big dog's bollocks.

When the school holidays arrived in late June, it was my first summer without any job prospects. My father had an idea that I should join him, my grandfather and Uncle Michael at the docks loading and unloading ships, or 'boats' as they called them. My mother thought he was crazy taking me down there but he got his way. First, I needed a pair of work boots and my father duly found me a second-hand pair that were ever so slightly too small.

When the day arrived, my mum gave us both a packed lunch and we set off in Dad's old, two-tone Morris Oxford to pick up the others. It was a beautiful morning and we drove all the way along York St to the docks and parked the car.

I don't know what my granddad and uncle thought when they saw me. There I was, 15 years old, skinny as a string tie, with a pinched look on my face from the grief those second-hand boots were giving me.

They walked, while I minced, towards a raised platform. Uncle Michael and two other men climbed the steps at the side that gave them an aerial view of the dockside. Men, real men, appeared out of nowhere until they were a crowd of 50 to 60 strong gathered around the three on the platform. Then, the selection process began.

It was a scene right out of 'On The Waterfront'. My uncle and the two others called out names and men stepped to one side to where the foremen were collecting work gangs of 15 or 20. The group of men to choose from shrank steadily until all that was left was me and one other scrawny individual.

My father finally came over and said, "There's no work for you today, son. Away on home."

On the plus side, the morning was warming up but that three mile hike in those boots was a killer. I didn't go back to the docks again.

My first proper job interview was at a tailor's on Clifton Street. Mum saw an ad in the window for a trainee and, because I was adept at adapting my clothes, she thought it would be a good idea. I went for an interview but didn't get the job. Maybe, it's because my mum insisted on coming with me but it could just as well have been the RC school uniform that I was wearing to look presentable. In those times, in Belfast, you just didn't know.

Over the summer months while Brenda and I dated, we met regularly at Clarke's. She worked in a chemist shop and, because I didn't want her to know my age, I told her that I worked full time in an off-licence. I soon realised that taking girls out was an expensive business so I soon needed another source of income.

I turned to a life of petty crime, no other word for it. It came to me one day while working in the office storeroom that the lady in the shop wouldn't miss the odd quarter of whiskey or vodka. I took one every other Friday to sell to some older guys - Tommy Donalson and his mate, Meaky, who were always at the dances at Clarke's.

I was 'flush' and things went famously with Brenda until my conscience got the better of me; not about the vodka, about my age. I eventually confessed to her the nearly two year age difference between us and that I was still at school. She said she needed time to think and consulted her friend, Anne McGinty, who was the girl I had first seen her with at Clarke's.

I really thought that that was the end of it. After a week or so, I rang her and she told me that the jury was in and the verdict was that we should carry on as we were. After a while, Anne began to go out with a nineteen year old English guitarist called John Cox, who had joined Just Five.

The lively Belfast music scene at the time was attracting people to the city. Another English guitarist on the scene, Roy Abbott, formed a great four piece called Cheese that did obscure stuff such as Sharon Tandy covers. Both Charlie McCracken and John Wilson played with Cheese and the two of them subsequently formed the second phase rhythm section of Rory Gallagher's band, Taste.

I spent the first time in John's company telling him how I had almost worn out Cream's album 'Fresh Cream' and how I could only dream of playing with a band like that. (I did eventually play with Jack Bruce when he joined Rory onstage. You can YouTube it.)

Anyway, after I had gone on and on about Cream, John told me about a new group hitting the UK that he thought were better than Cream. I thought he had lost his mind but he was, of course, talking about the Jimi Hendrix Experience.

The Blues and Jazz mix of both these great bands had a big influence on my musical awareness. It was because of Cream that I got to know about John Mayall and Graham Bond, and the Blues and Jazz that was the source of their musical lineage.

The Sixties in Belfast was a time of a great confluence of musical styles that unashamedly fed off each other. Nothing was considered niche. We were as much in awe of the Hollies as the Small Faces or Buffalo Springfield. The post-war impact of the US servicemen, who had brought their Soul and Blues sounds with them, added to the richness of Belfast's music scene.

Van Morrison tells how he first heard Sonny Terry and Brownie Mcghee on the street where he was born. In fact, Van's father had one of the largest record collections in the North at the time. He'd gleaned the music from his time living in Detroit, Michigan.

This kind of diverse music scene was not represented anywhere but in the record stores and people's record collections. It wasn't widely played on the radio or the television, so kids would spend their days browsing the record shops and hearing the latest stuff in the listening booths.

Checkpoint

We were just kids and practical jokes between us were commonplace. There was always mischief with Ferg around or some witty comment of his that would make us laugh. Once, he threw Jim's schoolbooks into the luggage rack of a Routemaster bus as it was pulling away and heading for the Short Strand Bus Terminus. Jim was so upset that we all agreed to take the next bus to the depot to retrieve them.

As Jim went up to the top deck, I grabbed hold of his legs for a lark. Fergie grabbed his arms. The arm of his coat came off in the struggle. Jim was mad with us but he never could swear. All he could say was 'Good frig, Ferguson! Good frig!"

Years later when Gerry and I were in Belfast to help produce a single for a young band called the Bank Robbers, four of us headed to the studio in Bangor in Ferg's little, two-seater, sports car.

It was a lovely, warm, dreamy day, the soft top was rolled back and there was no pressure from anyone or anything, Gerry and Ferg were sitting in the two seats, Tony Heading, an old mate, and I were perched on the rolled back roof. Shades on, hair in the wind, we might as well have been on the French Riviera, we felt that good. Just before we hit the dual carriageway going towards Bangor, there was an impromptu British Army and RUC road block. These were the heavy times in Northern Ireland and every car up ahead was being stopped and searched.

When we reached the checkpoint, we were approached by two grim-faced, middle-aged police officers carrying machine guns. In the low slung car, we came up to their knees. They took one look at us with the hair and the attitude and we knew we were off to a bad start. They checked Ferg's licence, asked us our business, where we were heading and why. They were deadly serious. It was pretty tense.

After all that, one of them asked Ferg if he knew that it was illegal to have three passengers in a two-seater car. We had no answer to that. He then asked Ferg what the engine capacity was.

"One thousand cc, officer," Ferg replied. The officer suggested that he'd be better off with a motorbike to which Ferg breezily replied, "But you couldn't get three passengers on a motorbike, sir." Miraculously, they waved us through.

Roddy Hasan and Liam Corr were two friends from the Scouts. Liam's brother, Eamonn, played the bagpipes in the Scout band. I got on really well with him. I didn't realise at the time but their dad, Arthur Corr, had been associated with the old brigade IRA along with Joe Cahill, who had been prominent in the brigade in the 1950s.

Roddy lived with his mother in Victoria Flats, next to the British Army and Territorial Army barracks off the Antrim Road, where, once upon a time, I delivered newspapers - a job that soon would be too dangerous to do. We had all been good mates for a while but I hadn't seen much of him or Liam since the Scouts. Then, they started coming to Cecil Clarke's.

I'm sure among a group of lads, there is always a girl that all the boys fancy. Jeannie Macken was that girl for us. She was 14, gorgeous and bubbly, long dark hair, five foot four and with a lovely figure. Before I met Brenda, I went out with her for a while. I was gutted when she dumped me after about a month despite my best efforts to seduce her. More upsetting than that was the fact that she started going out with Roddy Hasan.

Time passed though, hearts were mended and things moved on. One night, by chance, Don Doneghy, our bass player, took this girl to a party that Roddy and Jeannie were at. I don't know what the state of play was between Roddy and Jeannie but when Don met Jeannie, it was lust at first sight. Don ended up walking her home that night.

The band was due to play at Cecil's a few weeks later. It was a really busy night at the club and after we had finished our set, we were all sitting around the bar area drinking Cokes and Fanta, Don and Jeannie included. Spirits were high. We were six months in and getting the hang of performing.

Out of the blue, Roddy, Liam and some mates turned up and the atmosphere changed for the worse. When Jeannie saw Roddy, she made for the Ladies' toilets, but this didn't put our Roddy off. Fired up with jealous rage, he charged in after her. All Don could do was hover tensely at the door.

It was like a moment suspended in time until Roddy burst back out through the doors and rained blows on Don's head and face. Don was rendered completely defenceless. When Liam Corr joined in the beating, I jumped up and ran over to help Don. Within seconds, the rest of the band piled in followed by Roddy's mates and a few reckless bystanders who fancied a scrap.

In the end, there were eight or ten people punching the crap out of each other. Hands were grabbing and gouging, arms swinging and fists thumping when suddenly it all went quiet. DJ Jim Clark had pulled the music and Cecil and his right hand man, Oliver, a lean, fit guy, started peeling us off one another. Everyone in the place was watching us. The atmosphere was awful. No one had any lasting injuries but Roddy and his crew were chucked out and barred.

We were afraid that we would not be able to play there again, but we did. Roddy and Jeannie got back together and are together to this day. Years later, Don told us that he was driving down the road when he saw this woman walking on the pavement that he thought was rather attractive. When she turned around, it was Jeannie. So, there you go, Jeannie hasn't lost it and Don definitely still fancies her.

Judased

Another band, the Yaks, had begun to build its reputation at St Gabriel's. It comprised: Brian Donaghy, who was a great little drummer (rumour had it that, eventually, he moved to Dublin to help people keep to the beat there by opening a porn shop); Rab McCollough on guitar, who, like me, had a stammer but sang and played like Steve Winwood; Mo Toal, who was Gerry's cousin and a really nice bass player.

The Yaks did great covers of the Spencer Davis Group's 'Gimme Some Lovin'' and Small Faces' numbers. We did a gig with them in the hall next to Holy Cross Chapel. It turned out to be a great night. These were guys we could relate to and were a bit of competition, which is always a good thing.

We kept on rehearsing. Such was our commitment that on one occasion, Gerry and I pushed an amp two miles from our school to the rehearsal rooms at Don's house, while we were supposed to be sitting exams - GCE Maths, I think it was. We transported gear in the luggage compartment of a Routemaster bus and even in a black taxi - that took some persuading.

After hearing Rab sing though, we realised our man, Spud, wasn't cutting it. Since, Gerry and I were most likely to see him at school before rehearsals, we were given the unpleasant task of throwing him off the good ship, Pride, his stinking boots and all.

We spied Spud in the playground at break and took our chance. As we approached him, I became aware that I was alone. The coward McAvoy had done a runner. I had been 'Judased'- our gang's term for being betrayed. I broke the bad news to Frank that his services were no longer required. Needless to say, he didn't take it well. He didn't exactly cry but he did swear a lot. This early experience in broken deals may have led Spud to choose a career in law, at which he is very successful.

We found another good singer pretty quickly. His name was Tom Kidd. He was a few years older than us and a much more experienced performer. He was good looking, which the girls liked, of course. He fronted the band with some style.

We raised our game from then on and, playing up to three gigs a week sometimes, got more proficient. The highlight with that line up was playing at 'Inst. College', i.e. The Royal Belfast Academical Institution, in the centre of Belfast. It was a packed gig and we went down a storm. Things were going great until the usual personality clashes and 'creative differences' got in the way.

Tom and Don 'The Butcher' Donaghy clashed. Tom decided to hang up his microphone and another front man was required. We heard about Danny Watt, who lived in Hollywood, halfway between Belfast and Bangor on Belfast lough.

I thought he was by far the best singer that we'd had to date. He had a great, soulful voice but, unfortunately, his time with us was short lived, even though we were getting gigs and our reputation was slowly growing. With Danny gone, we needed to fulfil a booking at the Parochial Hall, next to Holy Cross Chapel. Someone - Fergie probably - had the brainwave, and the front, to ask the great man, Sam Mahood, to play with us. Sam had just parted company from Just Five and, incredibly, agreed to do the gig.

Sam was a gentle and polite man, nothing like his stage image. He came to Don's cellar to rehearse the day before the show and was ever so grateful when we presented him with a whole plate of cheese sandwiches when we had our break.

On the night, the gig was pretty packed and Sam put on the full stage show that he was famous for. There was a little extension to the front of the stage for the singer to promenade and strut his stuff. When some girl tried to grab him, he seemed to stagger as if he were being pulled into the audience. Gerry went to save him but Sam turned to Gerry and mouthed, "It's all part of the act." We had a great deal to learn.

A little while later, we played that venue again, with the Yaks, our old pals from school, headlining. They weren't as pally as we thought. Rab McCullough asked Don, our bass player to join them as their man, Mo Toal, was emigrating to Canada. Don, the traitor, accepted the offer.

We quickly recruited a new bass player, another friend of Fergie's from school, Adrian Kennedy. With Adrian came a name change. Many suggestions were put forward, including 'Traffic', but we decided on 'Deep Joy', a name suggested by Tony Heading. It was the catchphrase of surreal comedian, Stanley Unwin, who was popular at the time. He had a show called 'Ogdens' Old Walnut Flake' on which the Small Faces based the name for their album 'Ogdens' Nut Gone Flake'.

Deep Joy did some gigs at Cecil Clarke's, which went down very well. So much so, that Cecil organised a photo shoot with the local press for us. The shoot was in the car showroom beneath Cecil's dance studios. It had a plate glass window the length of the showroom. One night, Gerry witnessed a fight in front of it. One teenager was pushed through the glass and fell as if a chair had been tugged from under him. He ended up sitting among stalagmites of glass, cuts everywhere. Gerry pulled him up and the kid, bleeding profusely, ran as fast as he could towards the Mater Hospital.

As it happened, Mo's Canadian offer fell through and Don was left without a band at all. He thought there would be no hard feelings about him leaving us in the lurch and called round my house one day, for old times' sake. He wanted to come back and he expected us all to be there, as we often would be. Instead, Don was greeted by my father, who hadn't taken kindly to him walking out on his comrades. He gave Don short shrift and called him some very unpleasant names, poor bloke.

Alas, Adrian Kennedy didn't last very long, either. He wanted to move to London. He 'got real' there and became a London bobby. With Adrian gone, we were now at a crossroads trying to be a Blues band with nothing to sell. There were so many really good bands across every genre in the late Sixties in Belfast. The competition was fierce. You had to keep one step ahead.

The benchmark song in 1967 was 'Hey Joe' by The Jimi Hendrix Experience. It was a hard one to emulate because of the sheer virtuosity of that band. Billy McCoy, guitarist of Just Five, was in Cecil Clarke's one night when we launched into this song. He walked down the steps and stood in front of us to check it out. Billy could play it perfectly, of course. He listened for not very long, slowly shook his head before walking sadly back up the steps. We could hardly face each other after, never mind him. I don't want to point the finger or anything but Gerry was doing Hendrix's bit.

Following the lead of Cream and Jimi Hendrix, Rory Gallagher's Taste were making waves all around town with their own unique style. Our confidence in our own abilities was somewhat inflated at that time. If *they* could do it, we thought, why couldn't *we* take on that challenge? We determined to continue playing Blues-orientated music, with some 'underground' influences and sprinkled here and there some obscure pop. All three of us would share the singing duties.

The first major problem we had to overcome - a not insubstantial one in view of our competition - was the fact that we had no bass player. So, with a little bit of verbal prodding and out and out threats from Fergie, young McAvoy was persuaded to give it a try. Unfortunately, Gerry didn't have a bass guitar and his Dad wasn't keen on the instrument change. Gerry had been having electric guitar lessons from a jazz musician and his Dad had high hopes of Gerry being the next Wes Montgomery. In the end, he fell in line and agreed to buy Gerry a bass guitar. I asked my mum and dad to sign the HP agreement so we could get him a bass amp.

Gerry, Fergie and I went with my parents to Crymbles Music Store one Saturday afternoon to sort things out. As we left the store, I looked back to my parents and saw them skipping along hand in hand. It was a lovely, tender moment and it was like a ray of light breaking through the dark. I saw the innocent sweethearts' love that they had once had and I felt really happy that day, for them, and for me.

Frustration

Early that summer, Gerry and I were asked to do a couple of gigs with a band called the Carpetbaggers. They comprised a keyboard player, Norman Fusco, a bass guitarist, Derek Thompson, and the main man and singer, Paul Little, who also played guitar. We were to play in their rhythm section - Gerry playing rhythm guitar.

It was something we did regularly in our future careers. On a much bigger scale, a lot further down the line, we did this while working for the British blues band, Nine Below Zero, myself on drums and Gerry on bass.

We spent seven weeks in Canada with NBZ rehearsing and touring with Alannah Miles, who had the hit 'Black Velvet'. She was being managed by Miles Copeland, who also managed Sting, and to whose label we had signed in 1994. NBZ were the opening act and then Gerry and I formed the rhythm section for her band.

We came back home for nine days, rehearsed with Alvin Lee and went back to the States to repeat the same formula with him for a month. Miles thought it would be a great way to break NBZ Stateside. One of the highlights of the Alvin Lee tour was when Bruce Springsteen's sax player, Clarence Clemons, came along and jammed with us in San Francisco.

Back in Northern Ireland in 1968, the two dates with the Carpetbaggers were in the Stella Ballroom, Dublin, and good old Cecil Clarke's in Belfast. The Carpetbaggers were more pop orientated than we were in Deep Joy but they were still a good band. It would be our first trip to Dublin to play and we were all on a high.

After a quick rehearsal, we arranged the place and time to meet the Carpetbaggers. Unfortunately, they told Fergie that he wouldn't be needed even though we had assumed that he would be playing. (Fergie took the news pretty well considering. Anyway, the next morning he turned up anyway.)

When we arrived at Concetta's Fish and Chip Shop in Carlisle Circus - or The Last Supper Saloon as we called it because so many people had got shot coming out of it - it was clear that things were not going to go as smoothly as we had anticipated. For a start, the band's hired van wasn't big enough for our entourage - Clarkie, Fergie and Brenda - and all the equipment. This was mine and Brenda's first illicit weekend away together so she was *definitely* in the van. (Gerry had no girlfriend but he was always optimistic that he would find one at the gig.)

The Carpetbaggers decided that, since the two Jims were not playing, they needn't come. So, we waved our mates goodbye, no hard feelings. Not to be defeated, they managed to get some money together and got to Dublin by train.

We arrived at Mrs Heaney's guest house in Stillorgan in the late afternoon and were allocated our rooms. Brenda and I were very nervous about checking in together just in case Mrs Heaney sussed our marital status, or rather, lack of it. I was only 16 (and a half) and Ireland was a very Catholic country back then. It went surprisingly smoothly. Mrs Heaney had a lot of bands from the Stella stay so she was probably more broad minded than we had given her credit for. The bags were dropped off in our rooms and we had to rush off.

The Stella Ballroom was one of the few places that booked Pop as well as show bands. The latter did mostly material from the Top Twenty. Pop groups played more varied music and even had original material. The Carpetbaggers' big tune was 'Frustration', which was ironic as the cards were to fall for me that night.

When the chorus came around, Paul Little would hold his guitar on his right hip and thrust his pelvis forward three times to each syllable of the title. This was considered cutting edge. You have to remember that this was a time when Dave, Dee, Dozy, Beaky, Mick and Titch, were at the height of their fame. They most definitely did not do pelvic thrusting.

The show went well - five to six hundred kids, to be conservative, turned out - and we trooped back to Mrs Heaney's in high spirits. Gerry and Norman had got their hands on some booze and it took some time for us all to get settled in our rooms.

Brenda and I had only just got into bed, got our clothes off and our hands on each other when there was a rain of pebbles on our window. When I looked outside, there were the two Jims with a Belfast band called Sunshine in tow. Instead of coming to see us, the two Jims had gone to The Five Club to see them instead. That was a really cool place to play and, as a bonus, somehow, they had blagged Deep Joy a gig there in a couple of weeks' time. I had to let them in.

The commotion stirred everyone into life again and, before we knew it, mine and Brenda's small love nest was packed with the two Jims, the Sunshine Band and the Carpetbaggers.

Gerry came in with some girl and sat on the end of our bed. Sunshine's roadie, Eric Knight, sat on Brenda's side and I swear he had his beady eye on her. She had the bedclothes tucked up under her chin while I remained vigilant. Gerry informed the Jims that there were two other girls staying so off they went to find them and bring them back to the room. Norman Fusco wandered about pissed.

Eventually, everyone paired up somehow and left us in peace only for another commotion to start up a little while later when Norman, disorientated with the drink, came crashing through the B&B.

There was no sleep till breakfast, which Mrs Heaney made us all the next morning and served it up with a straight face and no mention of the previous night's farce.

The journey home to Belfast was a quiet affair. On the downside, Brenda and I had not consummated our relationship. Neither Fergie nor Clarkie had succeeded in persuading their girls to step up either. On the upside, the band had a gig at the Five. Deep Joy.

Gig at the Five

As time went on, we began to attract some 'interesting' people or 'characters', if you will, who wanted to work with us. We had a manager, of sorts. His name was Raymond Boyd and he thought he was Brian Epstein.

Ray was just a bit older than us. He worked as an engineer on the ships in Belfast Lough. You would never have thought it from his appearance. He wore a mohair suit and always had a thick coating of 'Tanfastic' applied to his face. Possibly to hide the stench of engine oil, he made free with Old Spice aftershave. His hair was naturally thin and sprayed with 'Cossack' hair lacquer, which made it look as if a small spider had spun a glistening cobweb around his head. He didn't have proper sideburns so he grew his hair long in strips around his face. He had to keep pressing them down to make sure they didn't stick out.

Paul Nolan, a friend of Fergie's, nicknamed him 'Musty' because he looked as if he'd stepped out of an old wardrobe. His name from then on was 'Musty The Manager'. He would insist on counting us as we went on stage to make sure we were all present. The gigs were coming in anyway so Ray really wasn't anything more than a front and he didn't last long. He was happy enough to go considering the money he wasn't on.

Our next manager, Tony 'Eric' Heading, was Musty's fashion negative. He was pretty eccentric and always on the cutting edge of things new. When Cream hit the scene, Eric faithfully embraced the Clapton image including the permed hair. A busty girl called Della Feely was his hairdresser. (Gerry went out with her for a short while.) When 'Eric' first went home with his new Feely/Clapton hairdo, his granny instructed him to "take that hat off your head".

On one occasion, Ferg and Eric were on their way to a party in Brompton Park, in Ardoyne. On the bus, they met Van Morrison and Mick Cox, an English guitar player, who had been playing around Belfast. They were going to the same party. Van had had a massive hit with 'Here Comes The Night' in the UK and came back to Belfast to chill at the weekends.

So, there's Van and Mick in their long maxi coats, Van with a bow in the back of his hair and Ferg and Eric looking as they did. When they got off the bus at Ardoyne, some greaser geezer, who was hanging around the corner gave them the stink-eye and the foursome nipped off quick smart to the party. Fergie pulled someone else's girlfriend there and they had a bit of a snog and a grope. When Ferg went to the toilet, the boyfriend followed him in and pissed all over his flared jeans.

We had a roadie with very thin, pointed features. We called him Seamus The Greyhound - 'Seamie' for short. He drove a Morris 1000 car with some strange modifications on it including a bedside lampshade that hung from the interior light. The guy never stopped talking. One day, Gerry and I were with him on the way to Bangor for a drive - we'd probably bunked off school. He was talking and looking around so much that he drove under the back of a tipper truck that had stopped in traffic.

Our gig at the Five Club would be our debut south of the border and we needed to get it right. We had one drum kit, Premier, one six string electric guitar, Vox AC30, one bass amp and speaker - no cabinet - and one bass guitar, Fender. We just needed one PA system and one van.

Someone Fergie knew agreed to lend us a PA system but, with just three days to go, getting the van was proving problematic. The Greyhound told us that his uncle had a van and that he might lend it to us. So, Seamie, Fergie and I went all along to Old Ardoyne to see Seamie's uncle, 'Jungle' McBride.

The house was a two up, two down, terraced house, one of those where the front door led straight into the living room. A middle-aged woman was changing a baby's nappy on a table as we walked in. A young girl hovered in the background while a stocky man, closing in on 30, washed his feet in a basin by the fireplace. 'Jungle', his feet submerged in the water, stared at us menacingly, to put it mildly. We stood whey-faced by the door while Seamie asked about the van. To our surprise, he agreed, for a small fee.

119

It was all going marvelously well. Come Saturday morning at about nine, Seamie arrived at mine in the van. Someone suggested that it might be a good idea for him to fill up with petrol first so off he went again. On his return, we loaded up ready for the off. All we had to do was pick up the PA system.

With the engine on and in first gear, the van wouldn't move. My dad came to see what the problem was. His immediate assessment was a burned out clutch. It transpired that Seamie had been driving around with the handbrake on and had ruined what was left of it.

"This van is going nowhere," my old man announced.

He came to the rescue though and helped us find another van and agreed to drive it. There was one for rent next to my Mum's cafe in Victoria Square. Ferg's Mum put up the cost of the rental - which she never did get back.

It was 12.30 when we set off. Only then did we inform my dad that we had to go to Enniskillen to pick up the PA system. No motorway back then and Enniskillen is 65 miles west. Showing uncharacteristic restraint, all my dad muttered was "Holy Jesus".

Nevertheless, we arrived at the Five on Stephen's Green just after ten that evening and just over three hours late. Our very recently promoted manager, Clarkie, was dispatched to tell them we had arrived but we couldn't stop on the one-way system. We had to keep driving around the block. As we approached the club again, Clarkie was outside shaking his head from side to side.

"We're too late. They won't let us play," he shouted as we crept by. Fergie yelled at him most unsympathetically and sent him back into the club to tell them what's what while we went around the block again. He was back out minutes later with good news. It turned out to be our worst mistake of many that day.

The place was packed as we set the gear up. Ferg plugged in his brand new, and as yet unplayed, Harmony StratoTone, triggering a screaming feedback that never stopped. My dad chose that moment to leave for the pub. Unfortunately, we had to play immediately, feedback or no.

When Gerry hit the bass, the speaker bounced across the stage like a beach ball as Fergie's guitar wailed inconsolably. The drum set was fine but what could I do? It was a total calamity and our eclectic mix of material and experimental sound was just too much for the crowd, who backed away from us into the depths of the club as if we still stank of fish.

Gerry said the final nail in our coffin was our disastrous attempt at Skip Bifferty's 'On Love' - a classic West Coast underground tune. To our credit, with the help of Clarkie, we were always on the lookout for quirky songs for our set. We also did a version of the Casuals' 'Windy'.

Nothing, though, was going to save us that night. I can't remember if we even got paid. I do remember that it was a long, long, miserable drive home. Our troubles weren't over. Two days later, Jungle came looking for his van with a terrifying bloke for backup. We'd totally forgotten about his van. We had parked it out of sight on a junction round the corner from my house. When I answered the door and saw Jungle and his mate, all I could do was tell them where the van was and what had happened. There were some raised voices and my old man came down to see what the problem was.

For once, in a very controlled manner, he invited Jungle into our house, shutting the door in his mate's face. My father's approach had a calming effect on Jungle and the discussion that followed was surprisingly reasonable. I got a telling off afterwards for not telling Jungle about the van but that was it.

The review of our Five performance in Dublin's 'Spotlight' magazine appeared shortly after. It said bluntly that Deep Joy were nothing of the sort and should never return to Dublin.

We did some strange gigs around this time. On one occasion, we played the Orange Hall in Larne, a predominantly Protestant seaport and industrial town, which was a reckless band decision given the times. It turned out to be a really good night and we ended up bedding down on the stage to sleep after for want of a place to stay.

On another occasion, my dad agreed to drive us to Magherafelt, a very Catholic town near Lough Neagh, the largest inland area of water in the British Isles. Magherafelt is a small town but the biggest in the south of County Derry and the social, economic and political centre of the area. It suffered a great deal in the Troubles. Eleven people were killed there by bombs or shootings.

Dad decided to invite my grandfather, 'Big Charlie' O'Neill, along to keep him company. Once we had loaded out equipment into the gig, the two Charlies went down the pub.

The gig was in the town hall and it was almost full with a 200 strong crowd. We knew the equipment had issues but we hoped for the best. Things were going great until the PA amp started to play up. One of the valves wasn't seated properly but, if it was held in position, it worked perfectly. Clarkie sat on stage with his finger on the rogue valve munching his way through a packet of Spangles for the entire two hour show. Just before we finished, 'Big Charlie and 'Wee Charlie' bowled in.

Big Charlie was fully refreshed, shall we say. Like my father, he had been a bit of an accordion player in his day and decided that he would come up and sing a few songs with us for an encore. We watched in horror at his enthusiastic approach.

It was a wooden stage with wooden steps up and he was on the second rung preparing for his big entrance, when my Dad caught up with him. It took all his powers of persuasion to get Big Charlie to realise it would not be a cool thing to do and to save the singsong for the trip home in the van, which he did, thank God.

Apprentice

It had been a great summer but September and Short Brothers and Harland were approaching fast and I began to feel insecure and unsure. That summer, for once, I had been free, doing what I wanted. After the camaraderie of the band, what I now faced alone was all a bit daunting.

It sounds daft but all my friends seemed more confident, bright and dynamic than I was. I certainly didn't feel any of those things. I've spoken about it since to Clarkie and he was surprised. He had always considered me sound - "a safe pair of hands" - but the truth was, I drew a lot of confidence by being around the band. I felt I was losing that. Working for Shorts would be a real departure - an unknown quantity.

My stammer got worse. On a Sunday night at the Russell's, Jim would hold a family quiz based on the Sunday newspapers. It filled me with dread to be asked a question and I'd just shake my head even if I knew the answers. I just couldn't get it out. They tried to include me but I couldn't get involved.

No matter how I felt, it was time to get organised for my first proper job. I had to have passport pictures taken for my security pass. I had to buy a micrometer, vernier caliper, inside and outside calipers and a pair of green overalls to flag my apprentice status. I'd let my hair grow through the summer but that had to come off. Shorts had a strict short hair policy for those working machinery such as lathes etc.

Monday, the second of September, 1968, arrived and I caught the bus that dropped me off at the gates of the Apprentice School. There were 101 new starts that year and just eight were Catholics. Surprisingly, there was another boy from St Gabriel's, who eventually became a welder on the Rolls Royce engine cowlings for the state-of-the art RB211 engine.

The idea was to spend a year at the school learning every aspect of aircraft production before being allocated a job title. The school was next to the missile department, which was high security. Apprentices had security clearance and could walk through it on the way to the factory. It was like being in a Sixties spy film with all the comic book big dials, rockets, tools and gadgets. It was spick and span, a really cool place, all futuristic and high tech. I actually got a schoolboy thrill being part of it.

Inside the school was like a mini shop floor with different departments teaching all aspects of aeronautical engineering. It had a lecture room and in one corner an old WW2 Comet, which had been taken apart and put back together many times by green clad apprentices looking for stored knowledge from the past.

Mr Black, the head instructor and lecturer, looked like ex-RAF, immaculately turned out with shiny, black, side-parted hair. He appeared very strict but he had a sense of humour. Mr Boyd was the next in command and co-ordinated the day to day affairs of the school. He was a fresh-faced young man of about 30, the clean living type.

As the year progressed, Mr Boyd visibly aged and started looking tired and worried. The Troubles were beginning and it seemed to affect him deeply. He asked me on a couple of occasions what I thought about the Civil Rights Movement and Bernadette Devlin, in particular. He asked me if I supported them. I said that I didn't.

At that time, it was the truth. I was 17, politically uninformed and unaware of what was going on. Whatever political and religious persuasion he came from, he obviously felt threatened by this, to date, relatively peaceful rebellion. He had always been upbeat and down with the lads. It was strange that he asked me out of everyone but the conflict in his own mind changed him.

As for me, I was always treated OK at the school. There was never an atmosphere. Nevertheless, it may not have occurred to poor Mr Boyd that there was something in the numbers. There were, as I said, just eight Catholic apprentices and, even though I didn't think about it at the time, that was a clue to the discontent in the Province that Mr Boyd was picking up on.

The working hours were between 7.45a.m. and 3.45p.m. with a 40 minute lunch break. I was home by 4.30, washed and changed and ready for the evening. My first wage packet of four pounds, thirteen shillings and sixpence - pretty average for the time - was handed over to Mum and she gave me pocket money and bus fare in return.

Money was still very tight. My mum seemed to be using the pawn shop and the Old Lodge Road more and more. All the while, the news was dominated by the Civil Rights Movement. Whispered conversations were had everywhere debating the implications of it all. The Prime Minister, Captain Terence O' Neill, the fourth Prime Minister of Northern Ireland and Leader (1963-1969) of the Ulster Unionist Party was a moderate Unionist. He sympathised with the Civil Rights Movement. The majority of his party did not and the hard right wing, led by the Reverend Ian Paisley, campaigned for his removal, which, unfortunately, is what eventually happened in 1970. The political scene was fractious and increasingly more dangerous.

For us and Deep Joy, it was background noise. What was really important was playing music and getting the next gig.

Around this time, Gerry had been staying with us at Fairview Street a lot. He slept with me in my double bed. My sister, Bernadette, in particular, doted on him. She made him fried egg sandwiches and generally fussed over him. He had been going out with a girl from Ardoyne named Marty O' Kane. One night, he came back late to our house having been out with her. Luckily, everyone was in bed because he was most distressed.

Marty and he had been making out and somehow he managed to catch his skin in his zip. How he did it I don't know but he made the two mile journey from hers to ours with it still entrapped. In agony, he told me what had happened and asked me what to do. "There's only one thing for it," I told him, "Take a deep breath and unzip really quickly." He took some coaxing but he did it, eventually. There were no lasting consequences. Au contraire.

All the band had jobs. Gerry was working in a solicitors' office. Ferg was working for the Northern Ireland Biological Unit. I have no idea what he did there apart from steal pure alcohol for his own and our benefit. Clarkie went on to Higher Education - eventually he became Head Teacher of our old school, St Gabriel's. He turned it into a success, by all accounts. Ironically, he was also instrumental in closing it down in his next role working for the CCMS - the Council for Catholic Maintained Schools. He kept his interest in music and for many years worked, and still does, for Aiken Promotions, one of the biggest music promoters in all of Ireland. He's worked with bands such as Bruce Springsteen and U2. They also looked after Rory Gallagher in his heyday.

Alcohol started to play its part in our lives although I didn't indulge until I was 20. I'd seen the negative effects of it and it frightened me off. Had it not been for Jim Russell, I might never have started. Brenda and I would sometimes go to the pub with him and Maureen at the weekend. Jim would say, "Just have a wee half of lager and lime. It'll do you no harm." It was the starting pistol I needed to make up for lost time.

The Hercules Pub in Castle Street didn't seem to have any qualms about serving anyone under age. Gerry and some of the other lads would go there for a beer. It was coming near to Christmas and we had a gig in a club on the Shore Road out by the lough on the north side. On route to my house for the meet, Gerry made a detour to the Hercules and arrived at my house after the rest of us had given up on him and left. He was in a jolly mood and he brought a couple of bottles of Guinness for my old man. Charlie thanked him and Gerry made his way to the gig.

Everything was set up and ready to go when he arrived. We had a really good crowd and we thought we were in for a good night. 'Mac' was a wee bit tipsy but things went well until about three quarters of the way into the show when a fight broke out in the audience.

The advantage of a high stage is that you can see everything that's going on but be out of harm's way. As the fight progressed, the mosh pit looked like it was going down a plughole. As it gathered momentum, Gerry decided to put aside his guitar and jump in. I'm not sure whether it was concern for Marty, who was in the middle of the melee somewhere, or that the scene from our high vantage point had convinced Gerry's booze-addled brain that he was some sort of superhero, Guitarman, or whatever. He landed in the middle of the mess and got stuck in sorting the good from the bad and the ugly.

When the music stopped playing, everyone's attention turned to Gerry. Some of the crowd took a poor view at his getting involved in their shit. He made his way back on stage, the crowd turned on us and shouted abuse. We got going again but the last part of that gig seemed like an eternity. When it was over, we packed down very quickly and took our leave by the fire escape, armed with a cymbal and a mike stand as makeshift weapons. It had never felt so good to be heading to the centre of Belfast. I think we played the club again, so no hard feelings, but it was a lesson learned in band participation in crowd control.

The Belfast Buzz

The Belfast music scene, and R&B, in particular, were in rude health in the Sixties, spearheaded by Van Morrison and Them. The shows were legendary and their chart success in the UK gave them substance back home. The band went through a number of personnel changes as a result of management and financial problems but they were all local musicians. One had great relevance for me. John Wilson, the drummer from the Misfits.

John joined Them from September 1965 to March 1966. With Van Morrison, Alan Henderson, Jim Armstrong and Ray Elliott, he played on the second Them album, 'Them Again', which was released in January 1966. John missed the early gigs of the tour because he was too young to get the visas to play abroad. Dave Harvey replaced him and he went on to play with Derek and The Sounds, and Cheese. As I have mentioned, John eventually joined Rory Gallagher in the second line-up of Taste.

There were other bands, such as Brian Rossi and The Wheels, who followed Them to England, but without the vision and song writing talents of Van, it didn't happen for them in such a big way. Van and Them were instrumental in establishing the Maritime R&B club, which later became Club Rado, at the Maritime Hotel. It was the place to play in Belfast for local and international acts. There was an enormous amount of local talent to inspire us younger musicians but in 1967 Rory Gallagher came to town.

Once when Just Five played in Cork and needed a stand-in guitar player to replace Mervyn Crawford, Rory helped them out. Just Five's Billy McCoy told Rory that, if he was ever in Belfast or needed a place to stay, to look him up and Rory held him to his word. He turned up at Billy's house in the early hours of the morning with his new band from Cork, Taste, the bass player, Eric Kitteringham and drummer, Norman Damery, in tow. Taste made an instant impact on the Belfast scene and became the must see band in town anytime and anywhere they played.

I once saw them in Romano's ballroom, opening for the Foundation, a soul pop band, whose big hit was 'Build me up, Buttercup". Taste was just great. Rory had a harmonica in a harness, strapped around his neck and they played a mixture of Blues, their own original material with some Bob Dylan for good measure. Rory was dressed in what became his trademark image, a checked shirt, jeans and white pumps. He prowled the stage with a purpose, giving obvious signs of encouragement to other band members, to the drummer, Norman Damery, in particular. Damery had a Ludwig kit like Ringo Starr's as a lot of drummers did in those days. When the equipment was changed for The Foundation set, their drummer had the exact same expensive kit.

The Foundation show was going well until there was a commotion behind the drum kit. It turned out that the bass drum head had split. They asked for Taste's bass drum to finish their show. The lads agreed to this but it was a kick watching The Foundation playing with the bass drum emblazoned with Taste in front of it.

By 1968, Deep Joy was now playing regularly around Belfast and further afield. We played school hops and dances, including St Gabriel's. St Patrick's and Inst College. Once, we supported the Whatnots, a good four piece, at a Methodist college, known as 'Methody'. Ferg knew the singer, Tom Fox, from school. I really admired the drummer, Paul Ashford, who played in the style of Bobby Elliott from the Hollies. We upstaged them. We totally blew them off, in the musical sense.

We were now getting more support slots in ballrooms. There were quite a few around the city centre: the Orpheus, Milano's, Romano's, the Plaza and the Astor. We supported Cheese, who as I said before were attempting to emulate, Cream. They were our first supergroup, if you will, featuring Roy Abbott on guitar, Charlie McCrachen on bass and John Wilson on drums. So, it was a great buzz to open for them and it was definitely our landmark gig. We later saw Taste support Cream at Romano's. As the rhythm section on Rory's second reincarnation of Taste, Charlie and John also played Cream's farewell show at the Royal Albert Hall.

The Astor was a great place to play.
I saw Gary Moore play one of the
Wednesday night gigs there. He did a
fantastic version of 'The Weight' by The
Band. It was an unusual song for him to
do because he was considered a blues
guitar player.
The Astor was owned by the McMahon
family, who came from somewhere on the
lower part of the Falls Road. They had a
deserved reputation for being a hard
bunch. The Saturday night gigs were run
by a guy called Arnie Knowles and Jim
McCann, who would eventually open the
Marquee Club in Hill Street.
One night, we played on a three band
bill, us as the opening act. The next
band on was Heart and Soul and, top of
the bill, The Group, a covers band. They
did unusual Top 40 songs with intricate
harmonies not unlike the Beach Boys. They
were real pros and performed every song
to perfection. They were known as a
'heads' band. If you were 'a head' you
were a top player.
We got to know everyone at the
place. Louis Small was the DJ and he spun
great tunes - a real mix of Pop, Tamla
and Underground. If you were having a do,
Louis was the man. There was a guy we
knew only as Ashtar, a tall, dreamy guy
who was pretty 'mellow'. He operated the
lights. Gerry McDine looked after the
cloakroom. He was a little guy, who took
his job very seriously. He also had a
slight speech impediment in that he
couldn't pronounce the letter 't' very
well. If a person was unfortunate enough
to lose their cloakroom ticket, Gerry
would tell them plainly "No dicket, no
doat".

We did well and were asked to do a Wednesday night. After that, Joe McMahon asked us if we would play the following night. He said he would pay us for both shows after Thursday's gig. We were delighted with ourselves and agreed immediately. After the last show, we went looking for Joe and our money - a fiver or so. When we found him in his sober Irish suit and black overcoat, he paid us for just one night, insisting that that was the deal that we agreed to. I tried to be grown up and businesslike about it. "Listen, sir..." I said.

That was as far as I got. He lunged at me and roared at me never to call him 'Sir'. I was nimble enough to avoid his clutches and we all left at speed. I told my Dad what had happened, thinking that since he feared no man, he might sort it. All he said was, "Put it down to experience, son. You don't mess with the McMahons."

We had another manager for a while, a guy called Bobby Forsyth. He was about 35 to 40 years of age, well dressed with a nice car. He collected our fees but we didn't see any of the money. We tried hard to get it from him but we had to put that down to experience as well. We weren't in it for the money but I sometimes wondered why we were in it at all. It could only have been the buzz we got from playing music.

Blades

Our sense of style was starting to change. Unconsciously, we were looking for a band image. In 1967, when the film, 'Bonnie and Clyde' was released featuring Warren Beatty and Faye Dunaway, we thought they looked sharp. Gerry's dad tried to put a dampener on our stylistic aspirations by reminding us that Bonnie and Clyde were outlaws and had been nothing but murdering thugs. He was not to be persuaded by the romance of it all and we duly ignored him. Off we went to the markets to find second-hand, pin striped suits and old military greatcoats. We mixed them up with hippy scarves and Mod haircuts.

Gerry bought a cape from an ad in the back of the Daily Mirror and we both bought girls' high heeled boots from the Freemans catalogue. We would visit the music stores and second-hand record shops in Smithfield Market dressed in all this gear. We carried the current hip albums under our arms to set us apart from the norm, as if the clothes weren't enough.

One night, Della Feely, Gerry's hairdresser, painted a moustache on him with her mascara just before he went on stage. Under the lights, it ran and left a tarry mess on his upper lip. Imagine Hitler dressed as Count Dracula and you'll have some idea of the impression he made. The high heels added to our torture.

Gerry did have the knack - which he never lost - of pulling good looking girls. This tended to wind up the old green-eyed monster in Fergie. Ferg thought he should be the one getting the girls because, in his own mind, he was by far the best looking. Gerry had an indefinable something though that was like catnip for women. A rivalry developed.

One night after a gig in the community centre in Belfast, we couldn't find Ferg. It turned out that he and his girlfriend at the time, Marie, were going at it on the stage behind a couple of amps, hidden underneath a couple of our greatcoats. Ferg was always on the pull and, as is the way with some young men, crude terminology was used after their sexual encounters - for example 'did you get your hole?' or 'did you get a ride?'. Their way with girls wasn't my way. I was in a steady relationship and, in any case, I didn't have the desire or the bravado to join in with them or talk about women the way they did. It just isn't in my nature.

Belfast was a dangerous place at the best of times and the threat of being picked on or beaten up by gangs of young men was always present. Once on our way home from the Scouts, only a couple of years earlier, Clarkie and I were stopped by some guys asking us for money. The incident happened right next to a phone box. Clarkie ran inside it threatening to call the police.

These guys took no notice. One of them raised himself up and, while hanging from the door frame, repeatedly kicked Clarkie in the head. I dragged Clarkie to a police station after and they eventually caught the guys, who paid the price. Clarkie spent a few days in hospital with concussion.

Ferg had experienced such incidents himself and had started to carry a knife for protection. He also carried a machete in the back of his Vox AC30 amplifier for a short while. One night at a party with Gerry and Terry Canning, Ferg got lucky with a girl and they made their way to the bedroom to consummate their newly found lust. The others hadn't had as much luck and were keen to leave.

They kept interrupting Fergie and his girl to get them to get a move on. After the third interruption, Fergie lost it and chased after them. He punched, or so they thought, them both in the back. Unfortunately, Ferg had actually stabbed them. Gerry, in particular, was in a critical way and had to be taken to hospital asap while the guys concocted a story about being attacked by strangers. Obviously, the consequences could have been devastating but I remember going to see Gerry in hospital and it all just seemed a bit of a laugh. In the end, it only served to cement what has become a lifelong friendship between them. Boys will be boys.

Meanwhile, my old man had been getting fed up driving us around so he found a little van for us - a faded blue Bedford that cost seven quid. He told us it needed some attention and it had no tax or insurance. It was put in a lock up near our house while the repairs were done and we saved up for the tax and insurance. Under no circumstances, he told us, was it to be driven until then.

It just so happened that we were offered a gig in Strabane.

I don't know what possessed us but we convinced ourselves that it would be okay to take the van. Herbie, a new acquaintance, had a licence so he could drive. It was truly an undercover mission. We took the van and, with the gear, a mattress in the back, three band members, Clarkie, Herbie, the driver, and Seamie, the greyhound roadie, off we went.

The gig went well and we acquired some young ladies as extra passengers on the way home. Clarkie made himself comfortable with them in the back. It was midnight. Spirits were high and the craic was good on the way home. We appeared to be the only vehicle on the road until, in the distance, another car came towards us. As it passed by, we saw that it was a police car.

It had just gone a few yards down
the road behind us when Herbie panicked
and took the first left turn into a newly
built housing estate. We followed the
road to a dead end by a high kerb and
open fields. Herbie killed the lights and
we waited, and waited, and waited some
more until, inevitably, a pair of
headlights came round the bend in the
road behind us. Herbie's sudden left turn
had obviously raised the cops'
suspicions. Being local, they probably
knew we had gone down a dead end.

Herbie opened his door and tried to
make a run for it but Fergie grabbed his
collar with an "oh no you don't!". The
police ordered us out of the van and,
while we stood in line, they made a list
of the technical shortcomings of our
vehicle: bald tyres, no handbrake, faulty
windscreen wipers, no passenger seats, no
tax, no insurance. Finally, they tested
the horn, which bounced out on its spring
like a jack-in-the-box. It lit an 'oh
fuck' moment in our tiny minds.

Surprisingly, after this terrible
litany of road unworthiness, the police
merely took our details and sent us on
our merry way home with an "all the best,
lads, and make sure the young girls get
home safely".

Inevitably, the court summons
arrived. We were to attend court in
Lisburn, the capital of Lagan Valley in
Antrim. On the day, some of our mates
came along to lend moral support. We
dressed soberly for the occasion but they
didn't. For example, that permed
pompadour, Eric Heading, arrived with
multiple scarves around his neck, a
greatcoat and trousers tucked into a pair
of brown riding boots.

We were in there minutes. It turned out that Herbie only had a provisional licence, which explained his haste to flee that night. The outcome was that he lost his licence for a year and hadn't even passed his test. We all chipped in to pay his £28 fine.

On the way home from court, Gerry, Ferg and myself visited the Evans music shop in Lisburn. Jack Evans was a family friend of the McAvoys and Gerry affectionately called him, Uncle Jack. We had been there a short while looking at instruments when Jack asked us to look after the place while he popped out on an errand.

'Not a problem, Jack," we said.

You would have thought that our recent appearance in court would have made some sort of impression on us. However, we were convinced that Jack would never notice the irresistible musical accessories, which we nicked and secreted about our persons.

I put a couple of drum heads up the back of my jacket. Fergie put a mike stand down his trouser leg and a microphone in his pocket, while Gerry helped himself to whatever. On Jack's return, we exchanged more pleasantries before walking robotically out of the shop with our booty.

Gerry was staying at my house that night and, at around 6.30 in the evening, there was a knock at the door. I went to answer it. Sean McAvoy, Gerry's dad, was standing outside. He did not look happy at all and, before I could say a word, he said, "Is Gerard there?".

The game was up. Gerry and him stood in our vestibule with the door shut while gruff mumbling ensued. (I don't recall my dad getting too upset about the episode. Maybe, my mum kept it from him.) We had to give everything back. Fergie was the only one to make on the deal. He had already sold the mike and stand so we had to all chip in to pay Uncle Jack back.

Interestingly, Jack had a stocky guy working for him named Ernie Hunter, who eventually emigrated to New Zealand with his wife, Jane. They founded Hunter Wines, which became world renowned. Sadly, he died in a motorbike accident a few years after winning many awards and accolades for his wine. When he worked for Jack though, he repaired amps and doubled up as 'The Enforcer'. He collected unpaid debts on instruments from slippery musicians, who were, as ever, in plentiful supply.

One time, Ernie had to repossess a saxophone from Hugo 'The Hound' Anderson. (I worked with Hugo years later in a couple of outfits.) He was working in a boutique in Pottinger's Entry when Ernie paid him a visit. Confronted by Ernie, Hugo confessed that he did not have the sax. Ernie left, Hugo locked up the shop and headed for The Marquee, where he had been keeping the instrument because he had heard Ernie was on the hunt. When he left the club with it, lo and behold, there was Ernie waiting for him. Ernie grabbed the sax and there followed a tug of war over the instrument. Realising he was losing the battle, 'The Hound' let go and poked Ernie in the eye. Ernie fell on his backside with the sax and Hugo gave him a two finger salute before legging it.

Get Clarkie

Most weekends, if we weren't playing, we were going to watch other bands. If neither, I spent Friday night at Brenda's and I'd catch the last bus into town to meet up with the others. We slept at my house or Gerry's.

One night, Ferg, Gerry and I had to share a double bed so I got in the middle. In my mind, I might as well have stuck myself between two vampires. I lay on my back wide awake the whole night. It wasn't just me. Jim Ferguson's wife once woke up from a nightmare and told him she had dreamed that Gerry and he were gay. Apparently, she reckoned the whole chasing girls in dual competition was a cover for their latent homosexuality. To be honest, I hadn't thought it through that deeply back then but I didn't trust them with anything or anyone when it came to the old rock and roll.

Cecil Clarke's was going from strength to strength and had started to attract bigger names. Taste came to play and English bands such as Aynsley Dunbar's Retaliation. Aynsley was a fantastic drummer, who played with John Mayall and went on to play with Frank Zappa. Cecil rearranged the room so that the stage went from its position at the bottom of the stairs to the back wall. This gave the audience a better view of the bands. When we'd played for the first time on this new stage and the sound check was over, all of us, bar Gerry, went to have a soft drink at the bar. We were just seventeen so we still couldn't get served alcohol.

Gerry had got a new bass guitar and he had hung back to play around with it for a while. A few minutes later, we heard an almighty bang followed by a horrible drone like all four strings on the bass had been hit. We looked towards the stage and Gerry was lying on his back with the guitar straddled across his stomach.

No one moved until Ferg remarked that it had to be serious because Gerry wouldn't have done that to his new bass. At that, we all left our drinks and ran over to him. Gerry had touched a mike while holding the guitar and some of the gear wasn't earthed properly. He had had a huge electric shock. It had not only knocked him over but out. He came to after a minute or so and like the true trouper he is, Gerry played the show.

When Arnie Knowles and Jim McCann opened the new Marquee in an old warehouse in Hill Street, it caused a great stir and anyone who was anyone wanted to play there. For some reason, Arnie and Jim didn't stay long. Jim's young brother, George McCann, a guy in his mid to late 20s, took the place over. When we played there, he must have liked what he saw because he became our fourth manager in just two years. The Marquee, naturally, became our new home.

They were great days. The old Marquee at the Astor had a name for Saturday nights, but the new one had acts on most of the week depending on who was coming through town.

The entrance was a small door cut into two great big doors that were large enough for vehicles to drive through. There was a courtyard beyond which led to the main room on the left and offices on the right. The main room, which held 250 to 300 people, was an oblong and the stage was on one of the longer sides, which was opposite a set of steps when you entered.

Besides local bands, Dublin bands had started to make their way to the new Marquee. George had an eye to the future and his sights on bringing bigger bands to the club and to Belfast. He had ambition.

Ditch Cassidy and the News were a band that we were really impressed by. They were covering Buffalo Springfield and other West Coast acts. Gary Moore had moved to Dublin and returned on Christmas night, 1968, with Skid Row. (Deep Joy were the support band.) Phil Lynott was their lead singer, Brush Shields on bass and Noel Bridgeman on drums. I was blown away by them. They did a version of 'I am the Walrus' and Phil used a Phillips echo chamber to create weird and unusual vocal sounds to great effect. The great John Mayall himself also played there, supported by Taste.

Another young band called Creative Mind spent a lot of time in the Marquee and we had a friendly rivalry with them. To be honest, at that time, they were better than us. They were three Protestant lads, who were managed by a young sandy-haired Roman Catholic priest called Tony Marcellus. He wore a dog collar, a black leather jacket and jeans.

Tony managed a few bands and had a great way with young people. He crossed the divide between the two communities in Northern Ireland. Not everyone agreed with his cross-community approach. The Church didn't always back him and Ian Paisley called him 'The Hoodlum Priest'. Naturally, we thought he was great. He eventually left the priesthood, got married and raised a family.

Unfortunately, Deep Joy's progress as a three piece was stalling. We concluded that we needed another guitar player to move forward. Someone told us about a guy called Jimmy Carlisle, who had just come back from touring Germany playing at American and British military bases. He had played in Hamburg, which really impressed us.

He lived a short distance from our house off the Old Lodge Rd and was four or five years older than us. He had black shoulder length hair with a middle parting and almost always wore a lightweight crew neck, blue jeans, black boots and a green camouflage jacket. He spoke about exotic foods, such as Frikadelle, a kind of German/Dutch burger, and 'Dubes' - uppers and downers. Combined with a really laid back personality, Jimmy was what we were not, i.e. hip.

The closest we had been to burgers was our local Wimpy and the closest we had been to drugs, soft or hard, had been when Peepsie, the guitar player from Sunshine, dropped a tab of LSD one afternoon in the Marquee. Walking through town with him had been a nightmare. He kept trying to jump in front of buses thinking they were balls of red wool.

Jimmy came along to our rehearsals after the Friday night show at the Marquee. We would set up our gear and work through until four or five, sleeping in the office until late morning. Our parents were OK about it because they knew where we were.

One time, I forgot to tell mine and as we were locking up to leave, my father arrived and, with no introductions, gave me the most almighty punch in the jaw. I went down and I could hear Clarkie saying, "Cool it, Mr O'Neill. Cool it!" to which my dad replied, "I'll cool you, you wee bastard!" before chasing Clarkie up the street. Clarkie got away but my father came back and I had to walk behind him all the way home in all my bedraggled band finery while the guys drove past me, their eyes looking straight ahead.

The new location at the Marquee didn't diminish our appetite for juvenile practical jokes or 'Judases'. Jimmy was far too laid back and mature for all that stuff. Clarkie was the usual mark. He would be walking through a slightly open door before realising that a heavy base of a mike stand perched on it was about to fall on top of him. Or he'd turn a handle only to find we'd wired it to the electric mains.

Once, in early Summer, after a late night rehearsal, Gerry, Ferg and myself decided to investigate a possible route to the neighbouring buildings via the roof. All very exciting. On the return journey, we could see Clarkie sitting in the courtyard below on a bench, enjoying the first early morning rays of the sun. We all thought it would be enormous fun to sneak onto the roof opposite and piss on him from our lofty position.

I took up the challenge and made my precarious way over. I stood unsteadily on the sloping roof looking down, my manhood in my hand. The urge to urinate suddenly eluded me. I could see the others laughing at me from the other side. After what seemed an age, the flow started and I rained a golden shower on Clarkie. Call it premonition but Clarkie jumped out of the way. Unfortunately, he'd been sitting on my jacket, a delightful, lightweight, military-style blouson from the market that I proceeded to soak with my own urine.

Jimmy coming along was the best thing that had happened to the band thus far. With his rock and roll influence and Clarkie's extensive record collection, we got a really great set together - a mixture of Blues and the West Coast music of the time.

The band took shape and gigs were plentiful. One night we did two shows, wheeling our equipment between the Marquee and the War Memorial Hall. It was an exciting and busy time. People were coming to see Deep Joy by this stage. We weren't just being booked for a hop. When Peter Green's Fleetwood Mac played at the Ulster Hall and we opened for them.

We returned to Dublin, driven by Deano this time, at the behest of St John of God's. It was a Church-based charitable organisation that ran a Sunday night gig on the outskirts of the city in a kind of sports complex. Jimmy, being Protestant, asked us, tongue in cheek, if we were going down to HQ. Clarkie wore a lovely new mohair suit for the occasion.

After the gig, Ferg thought it might be an idea to give poor Clarkie another soaking - with water. On guard as ever, Clarkie cottoned on when we tried to manoeuvre him into the shower and he put up one hell of a fight. I got a whack on the head with a plunger. It drew blood and I still have the unheroic scar. The struggle carried on into the car park and into the van. Someone wound a rope around Clarkie's neck and tied it to the back of the van. Deano drove off before realizing poor Clarkie was running for his life behind him. Deano eventually stopped, Clarkie was released but Deano drove off again at speed as we were all still scrambling into the van. Gerry couldn't get a grip and fell off into the road. He had to walk for 10 to 15 minutes before catching us up at a petrol station where we had stopped for him.

Yes and Bonzo Dog

George McCann made his first move into promotion in May 1969. He booked Jethro Tull to play three shows in Ireland: Dublin's National Stadium on the 28th, Belfast Ulster Hall on the 29th and Cork City Hall on the 30th. Ferg went with George to meet and greet the band when they arrived. During the introductions, George made what was the common mistake of asking which one of them was Jethro.

It wasn't his only one. Aiken Promotions had booked Peter Green's Fleetwood Mac to play Dublin the same week. The two bands played on the same night and Fleetwood Mac cleaned up.

It couldn't have hurt George too much because, undeterred, he was already in negotiations for his next venture. It was a package of three bands: Bonzo Dog Doodah Band, The Nice and Yes. The venues were: Belfast Ulster Hall, July 18th; Dublin National Stadium, afternoon and evening gigs, the 19th; and Cork Hibernian Football Stadium, the 20th. Creative Mind were the local support band in Belfast. Deep Joy got the opening slot for the next two shows.

The National Stadium, Dublin, was 2000+ capacity with a purpose-built boxing arena. It was by far the biggest venue that we had played to date and we were a little overawed. We arrived on Saturday in plenty of time to load in and set up our gear. However, things didn't go to plan.

Ticket sales for the matinee were poor and George decided that only Yes and Deep Joy would play for the small crowd. It didn't bother us. We had a ball just being on that stage. The evening show sold well and we couldn't have been in a better place. The next morning, a big coach was waiting outside the Gresham Hotel to take the Bonzos, Yes, the management and us to Cork.

We arrived from the good old Ashling B&B, where the show bands used to stay, and took our places at the back of the coach. Brenda had also come along for the trip.

Everyone was on board except for Clarkie, who was approaching the bus from the rear. When the driver asked if it was OK to go. Ferg yelled, "Yes!" and the driver closed the door and pulled away. Clarkie gamely gave chase along a very busy O'Connell street. Someone saw him running and waving and alerted the driver. Clarkie had begun to flag but as soon as he saw the bus slow, he picked up speed again and caught us up.

I think the freaks on the bus thought, correctly, that we were a bit childish. It was a bit like inviting the Bash Street Kids to take part in University Challenge. On the other hand, to us, the long haired hippies in these bands were pretty eccentric. For example, Viv Stanshall, the Bonzo's lead man, wore a beret and knee length khaki shorts. On the way, he took out his knitting to pass the time. We traversed rural Ireland like a caravan on the 'The Silk Road'.

As the hours began to drag. Clarkie made the schoolboy error of nodding off. As he slept, Ferg filled the hood of his coat with toothpaste and chocolate and it melted into a minty goo as the bus got hotter, sweatier and more unbearable. Mercifully, the driver stopped in a tiny village with a pub. We trooped in and the landlord was tasked to pull eighteen pints of Guinness.

We arrived in Cork at about three or four in the afternoon to a disaster that had already happened. The 'stadium' - a run down football pitch with a surrounding wall - was deserted. What was supposed to be the stage was a heap of abandoned, rickety scaffolding. A single cable led across the scrubby field to a solitary, wooden ticket office where there was one electric socket. Attached to it was an electric kettle flex held in with matchsticks. When the roadies tried to plug the equipment into it, the lot fused. There could be no Keith Emerson stabbing his keyboard after that.

We sat down in the field while the other guys started chasing their manager. Roger Spears, Bonzo's sax player, let off an incendiary device that rattled the grandstand. Later, a handful of people turned up and, by a democratic vote, it was left to Clarkie to announce that, due to unforeseen circumstances, the show had been cancelled. He showed the disappointed group the cable, the kettle and the plug and they all shook their heads as if this was a poor excuse indeed.

Melody Maker journalist, Chris Welch, documented that tour and wrote amusingly about it and its aftermath in a local pub in his book: 'Yes. Close to the Edge'. For our part, our first venture into the big time was a crushing disappointment. To put our technical misfortunes into some sort of perspective, as The Bonzos flew back to London, the Americans succeeded in putting a man on the Moon.

Andwella's Dream

Sunshine (not the Pop band) was a Soul band that was around from 1967 and played regularly at the Marquee. It comprised some of the best players from some of the best bands around in Belfast: the Luvin' Kind, the Interns and The Set. Their rented house off the Antrim Road had a reputation for being a 'free love and drugs' den.

'Peepsie' was the guitarist and 'Beechy',the drummer. Beechy was a great player but his future success lay elsewhere. He was to become 'Therapist to the Stars', treating celebrities for drink and drug problems in his Harley Street clinic. Both Elton John and Michael Jackson were clients. Unfortunately, his sexual predation of female patients led to a scandal that ruined him. It was in all the papers. I think he rekindled his drumming career after that.

Sunshine's manager was one George Mechin, who lived two streets away from me in Twickenham Street. He had a van painted with flames on the side panels courtesy of Ashtar, who did the lights at the Marquee.

George lived with Sunshine's bucktoothed roadie, Bee Gee, and pet dog, Skipper. Once, when George went to London to visit his Playboy Bunny sister, he left Bee Gee in charge with enough money to feed Skipper. Bee Gee did not manage the household budget well and ended up sharing Skipper's tins of Pal for his supper.

George also managed a three piece called The Method, fronted by a guy called Dave Lewis, a very talented guitar and piano player, singer, and songwriter. Paul Hanna played bass and the drummer was Wilgar Campbell. Wilgar would become Deep Joy's drummer when I eventually left. He subsequently went on to join the Rory Gallagher Band.

If I hadn't left our band would I have got the Rory gig? The way I see it is that Wilgar was five year older than me, he'd been to London, and, I believe, he was a much more experienced and proficient drummer than I was. Even so, I reckon my chances would have been 50/50. That's life though. I'd chosen another fork in the road.

I'd seen The Method play in clubs around Belfast and they really impressed me. They went to London in 1968 and changed their name to something a lot less Mod and a lot more trippy - Andwella's Dream. The first album 'Love and Poetry' was penned by Dave, who was barely 18 years old, and released by CBS. It wasn't a commercial success but has become very collectable over the years. Gerry tells me there was a copy on eBay selling to collectors of psychedelia for between £300-£350.

Wilgar split from the band in 1969 and came back to Belfast. We met up with him when he came to jam with us at a gig we did in Victoria Park on the eleventh of July. He was a bit droll was Wilgar and when we asked how Dave was, he replied that Dave believed the new album that he had penned was his 'Abbey Road'.

Wilgar had come back with a superior attitude and the erroneous impression that he could just rest a wee while on my bass drum while he played the harmonica. He was a lovable guy but he had a high opinion of himself. When the Beatles' 'Abbey Road' first came out, Deep Joy did a version of the segway tracks at the end of the album. Wilgar actually refused to play Ringo's solo - he considered it 'beneath' him. He went ahead and played his own.

Gerry tells the story of a gig at Queen's University when they had the audience in the palm of their hand until Wilgar had a moment of 'serenity'. He placed a dismantled clock on top of the tom tom and led the band into some psychedelic fandango while the stunned audience watched a perfectly good gig disappear up its own arse.

We continued to meet Wilgar around town. He was trying to get something new together to head back to London. We were a bit immature for him, to be frank and he was right. Friday night rehearsals still often ended in a puerile farce. One time, at about two in the morning, we ordered fourteen cabs to turn up at George Mechin's. He was awake, of course, but did not see the funny side of it. Thereafter, he complained to everyone he met about it.

Another time, at a similar hour, we came across a Mr James Bond in the telephone book. Naturally, we gave him a call. When he answered, we all sang the James Bond theme down the phone to him. He gave us the impression that he'd heard it before, many, many, times.

One night in the 'Venice Café' i.e Concetta's, Clarkie was suffering from a very bad cold. Ferg suggested that he had a possible cure that Clarkie could try. Ferg worked next to the RAF Medical Centre at Aldergrove Airport and had become friendly with two lab assistants there. He had acquired from them a tube of something or other with an applicator attached that had been developed to treat pilots' piles. They told him that it could also be applied to the end of your knob to prevent premature ejaculation. A product called Stud was the only one on the market for that at the time.

Ferg happened to have the medication on him and said if Clarkie stuck it up his nose, it would clear his sinuses. Without a thought as to where it might have been, the desperate Clarkie did so. Poor Clarkie's face froze in horror and as he ran outside to be sick, he lost the plate to which his two false front teeth were attached. He came back in the café without them and had to go back and rummage in vomit to retrieve them.

One Friday evening, we met at The Marquee and headed to Comber, a small town about 20 miles southeast of Belfast, for a gig. As we approached Queen's Bridge on the one-way system, the van broke down. George McCann opened the bonnet to see what was wrong and found the accelerator cable had snapped. Back then, this area was a dodgy part of town. Opposite us was a notorious brothel called DuBarry's. While George was trying to repair the cable, a cat fight began outside that establishment and two gaudy gals ripped shreds off each other.

Fifteen minutes later, George popped out of the innards of the van to announce he'd fixed it. He had managed to reconnect the cable but because of the break, it was now considerably shorter. The more mechanical among you may have already guessed what this meant. When he started the engine, it revved like we were already going 45 miles an hour. When he selected first gear and engaged the clutch, we took off like a firework. George tried to change gears as smoothly as he could but he was on a hiding to nothing.

When we reached the outskirts of the city, we had to stop for petrol. Jimmy and Fergie decided to opt for more thrills by continuing our journey on the van roof. Jimmy, pretending to be the Michelin Man, assumed the position at the front with his skinny legs dangling over the windscreen and his jeans around his ankles. This way, he managed to obscure most of George's vision. Seeing an arse-shaped dent in the roof, Gerry kicked it, almost sending Ferg off the back and onto the road behind us. (He may well have been acting out of revenge.)

The gig was at The Thomas Andrews Hall. The eponymous Thomas Andrews was from Comber and was the principal designer of the Titanic. He went down with his ship.

The support band that night was called Volume Road and the singer was Davy Hamilton, who later became a cabaret singer. Davy and I have played in a few bands together since and are lifelong friends. Davy's son, Paul, now plays drums with Foy Vance, touring with Ed Sheeran as well as working with Elton John. Our opening number that night was 'Born to be Wild'.

By 1969, we'd been playing for two years and on Easter Friday of that year we went into the black for the first time. We got paid five pounds each for the gig on that day. So, instead of having to pay our expenses, Gerry and I made plans to take our girls to Dublin for the weekend. Unfortunately, Gerry almost did not survive that gig because the bass stack fell over and nearly flattened him. That guy must have been a cat in another life.

We were busy doing gigs all over the place. We did a show in Cookstown with Sam Mahood's new band, Soul Foundation. They were a great, up-tempo soul band and a pretty unruly bunch. After we'd set up the gear, the organisers brought two big platters of sandwiches to the dressing room. They only just managed to get their hands out of the way before the Soul Foundation fell on the food like wolves and scoffed the lot. Sam was furious and tore a strip off them.

Another time, while Sam and the boys were touring the North of England, dep drummer Gerry McIlduff, claimed that he had to go home urgently to sit an Irish Language exam. The roadie, Neam, who had been a drummer back in Belfast, was forced to dep for _him_. The guys weren't happy with the situation.

After the show, they undid the skin of Gerry McIlduff's bass drum, took a shit on it and replaced the skin. By the time, Gerry came to use the drum again, there was a distinct, mysterious rattling coming from within. Gerry couldn't work out what it was and no-one had anything sensible to say about it. When the stage lights shone on the drum, the dried crap could be seen bouncing around inside.

All these characters and bands kept the Belfast music scene on the boil. Our adolescent bubble with its childish pranks and energetic gigs distracted us from clear and present dangers. Behind it all, Northern Ireland was vibrating with bad news.

THE TROUBLES

Fear

On New Year's Day, 1969, a civil rights protest march set off from Belfast to Derry. It was led by a group of university based activists, People's Democracy, unhappy at the Government's limited civil rights concessions. We did not have one man/one vote in local elections.

The march was attacked by some 200 hardline Unionists at Burntollet Bridge, while the Royal Ulster Constabulary (RUC) stood by. Some of the assailants were actually off-duty police. The attack sparked riots between the RUC and Catholics in Derry and in Newry. By April, there would be riots ongoing in Belfast and Derry and sectarian violence erupting, from both sides.

It was not strictly a religious nor a nationalist conflict although it fell along those lines. It was rooted in the discrimination against Catholics. However, the Unionists, mostly Protestant and Loyalist, suspected Irish Republican motives behind the protests and rioting with the ultimate goal of reuniting Ireland.

In March and April 1969, loyalist paramilitaries, the Ulster Volunteer Force, bombed water and electricity installations in Northern Ireland. As a result,Belfast was left without water or power. The perpetrators blamed the bombings on civil rights activists and the Irish Republican Army (IRA), hoping to end concessions to Catholics. Prime Minister O'Neill resigned his leadership of the Ulster Unionists and of Northern Ireland at the end of April.

Catholics rioted in Belfast splitting the resources of the RUC and 'B' Specials - part-time, unpaid, police reservists - and alleviating the pressure on the Bogside, Derry. Even though unrest was generally limited to a handful of towns and cities, the whole province was on tenterhooks. Civil unrest had not been seen on this scale since Partition in 1922 nor the street riots in 1935. Everyone was afraid.

By August 1969, Northern Ireland was ready to blow and it did. The fallout would last for thirty deadly years and would become known as the Troubles.

Since I spent a lot of time at the Russell house, I got two very differing points of view. Jim Russell was very pro-British and Loyalist. My own family's stance was Irish and Nationalist. I was also working at Shorts Bros and Harland's with all my new Protestant friends. My grandparents on both sides were born into an Ireland that did not have a border. To say I was conflicted and confused was an understatement.

As a band, we didn't really talk about it. It just wasn't on our agenda. I didn't know anyone among my friends, Protestant or Catholic, who were openly part of any paramilitary organisation or political movement. We were kids, we thought it would be sorted out but, between August 13th and 16th, the whole hate machine went into overdrive.

Mistrust and fear on both sides had reached fever pitch. On the 13th, a large crowd of Catholics handed a petition into the Springfield Road RUC station in protest of the events in Derry, with its larger Catholic population, where marches had been attacked by Loyalists, supported by the RUC.

They marched along the Falls Rd where a group of youths attacked another police station causing terrible damage to property and vehicles. Shots were fired for the first time between the RUC and the IRA. Families living on the fringes of Protestant and Catholic communities were nervous and began to move away from the flash point areas. Barricades were erected for protection.

We were only one of a few Catholic families in a Protestant area. My father and grandfather thought it would be best if the four youngest kids were sent to the Ardoyne to live with my grandparents O'Neill for safety until the situation blew over. I was to remain living in East Belfast at Brenda's so I could get to work.

On the evening of the 14th, Nationalists marched to Hastings Street RUC station and this time were confronted by a Loyalist crowd throwing petrol bombs, stones and sharpened sticks. Intense fighting broke out with the police side by side with the Loyalist crowd. The conflict continued unabated from Divis Flats to the Ardoyne, a distance of at least two miles.

When rioting broke out in Ardoyne, police and Loyalist crowds broke through the makeshift barricades and houses were set on fire. The area was defended by a group of ex-servicemen (British Army, of course) with shotguns. My sister, Teresa, who was about 13, still remembers the sound of machine gun fire as she hid under the bed.

Ardoyne was probably where Catholics were most vulnerable. I remember watching the evening news with Brenda at her house and being left absolutely speechless at what was happening on the other side of Belfast.

The Irish Taoiseach, Jack Lynch, condemned the RUC and said his government could "no longer stand by and see innocent people injured and perhaps worse". He called for a UN Peacekeeping Force. Lynch's statement fuelled rumours of an invasion by the Republic. The new Prime Minister of Northern Ireland, Major James Chichester-Clark, responded by saying neighbourly relations with the Republic were at an end and that British troops were being called in.

Troops from the 1st Battalion, Prince of Wales's Own Regiment of Yorkshire, occupied the centre of Derry, replacing the exhausted police officers, who had been patrolling the cordons around the Bogside. The Catholics initially welcomed the British Army but, ominously, the period of calm was described at the time by the British military as just 'a honeymoon period'.

In three days, six Catholics and two Protestants had been shot dead, 750 people injured, 133 from shotgun wounds. more than 150 Catholic homes had been burnt and 275 businesses destroyed, 83 percent of which were Catholic. The Irish Army set up refugee camps on the Republic side of the border.

Catholics believed that the RUC and B Specials had worked hand in hand against them. Almost immediately though, some also pointed the finger of blame at the IRA for not protecting Nationalist areas. The IRA were accused of being unprepared for such events and, as a result, the Republican movement fractured. The two factions - The Official IRA and the more militant, Provisional IRA - were from that point deeply divided. The Provisional IRA (PIRA) were to become known as the Provos.

The Provos demanded the unification of Ireland and civil rights for Catholics. Unlike the IRA, it was prepared to use violent means to achieve its ends. The Official IRA wanted a political solution and the Provos wanted military action.

For us kids, it was business as usual. Deep Joy had two shows on Friday, August 15th, at St Anne's School and Penny Lane. I'd been working all week and hadn't been home. We all met at the Marquee and with passing chit chat about what had happened, our main concern was whether we'd be able to play or not. We duly set off towards West Belfast in George McCann's van to pick up a PA system.

The eerie atmosphere as we drove through was unlike anything we had experienced. There were few people on the streets even though we were on the other side of town from the fighting. As we drove along, the severity of the situation began to sink in. It was a strange sensation for me. Was it the end of something? Or the beginning?

An unfamiliar feeling of uncertainty and doubt began to set in between us all. George probably was the one who asked the question that we were all thinking. Should we go through with the night's gigs? The vote was unanimous. We turned around and despondently took our gear back to the club.

As Gerry, Ferg and I walked along Clifton St back to my house, we had just passed Carlisle Circus when we saw two guys throw petrol bombs through the window and alleyway entrance of the Cherry Mount pub. Fortunately, the place was closed because of the situation.

We ran to the phone box to report it to the police and, naively, we left our names and addresses. When we got to ours and told my parents what had happened, my dad was adamant that we shouldn't have got involved. But, it was done. Ferg went home. Gerry stayed and we all went to bed. It was a shock to be told that we had done wrong by doing right.

Saturday morning felt different again.

Normally, it was my mum's shopping day, a visit to the Shankill Rd for bargains and after tea, the tin bath would be filled with water and the kids would all have a bath. Mum would have made stew and beef tea and bread to dunk in it. Bernadette and Teresa used to really look forward to this. The old man would come home after a few pints and they would all sing Minstrel songs together.

Not that Saturday. That morning, Gerry left to go to town to meet his girlfriend, Marty, and her friend, Margaret. He brought them back to the Ardoyne and later that day, Gerry's father came and took Gerry and Marty away. Some time in the afternoon, a handwritten note was posted through our letter box. It read "You have twenty four hours to get out or be burnt out."

I'm sure my grandfather's words of warning resonated in my father's head but who could have foreseen this? It had been over 30 years since my Grandfather O'Neill had fought hand to hand in riots at the docks and things had seemed to have been improving over the years. My dad went out for a few hours, probably to the pub, to find out how genuine the threat was. My Aunt Sally came to the house later that day because she and my Uncle Sammy were in the same predicament. They had decided to go to Granny Lagan's house in Ardoyne.

We didn't know what to do with all our furniture and belongings. I don't remember whose idea it was but we decided to ask George McCann if he would help move our stuff in his van and store it at the Marquee. We didn't have a house phone then so we had to walk to the phone box by Carlisle Circus to call him. It was a five minute walk but the air was thick with danger. We felt very vulnerable.

The next morning a crowd of between 20 or 30 had gathered at the end of our street at the junction with the Old Lodge Road. We panicked at the sight of them. Were they there as sick onlookers or had they come to menace us? Rumour reached us that some had petrol bombs. Our neighbours stayed behind closed doors. Eventually, the police arrived.

The Old Lodge Road with its parade of shops had been our patch for the past seven years: the fish and chip shop, the sweet shop where we spent our pocket money, the launderette, the pawn shop, the pub on the corner, the butcher's and Hagan's Drapers shop where I went with Bernadette to buy her first pair of woolly tights. They were all closed to us now.

We wrapped clothes in sheets and rolled the mattresses with the bed linen still on them. The beds were dismantled. The accumulation of twenty years of marriage and family life had to be out the door in hours. George arrived and the van was loaded for the first trip.

My poor mother was starting to show the strain as the crowd on the corner grew. I walked back into the house after the van left and found her standing with her back against the kitchen wall. She had the strangest look in her eyes before she went limp and collapsed onto the floor. We rallied her with words and glasses of water. The situation was dangerous. She, everyone, everything, had to go on, no matter how we felt. My mother never came to terms with it. After the incident, she was eventually prescribed Valium, which became a problem for her as time went on.

When we had taken what we could - some larger things had to be left - my dad locked the front door. As we left, we saw a man running with a side of beef on his shoulder. The crowd had begun looting the shops of the Old Lodge Road.

Mum, Dad and Bernadette went to Ardoyne. They did not want me to be there. I was a young male and at too vulnerable an age. I had to go to the Russell's and I duly went in the opposite direction with George to the Marquee to unload the rest of our things. The contents of 45, Fairview St were piled against one wall of the outside room. I felt numb as I went to Brenda's house.

My father went back to Fairview St a few days later and found the house had been broken into. What we had left behind had gone. They even took the lead from the roof.

It is a terrible thing to be driven from your home. These events happened to families on both sides and I wouldn't wish it on anyone.

The Gun

Going to work on Monday felt very odd. There wasn't time to digest fully what had happened at the weekend. My world had been turned upside down and I was unsure what the future had in store. At the Apprentice School, no-one mentioned anything, nor asked, and I didn't let on as to how it had affected me. You'd think it would have been the talk of the place but it wasn't. There was no hostility, none whatsoever, which was a relief.

It was almost the end of the year at our school and we would soon be going to the main factory with our qualified job titles. I would become an airframe fitter and start building aircraft.

The apprentices weren't just excited about their job prospects though. I remember one lunchtime, the week after the Troubles had started, a group of us enthusiastically chatting about Taste. News of their success was constantly in the music press. After every festival or gig they played, the band's reputation grew. At the end of the day, we were all normal seventeen year olds and music fans. Taste was from our neck of the woods, our champions. With them, our troubles drifted out of sight for a while. It's worth saying that Rory was a Catholic from the South, John and Charlie were Protestants from the North. Together, they created one great band and they were our heroes.

For the next month, the rest of the family stayed in the Ardoyne, in very cramped conditions, with my grandparents. On occasion, some of the younger ones stayed with neighbours. My parents knew this could only be a temporary solution. They had a mortgage on Fairview St so their difficulty was enormous.

The number and needs of displaced families in Belfast was growing. People tried to find short term or permanent accommodation where they felt safe. Paramilitary groups commandeered housing in various districts for their own. My father heard about an empty, boarded up property in Spamount Street in a small Catholic enclave off the Antrim Road. He wasted no time in securing it for the family and as my parents had already applied to the Housing Executive, they didn't expect to be at Spamount Street for long. They collected just enough things from The Marquee to tide us over and there we went.

It didn't take us long to realise why it was empty. The rooms were very small and the whole place reeked of mildew and damp. It didn't have a bathroom and the outside toilet was a health hazard. As winter drew in, so the damp got worse. Fortunately, the gas meter didn't have a lock on it so it could be fed with coins to provide us with hot water, which came from a small geyser in the kitchen. The house had a couple of open coal fires but the room I slept in couldn't be heated because the bed filled it. The bedclothes always felt damp.

Worse, we all felt jumpy and insecure. Bernadette remembers that on one Saturday evening, herself, my mum and young brother, Martin, were huddled around the fire watching Hitchcock's 'Psycho' on the TV. At the scariest part of the movie, when Anthony Perkins came out of an upstairs bedroom with a great big knife and dressed in his dead ma's clothes, they all screamed to high heaven. My father leapt out of bed, bounded down the stairs wielding the family shillelagh and went running into the street thinking we were under siege.

We squatted in this hovel for just over six months. My old man was never one to take things lying down. He made it his business to find out who had betrayed us with the result that we were forced from our home.

The O'Neills had a long connection with the docks and the Royal Navy and the Merchant Navy. Two of my uncles, Michael and Kevin, joined the Merchant. Michael and my Dad had always been pretty close. My uncle Norman joined the Royal Navy in 1961, straight from school. He signed up for 22 years. By the end of the decade, he was an electrical engineer and petty officer. Norman and Kevin were late additions to the family and are only six and three years older than me, respectively. My uncle Kevin was still at St Gabriel's when I went there.

Before the Troubles, I remember
seeing Norman, in Ardoyne, home on leave,
wearing his uniform and looking very
proud. Many Irish men from the Republic
of Ireland joined the British Army and
the Royal Navy during the Second World
War despite the enmity towards the
British. They were considered deserters
and traitors for fighting for them.

By August, 1971, Norman found
himself on the internment ship, HMS
Maidstone, docked in Belfast Lough. The
crew comprised English and both Southern
and Northern Irish guys. The Army was on
board watching over the internees, who
had been arrested, by way of the Special
Powers Act, on suspicion of being
involved in the Republican Movement.
Norman found the experience so
overwhelmingly negative that he left the
Navy soon afterwards and went to
Manchester. He had lived for the Navy and
he was very cut up about the loss of his
career but he felt he could no longer
serve with pride.

Anyway, my father tracked down the
person whom he believed had been
instrumental in having put us and other
families out of their homes that fateful
weekend. His name was Tommy Orr and he
was a Protestant, who lived on the Old
Lodge Road behind the Courthouse. My
father knew him and the two men had never
got on.

The story I remember being told was that my father and one of his brothers, whom I assumed to be Michael because they spent so much time together, had gone to Orr's house looking for him but he wasn't at home. His mother answered the door and they asked where her son was. Just as things got a little heated, a police Land Rover drove by and my father and his brother left.

Some months later, my father received a summons to appear in court accused by Orr's mother, of carrying a firearm and trying to get Tommy Orr to shoot two Catholics. It made no sense but the summons stated that the incident happened on the day we were put out of Fairview Street. That date was later amended.

When the case came to court, it was my father's word against Mrs Orr's. The court believed her and my father spent two months in the Crumlin Road Gaol. My poor mother, on top of everything else, this had to happen. He was imprisoned at Her Majesty's Pleasure just as we were moving house again. At least, Mum didn't have to make excuses as to why he wasn't at home. Myself, to be perfectly honest, I had mixed emotions about him being away. I certainly spent more time at home while he was.

Years later, I asked him if he had had a gun that time. My father said that he didn't, categorically "No". A couple of years ago, thanks to good old Facebook, my Uncle Norman contacted me. I hadn't seen him for 45 years. We eventually spoke on the phone. He told me that it was him who was with my Dad on that day and not Michael and it was he who had been carrying the gun.

Norman had got the gun for protection when he was in the Far East. He told me that the incident with Mrs Orr was very brief and that they had gone there to give Tommy Orr a taste of his own medicine. They hadn't wanted to do him any permanent harm and definitely did not want him to kill two Catholics. My father had taken the blame so that Norman wouldn't be court martialed.

Norman reunited me with some old tapes of my parents singing along at my grandparents' house. The tapes were sent to him by my father while Norman was stationed in Hong Kong for the Christmas/New Year 1970, just months after these events took place. Apparently, the whole crew sang along to my parents' beautiful duets.

Shorts

On week nights that I spent at Brenda's house, we would often go into the front room to listen to music. The room was a kind of a parlour and was mostly used at the weekends for entertaining and the like. Jim's record player was in there.

We played John Mayall albums - I toured with him not long ago with his Bluesbreaker guitarist, the great Buddy Whittington, and my friend and bass player, Peter Stroud - Fleetwood Mac, Duster Bennett, The Rock Machine Turns You On, Hendrix, Cream and the Small Faces.

Of course, it wasn't just the music that drew us to the front room. Our youthful urges demanded attention. We would turn down the lights, listen to music and try to get to it. The lulls in conversation must have raised Jim's suspicions for, on occasion, he would just barge into the room pretending to be looking for something and almost catching us in the act.

While I was working on the shop floor, I would sometimes see Jim walking around the factory. He was a different person there and had no time for small talk. In fact, he wouldn't acknowledge me or anyone else who wasn't involved in his day to day business. At home though, he would tell us what he had encountered at work. Problems or arguments that he had had with colleagues who didn't agree with his decisions. He even repeated jokes from the factory floor. He liked to recap on his day.

After leaving the Apprentice School, each lad was placed with a journeyman, an experienced tradesman. I was apprentice to two fitters, Mickey Flanagan and Jack Chricton: one Catholic, one Protestant. They were great mates and Jack knew Jim Russell very well. They agreed on virtually everything, even social conditions (everyone entitled to their dues) and trade unions (everyone entitled to representation). There was always a healthy debate going on when you were around them.

I just listened, fascinated. I had never heard anyone of either side openly debate together. I was learning all sorts of things about the other point of view. Over the next couple of years, as the Troubles intensified, they couldn't agree as to how to resolve the situation. Before, it was always about the working man and looking after your family but after, sides were definitely taken.

Mickey and Jack were great guys to work with but one drawback was I ended up smoking 40 fags a day. I think, between us, we kept Gallaghers alive while slowly killing ourselves. Each time either of them took out a packet, they passed them around. I had my own and did the same. I decided to give up smoking when I was 21 and coughing up black tar.

My best mate then was a guy called Bobby Ray, or 'Daz', because Jack said he was always so white, neat and shiny. Jack called me 'The Vulture' because I brought the biggest lunches and ate everyone's leftovers.

One day, Daz got pretty annoyed with me and told me so. He was a Protestant and, at that time, I was really starting to reject Catholicism, the Church and its practices. I probably went on about it a lot. He told me straight out that I shouldn't criticise my own and that I should side with my own people. He had misunderstood me. Maybe, I wasn't articulate enough because it was the religion I was knocking, not the people.

Despite the political situation in Belfast, there was a pretty good atmosphere on the shop floor. We were working on a new project that wasn't in production - the cowlings for the Rolls Royce RB211 engine, which was pretty advanced technology back then. Made from perforated titanium, new ways of drilling and welding the material had to be found. The inside diameter was big enough for a model to stand inside for the publicity photographs. Ferg's dad, a lovely man, also worked at Shorts. He built wings for the German/Dutch Fokker.

Everyone got on with the job. Targets had to be met and the work was highly skilled. The machine shop was at one end of the factory and, at the other, were the completed aircraft. Shorts built the Skyvan, a small freight carrier, and were developing the SD3/30, a small capacity passenger aircraft. The unique thing about them was that they could take off and land on a very short runway.

I never thought about what the future would bring. Years later, I took an SD3/30 from New York to Philadelphia on the Rush tour with Rory. I had met a girl in Chicago and she agreed to meet me in Philly for the last three shows of the three and a half month tour. I woke up in New York in a fancy hotel room the day I was leaving and, looking out of my window, I could see Central Park covered in snow. My future was to be so different but I will always remember the sound of an SD3 turboprop engine. I'd heard so many being tested on those large forecourts next to the Belfast Lough.

The Passenger

Riots and confrontation were commonplace now in Belfast and the atmosphere in the city was crackling with tension and ready to blow.

We were rehearsing, as usual, one Friday night in the Marquee when Father Tony Marcellus, the rock and roll priest, turned up with some Catholics from Ardoyne, who needed to be rescued. They made us feel decidedly uncomfortable but we kept on playing until one of these guys demanded that we play 'Jo Jo'.

We said that we didn't know it. He then began to sing a bastardised version of the Beatles' 'Get Back'. We knew it, of course, but his manners were bad so we pretended that we didn't just to piss him off. In that, we were successful. He ordered us to "Play Jo Jo" and made it clear that we had no choice in the matter. We did as we were told and promptly left.

We were playing bigger gigs, opening for bands such as Ton.E.King and the Ray Dots and the Plattermen. The latter were a show band that had crossed over doing Blood, Sweat and Tears' material. In the film, The Commitments, based on Roddy Doyle's novel, the band's vocalist, Deco Cuff, was, in fact, played by Andrew Strong, the 16 year old son of the Plattermen's singer, Rob Strong. We played the Ulster Hall with the Plattermen on one occasion.

Despite these good gigs, we were unsettled. I remember Ferg threatening to leave over something or other at a gig in the Jazz Club. There was a feeling in the band, with George McCann's encouragement, that we should move to London. Decisions had to be made.

I spoke to my dad about it and his response was categorical: "No way. You must finish your apprenticeship, Get something behind you".

My father's attitude and my relationship with Brenda made my mind up for me. I took the easy option and said "No" to the move to London. Whether it was the right choice is anyone's guess. Life takes its course and every experience makes you what you are. My decision, then, mapped the rest of my life and I have no regrets.

We rolled into 1970 unsure of how things would pan out but when Wilgar Campbell agreed to join the band, it was settled and the band made its move to London. I did all the gigs until late February, while the others rehearsed with Wilgar. We all hung out together, good mates, and Wilgar came along to one or two of the gigs I did before the changeover. I really wasn't sure whether I was doing the right thing or not.

It was winter. The nights were cold and dark. Belfast was in a state of chaos and my best mates were making plans to split. The last gig I did was at the Ulster Hall with Fleetwood Mac. I played the first part of the set and Wilgar played the second. Then, it was all over.

It didn't surprise me when, a few weeks later, Ferg left. I don't think he liked the new direction the band was taking. He was replaced by Dave Harper on keyboards, who within five or six weeks was replaced by Chris Morrison. Clarkie wasn't around as much either. Funny enough, George McCann asked me to come back, two or three weeks before the band left for England. I said that I couldn't do it.

On the fourth of May, 1970, Deep Joy left for London leaving a big empty space in my life.

Clarkie, Ferg and I didn't see much of each other in the following few months. The thing that bound us together had gone. I slipped into a domestic routine of going to work, Brenda's in the evening and at weekends. We started to go to the pictures regularly. I became friendly with more apprentices in Shorts.

Some lads travelled to work from Ballymena in the country in their own cars. Bobby Stuart, one of my mates from East Belfast, also had his own car. Not wanting to be left behind, I decided to learn to drive. I asked my dad if he would teach me and he said he would.

He agreed to meet me at a cafe where my mum worked in Victoria Square one Saturday afternoon at 1pm prompt. I was already there and waiting when he arrived in his car, a pale yellow Austin 1100, the pride of British Leyland. He'd already had a few pints by then.

We headed to Duncrue Street, which was part of a road network on a huge area of reclaimed land next to the lough. Trucks used these roads to deliver landfill material but, at the weekend, it was the perfect place to learn to drive. On this occasion, we were the only ones there.

Dad drove me around the circuit a couple of times to familiarise me with the lay of the land. We stopped and he talked me through the workings of the clutch and gearbox, how to change gear and when. It was time to give it a go. I nervously got into the driver's seat and adjusted everything to make myself comfortable. I followed his instructions and, before I knew it, we were moving.

It was unbelievable. I was in control of my slightly inebriated father's beloved car. He kept on telling me when to change gear, slow down, speed up, etc. We went around the circuit a further four or five times and I was just starting to relax when he told me to pull over so he could take a Jimmy Riddle. I was to drive around the circuit again, come back and pick him up.

He must have been more pissed than I realised because when I came back for him, he got in the passenger's side and directed me off the reclaimed land onto the shore road, leading onto Royal Avenue - Belfast's 'Oxford Street' - at about two on a Saturday afternoon. It was a baptism of fire.

We were back at Victoria Square within the hour. I was in bits but my father was pretty pleased and relaxed about it all. Years later, he worked as an HGV instructor in Dublin. His students invariably passed but my dad got the sack for insisting on taking them for a celebratory drink in the pub opposite the testing centre afterwards.

He was a hard act to follow but I never asked him for another driving lesson. I took 13 lessons from a qualified instructor at a pound a go and passed my test the first time. My father insisted on taking the credit for it.

One Sunday afternoon while I was learning to drive, we went for a family drive with the Russells. We were driving through Bangor, a busy seaside town with a big harbour and all sorts of boats moored up. It has a long harbour wall on one side and quite grand Victorian houses on the other.

Maureen got it into her head that Jim should let me have a drive to practise for my test. He wasn't keen but she, Brenda, and Brian kept on at him until he gave in. Jim's car was an old white 1958 Ford Anglia, the same shape as the Popular and the Prefect, with red leather upholstery and a three speed gearbox.

I got in the driver's seat and pulled away. Jim was obviously very nervous. For the first few minutes, things went well. Someone in the back asked me how it felt and I made the mistake of trying to speak and drive at the same time. Being a wee bit nervous, I started to stammer and, eventually, so did the car.

It was a real Michael Palin in 'A Fish Called Wanda' moment. We had a tankful of kangaroo petrol and were bouncing all over the road. Jim was shouting at me to depress the clutch and stop the car, which I managed to do. It was silent for a moment until laughter erupted from the back seat. I sheepishly got out and got into the passenger seat.

When I passed my test, Jim sold me his pride and joy for 18 quid. Within the first month of passing my test, I had three very close calls.

The first was when driving along the New Lodge Road and a little girl of about four ran out in front of me. I swerved and only just missed hitting her. I was really shaken up and it was about 10 minutes before I could get going again.

The second was when I was driving through the New Barnsley Estate and a little boy ran from between two cars, straight into the side of my car. He literally bounced back off as I slammed on the brakes. I took the boy and his dad to the Royal Hospital but thankfully there was no real damage done to boy nor car.

The third incident was on a Saturday night at around 10 on the Newtownards Road. As I was driving past a drinking club on the right hand side of the road, people were starting to leave after a night on the hooch.

Most people nipped across the road fairly quickly but one guy, the worse for wear, hesitated in the middle of the road and was unsteady on his feet. When I sped up, he stopped. When I slowed down, he decided to walk. Just as I gathered speed again, he changed his mind and stopped. He changed his mind again but I forgot the steps to the dance, and he ended up on the bonnet of my car. I braked hard and he rolled off onto the kerbside.

His mates thought it was highly amusing as their friend lay spreadeagled on the footpath. Unfortunately, the mood quickly changed when one of them accused me of driving too fast. I was on the wrong side of town to get lippy but the driver behind had watched the pantomime unfold and offered his services as a witness should I need it.

Nothing came of it.

The Quick and the Nearly Dead

The weekends were very different without the band. Not just the gigs but the social side as well. After playing, we would often go to the Venice Cafe at Carlisle Circus where we would meet up with other musos who had been gigging somewhere. Sometimes, we went to Ken's Fried Chicken (Gerry lived for this place, by the way).

My father was inside so my home life was less fraught than it had been. The fact that he was serving time meant the transition away from the band was easier because I spent more time at home with the rest of the family. My mum was still very stressed from the Fairview Street incident. She was getting up later. I had to make my own sandwiches for work, which was unheard of. She was on Valium and they don't call it Mother's Little Helper for nothing.

Brenda and I spent a lot more time together. The car gave me a new sense of freedom. Some weekends, Brenda and I would travel to Ballymena, next to Lough Neagh, to stay with Dennis McHenry, one of my apprentice friends. His father was a doctor and they owned a pretty big house there. When his parents went away for the weekend, Dennis would invite some friends to stay.

Dennis was a Catholic and his girlfriend was a Protestant. They got a lot of grief from some family members on both sides about it. As soon as Dennis finished his apprenticeship, they emigrated to Australia.

Dennis liked to drive fast. One morning when he was driving to work with a couple of other lads, he rolled his Ford Escort. No-one was seriously hurt. Bobby Stewart, another apprentice friend of mine, also liked fast cars. He had a Downton-tuned Mini, a flying machine. One lunchtime, we took it to Hollywood, five or six miles along the coast, for a spin. He was doing 105mph at one point down those narrow country roads, too fast for comfort but it sure was a thrill.

Dennis took us to a nightclub just outside the town. It had a big dance floor with tables and chairs on three sides and a bar on the other - a typical country dance place. I went there twice and disgraced myself both times.

The first time I was sick from smoking cigs and drinking Coca Cola, and the second from smoking cigs and drinking Pernod. I hadn't long been drinking alcohol. People kept buying rounds. I ended up drinking a couple of pints of beer and 11 Pernods. Considering a measure in Northern Ireland was nearly twice that of the rest of the UK at that time, I had consumed a lot of booze for a kid who was nine stone wringing wet.

I was in a mess, drunk, confused and feeling very, very, ill. I went outside to get some fresh air and ended up walking down some country lane. It was pitch black and, as I turned around and around trying to find my bearings, I stumbled into a ditch and passed out. The others found me about an hour later. When we got back, I was put to bed and they carried on. I never drank Pernod or went drinking with country lads again.

When my dad came home from his eight weeks in Crumlin Road Gaol, we tried to start living a normal life with his boots firmly under the table again. Our new home, 96, New Barnsley Park, was a housing association house in the New Barnsley estate, which had been a predominantly Protestant area until the recent upheavals. Being close to Catholic Ballymurphy, Turf Lodge and Andersonstown, Protestants had moved out. Our next door neighbours, Roy and Lily were Protestants and my parents developed a lifelong friendship with them. They eventually emigrated to Canada and my parents went to visit them there two or three times. It only goes to show that good people can always get along.

I would say that by the end of 1970, the segregation of Belfast was complete except for some middle and upper class areas where it didn't seem to be as much of an issue. A better off, educated, middle class Catholics had less to lose than a poorer, less educated, working class Protestant. The latter definitely had the most to lose from equality and civil rights in terms of access to jobs and power. As paramilitary groups hardened their positions and took more control over the working class parts of the town, so the presence of the British Army was more and more in evidence.

The Army set up barracks in the police station of the New Barnsley estate. The police shared it for a while but eventually the Army took it over completely. It was on the Springfield Road opposite the Ballymurphy estate. Army patrols on foot or in jeeps became a common sight but, by this stage, they weren't seen as protectors by the Catholics, far from it.

At night, the street lighting was limited for security reasons. Soldiers on foot would hide in the hedgerows and bushes, faces blackened, in full camouflage gear, watching for any unusual activity or cars driving through the estate. At about 11.30 each night, I drove from Brenda's in East Belfast, where things were comparatively normal, to an urban guerrilla war zone.

The first time a soldier jumped into the road in front of me pointing an SLR rifle at my head, I thought I was going to die of a heart attack, never mind the bullet. One wrong move and it would have been Goodnight Vienna.

I froze.

The soldier, a man in his late 20s, stood and waited. He didn't say a thing. I didn't say a thing. I didn't move a muscle until he felt comfortable enough to come to the driver's side and indicate with his gun for me to wind down the window. He interrogated me as to who I was and why I was there to establish that I really was from the estate before allowing me to go on my way.

These guys were nervous. We were nervous. Every living, breathing thing was nervous. In a weird, macabre way these events soon passed for normal. Every time it happened, you let them get on with what they had to do and, basically, sat on your hands and kept your mouth shut until asked to say or do something. The crazy thing was I never stammered in these situations.

I've lost count of how many SLR rifles I've had pointed at my head. Readers, it's made me the sane, calm, restrained individual I am today.

Deep Joy Unbound

Deep Joy came back to Northern Ireland from London to play some gigs and ended up being the fall guys for some drugs run involving their roadie, Chico. 'Narco' Chico had stashed the gear in some record decks but the police knew all about it and put them under surveillance. The band was duly stopped leaving a gig but the gear wasn't in the van. Even so, they were charged, given a suspended sentence and got a criminal record for it. I do believe the guys when they say they didn't know about the drugs. Thanks to this debacle, I didn't see much of them. After two gigs and the court case, they went back to London.

Things didn't go well for them there. By December, they had disbanded and Gerry and Chris Morrison were back in Belfast. Gerry wanted to form his own band with Chris and asked Ferg and I if we would join them. He wanted to call the band, Joy.

We did some rehearsals at Chris's house and fell back on our old repertoire, which wasn't very inspiring. Clarkie was at teacher training college and already honing his promotional and organisational skills. He set up a gig at the training college's female campus, St Mary's. After the gig, Gerry pulled me to one side and told me that he had had a call from Rory Gallagher. He was to go to London to have a play.

"What shall I do?" he asked me.

It was the easiest piece of advice I have ever been asked to give.

I said, "Gerry, get over there as quick as you can."

He went and came back after a couple of days, walking just a bit taller. He waited a week to hear he'd got the gig to record with Rory. Although Gerry was never *officially* invited to join the band that was the beginning of his 20 year career with Rory.

The good thing that came out of that short time with Joy for me was that I realised what had been missing from my life for the past 10 months. I loved playing drums and making music and I loved being around musos.

I'd met a couple of lads at Shorts who were players. Bobby Dyer was a drummer and we began to practice together at lunchtime on the wooden benches. Arnie, another drummer, lived around the corner from Brenda and had a kit set up in his house (lucky git).

'Stewardy' Stewart was a bass player and Terry Holland was a guitar player. Terry had been in a band called Richmond Hill and I saw them play in the Marquee. They did a great version of 'Something in the Air' - the Thunderclap Newman song.

I was slowly developing more of a connection with East Belfast so, when Terry asked me to come along to a rehearsal for a new band, M.A.S.H., he was setting up, I didn't have to think twice about it. The repertoire was leaning towards Rock: songs like Deep Purple's 'Black Night' and Free's 'My Brother Jake', which I ended up singing.

I think the guys liked the fact that I wanted to get things right. We went over the drum parts in 'Black Night' until we couldn't get it wrong. We worked hard and got a real good set together. Terry Fagan, was on bass, Raymond Donnan doubled on tenor saxophone and flute giving our sound a lot of variety, and David Hamilton was a great singer/front man.

The rehearsals for M.A.S.H took place in Newtownards, a small town just outside Belfast. Raymond's father owned a coal merchant. We rehearsed in a lovely big garage at the back of his house - a proper garage band, you might say.

We started doing a few small gigs around town, which went well and led us to working with D.L.P. Promotions, who had some clout and eventually became our management. Gigs got better and we were being paid - a tenner a gig in 1971 wasn't too shabby.

One night we played at the Plaza Ballroom and the next day, we headed to Dublin to play the Stella Ballroom once again.

Terry drove a Morris Oxford at the time, a wonderful, big, sturdy old vehicle. As he was driving home from the Plaza, a drunk driver jumped the lights and crashed into him. His little tin can bounced off Terry's pride and joy, which was built like a tank, and careered through the window of a ladies' clothes shop. The car, the driver and mannequins, some clothed and some, now, unfortunately, naked, were strewn across the shop front and pavement. A picture of the ghastly scene was used in the anti-drink driving campaign on the lead up to Christmas that year (1971/2).

We drove to Dublin the next day. With the extra money flowing in, I decided to upgrade my car and found a Ford Anglia 105E in the classifieds. I didn't have all the 85 quid for the cash sale so Clarkie lent me the balance and I paid him off in instalments. When I had settled my debt to him, I asked him for the lend of some more for something or other. He wisely declined.

I gave my old car to my father. I don't remember why he didn't have one at the time. I had driven it for over a year without putting a scratch on it. He only had it a few weeks when he pulled out in front of another car after having been in a pub and wrecked the front wing.

M.A.S.H. was a great little band, but when Raymond was offered a job with the Freshmen, one of the biggest show bands in the country, it petered out. In early 1972, I joined the Regency Showband. Mervyn Crawford from Sam Mahood's Soul Foundation was the sax player and it had a lot of potential. I was only with them for about a month when Davy Hamilton turned up after a gig one night and told me that he had a new band and that I was going to be the drummer.

Davy and Terry had joined CSF together after M.A.S.H. and replaced two of the existing members. CSF stood for the City Skinhide and Fatstock Company. Alexis Korner had a band called CCS, which stood for the Collective Consciousness Society. It was Gordon Craig, who thought to steal Alexis' idea to abbreviate our name.

The band had been formed by Colin McClelland and Dougie Vance. Colin worked for City Beat magazine and had a lot of contacts. He wrote for NME and eventually moved into mainstream journalism when he became a features writer for the *Belfast Sunday News.*

The bulk of the band came from a four piece called Profile. Gordon Craig came from Headband. The drummer Malcolm Hill left and I was his replacement. Terry told the rest of the band that Davy, himself and I had already worked together and were a good unit. It worked out really well.

We rehearsed on the top floor of a Sixties office block opposite the Albert Clock, a Belfast landmark near the docks. Someone knew Joe the caretaker and we gave him a bung to let us use it in the evening when all the workers had gone home. We were also supposed to put money in the electricity meter but Davey was an electrician and he by-passed it so we had free power. We got our comeuppance. We sometimes stored our equipment there overnight and someone stole it. I lost a Ludwig snare drum. It was worth a good few pounds then and it would be just as pricey today.

Uncomfortable Unions

Jim and Maureen Russell were always very welcoming, understanding and patient. After internment was introduced, I stayed with them but being there on a full time basis upset the family routine. I slept in Brian's bed, which meant that he had to share with Brenda, which wasn't an ideal situation. Although Jim was the breadwinner, Maureen was the one who called the shots and Brenda and her mother didn't always see eye to eye.

Brenda and I had been going steady for six years. Our families had gotten to know each other. My parents had been to the Russell's on a number of occasions for drinks and supper. I would sometimes bring my young brother, Martin, on a Sunday. Everything was becoming very homely and familiar. People said we made a lovely couple. Even our names were similar: Brendan and Brenda. They all said it was meant to be, and so did we.

We went to a jewellers in town in June 1972 and picked a ruby engagement ring and set the day of our wedding for March, 2nd, 1973. It didn't occur to me, or anyone else, that I was only 20 and I would be 'Happily Married' by 21. My life had been mapped out in front of me: job at the aircraft factory, car, wife, next thing, a mortgage and, inevitably, children.

It wasn't long before there was trouble.

Brenda was a very attractive young woman and drew a lot of attention from other men. One night, we were playing at The Boat Club to a packed house and Brenda was dancing near the front with one of her friends.

As happens at dances, guys will ask girls, who were in pairs or on their own, to dance. We hadn't been engaged very long and, as I played, I saw this bloke ask Brenda to dance. I didn't like the idea of him dancing with her, and also, I didn't like the idea of others in the band seeing it either. It created in me a lethal mixture of testosterone, jealousy and male pride.

What should have happened was that she should have danced the one dance and then walked away with a "thank you" but she didn't. Dance number two and he was getting very chatty and I was getting very angry. Dance number three and he started touching her. Generations of stewed O'Neill rage surged through me.

I jumped up from behind the drum kit and rushed to the front of the stage, yelling and screaming at this bloke. The band kept on playing, as you do, but the whole gig fell apart. Davy put a gentle hand on my shoulder and told me to "Leave it."

The bloke with the dancing feet and the wandering hands looked up at me first, then, at the rest of the seven-piece band, and hopped it. Brenda felt humiliated and furious and, after the show, we had a blazing row. She ended up leaving with her friend and swore that she would never see me again. Our engagement seemed over before it had hardly begun but, after a week or so, predictably, we made it up.

The whole episode was obviously a bit childish and silly but, in truth, I think it exposed the way I was feeling about a lot of things then. I would wake up some mornings feeling very down. It seemed like a heavy black cloud hung over me. Some unnamed thing was weighing on my mind. At first, the feeling would last only a few hours but, as time went on, it lasted for days. I felt like I was in a hole and the longer I felt this way, the deeper and darker the hole would become, with less and less light reaching down to comfort me. I would sometimes lie in bed at night talking to a God I didn't believe in and asking him to not let me wake up the next morning.

I would always rise out of that black pit eventually but these feelings to a much lesser degree have stayed with me all of my life. I can detect when the gloom is coming now and take action to avoid it. It didn't occur to me at the time that I must be suffering from some kind of depression.

I had been working night shift - apart from weekends - for a month and I hadn't seen Mickey Flanagan or Jack Crichton in that time. On that first Monday morning back on days, things had changed.

A vacancy for the shop steward's job at the trade union had come up and I knew Mickey had applied for it. The majority of union members in Belfast were Protestant but the workers at Shorts elected Mickey as shop steward. The fact that he was a Catholic wasn't a concern. He was the best man for the job and would look after the interests of all concerned.

Recent events in Northern Ireland, however, had changed the nature of unions. There was a new organisation called L.A.W. - the Loyalists Association of Workers - which was led by a Protestant trade unionist called Bill Hull. He wanted to create an organisation that represented only Protestant workers. They were a heavyweight group and, later, it was learned that they had connections to the Ulster Defence Association, a Protestant paramilitary group.

They didn't like the idea of Mickey being elected. They overturned the decision and replaced him with a L.A.W. member. The dynamic of the shop floor changed from that moment and relationships were affected. It was the first time that I experienced religious and political tension there, which I was now beginning to understand. In Northern Ireland, they were one and the same thing.

L.A.W became so influential that on March 7th 1973, they called for a day of action in protest against the abolition of Parliament in Northern Ireland. They ensured that supplies of electricity in Belfast and surrounding areas were stopped, forcing the closure of industry and many shops. Apprentices in Shorts weren't expected to join the protest but, on the day, I found myself walking around a silent factory. Everything had come to a halt. The shipyards, everything, were closed.

There was a lot of violence that day. A gun battle with the Army ended with two Loyalists being shot dead and five people in total dying over 24 bloody hours. It was a frightening time.

Mainstream unionism, however, got a grip and rejected this approach. L.A.W., with its murky political and paramilitary connections, faded away by the middle of 1974.

What Religion Are You?

The first time I saw a road ramp, aka a 'sleeping policeman', was on the Springfield Rd outside the old police station, now a British Army barracks. They were there for security, to prevent drive-by shootings and the like. There were about six of them and they were so high, you had to drive very slowly and carefully, so as not to scrape the bottom of your car.

I was then 19 and driving by, as usual, at about 11.30 at night. Ahead of me, two cars were crawling over the ramps when the gates of the barracks opened and a patrol of soldiers filtered out. These patrols liked to get onto the main roads and off quickly onto side roads for safety. It was unusual for three cars to be on the ramps at that time of night so the patrol may have thought we would be good cover for them.

No sooner had the gates closed behind them than there was gunfire from the direction of the Ballymurphy Estate on the opposite side of the road. Some of the soldiers immediately dropped to the ground and crawled. Others ran to the side streets.

The drivers in the cars in front of me halted and we were stopped there for what seemed like an eternity as the bullets flew. The soldiers could not return fire because we would have been caught in the middle of it. I felt like a sitting duck.

When I came to my senses, I hit the accelerator of my little Anglia and overtook the cars ahead at speed. As the car hit the ramps, it became almost airborne but I raced on until I got to straight road and the New Barnsley turning. I hadn't looked back until that point and when I did, the other cars were moving but a long way behind. Maybe they had done the right thing. In retrospect, the soldiers might have thought that I was part of the ambush because I sped off so quickly. It's hard to know. I acted on instinct that night and it worked for me.

Confrontation and violence across the whole of Northern Ireland had reached new levels since internment was introduced in 1971. Individuals, who were suspected of being involved or connected to the IRA, were arrested in a series of early morning raids conducted by The British Army across the province. There were a lot of arrests in Ballymurphy and Turf Lodge.

On the morning of the raids, it was impossible to get out of the New Barnsley Estate. The whole area was in lockdown. I heard, for the first time, bin lids being hammered as a warning, which, in itself, was very primal and intimidating.

My mum was in a terrible state. For as sure as there were many arrested who were involved in the IRA, there were many who weren't involved at all. She wanted to get me out of the estate as soon as possible. I was nineteen at that time, the perfect age to get picked on and picked up.

I was meant to have gone to work that morning but was unable to go. My parents and I discussed what we should do and decided that I should wait until 10 and try to get through the army cordons then. I should make my way to work and stay with Brenda until things calmed down.

As I drove through the estate and on to the Springfield Rd, there was no-one to be seen. It was like a ghost town. The road looked wide and empty as I made my way to the checkpoint. I remember it so clearly: the light of the morning sun shone on a world in slow motion. Things that I had never paid attention to before, the hedgerows, the street lamps, came into sharp focus. When I arrived at the checkpoint, there was no queue. It was just me and a barricade of army vehicles and soldiers, guns at the ready.

A soldier came to the driver's window and asked me my name and where I was going. I delivered the answers as calmly and clearly as I could. He checked my driver's licence. We had had photo driving licences in Northern Ireland since the Sixties. Everyone carried them for ID.

The soldier handed my licence to another soldier, who got on the radio to see if my story stood up. The soldier, who had taken my licence, searched the car meticulously.

It probably took minutes but it seemed a lot, lot longer to me. When he had finished, the other guy had handed my licence back to him. He then came very close to the open window, put his hand behind my head and gave my long, shoulder length hair a really good tug. Maybe, he thought it was a wig. When it stayed on my head, he slowly handed me my licence and waved me through.

At any other time, in any other place, no-one would have pulled my hair and got away with it. In such circumstances as those, you just have to take it.

The journey past the barricade of New Barnsley was like a long, stifled sigh breathing out at last into clear air. It was a good mile or so before the streets felt normal. When I arrived at Shorts at gone 11 that morning, no-one said a thing to me. Over the next 48 hours, 17 people died. The Troubles were here and what was to come would be much, much worse.

January, 1972, began with an anti-internment rally. When the Army shot 27 people, 13 of whom died, it became known for ever more as Bloody Sunday. The IRA bombed targets in Northern Ireland and the rest of the UK, killing and maiming scores of people.

Tit for tat killings were everyday news. My 18 year old cousin, Raymond Mooney, a clean living, good Christian man was abducted from a bus stop on his way to work and murdered. We never found out why. It was a random act, probably in revenge for another, or just because.

My good friend, Davy Hamilton's wife, Marian, lost her brother, and Gerry's old girlfriend, Marty O'Kane, also lost hers, the same way, senselessly. Belfast was now a shocking and terrifying place. The longer it went on, the more death and violence became commonplace and part of everyday life. You learned not to go to certain places, you followed the beaten path.

Through all of this, Gerry would come home on a regular basis between tours with Rory. Once when he was over, we went to see a local band and met Billy McCoy, the Just Five guitar player of whom we were all in awe. Billy enquired politely of Gerry, "Are you home for your tea?"

In late June, Gerry was back again for a few days but this time, he brought with him Rod De'Ath, Rory's new drummer. CSF were, by then, in full cry, playing Romano's as the main attraction, the Starlight, the Queen's Court in Bangor, the Town and Country in Newtownards, and the King's Arms in Larne - all good gigs to play.

We were rehearsing in Donaghadee on a Monday and Gerry and Rod decided to come along with me. The equipment was already there and set up when we arrived. Rod and I chatted about snare drums and cymbals, as you do, and the lads had a bit of a jam. Gerry's playing had obviously really come on with the regular touring. After a while, they decided to go to the pub and let us get on with our own rehearsal. We were just packing down when they came back in very good spirits.

Rod repeated a conversation he'd had with a couple of girls. They had bought the girls drinks and they were intrigued by his accent. One of them asked where Rod was from. He told them he was from Wales. The next question, inevitably, was, "What religion are you?". Rod replied, "I'm a Buddhist". There was a short pause, then one girl asked, "Is that a Protestant or a Catholic Buddhist?". Rod had nearly choked on his drink, but that was Northern Ireland for you.

After the rehearsal, we said our goodbyes and headed back to Belfast. It had been a good night and even though it was ghostly quiet driving into town, we felt good. Direct rule had just been imposed to clear the way for talks between the British government and the IRA. A ceasefire had been called at midnight to coincide with the talks. There was reason to hope.

We were the only car driving along the Castlereagh Road heading towards the MountPottinger Road - both Protestant areas - when a car came up behind us at speed. It overtook and swerved in to have us off the road. I braked quickly and we ended up with two wheels up on the kerb.

We sat in silence. Gerry in the passenger seat looked at me and I looked at him. We quickly gathered our thoughts and decided to get out of there as fast as possible. We passed the junction from MountPottinger Road into Short Strand, a Catholic area, and had to slow for the traffic lights. I had just started to pick up speed again when an army patrol came into view on the left hand side.

The soldiers were standing in the shadows of doorways and, as we drove by, I saw one soldier run behind the car to get to the other side of the road. In the quiet of the night, shots rang out loud and clear. This time, I did look back and I saw the soldier fall.

Rod came out of whatever Buddhist meditative state he was in and started to scream and wave his arms about. Gerry and I both yelled at him to get his fucking head down while we did likewise. I put my foot down hard on the accelerator and didn't slow down until we got to the Queen's Bridge. I only stuck my head up now and then to see where we were going. No-one said much as I drove the guys the 15 minutes to Gerry's house and then made my way home.

We found out the next day that the soldier, who had run behind the car, had died. He was the last soldier to be killed before the short-lived ceasefire. With hindsight, we realised that the car that had wanted us off the road, knew, or was part of, that ambush. It had been a warning to us not to go on.

A few days later, CSF played a gig in Cookstown Town Hall. It was at venues like this that the other lads in the band would call me 'George'. They were all Protestants but we didn't want to draw attention to ourselves by calling me Brendan or, indeed, Mary. Gerry - and Rod, amazingly - came with us. They bought a carry-out from an off-licence due to the venue being alcohol-free.

CSF had a big sound and had a good horn section. Almost as soon as we started playing, the dance floor filled. In the middle of the crowd, there was a big country lad dancing with a girl. He took one small step to the left then four or five steps right and left, rural fashion. A little guy started to laugh at him. The big guy thumped him right in the ear with barely a break in his fancy footwork. We'd been laughing at him too but, mercifully, he hadn't noticed us.

After the show, Rod, Gerry, Davey and I went to the car park to get Davy's car. We had just driven onto the main road when we were stopped by the police. Luckily, Davy hadn't been drinking but the police did their usual checks and busted him for having a bald tyre. I know they were only doing their job but, after what we had been through, and in the grand scheme of things, it seemed awfully trivial. One lesson from that, I suppose, is life goes on. Just because bullets are flying around your ears, doesn't mean you can ride around infringing traffic laws.

Child Soldiers

I finished my apprenticeship in September 1972 and became a fully fledged airframe fitter, ready to build fuselage panels for the Skyvan.

As a reward, we were given a voucher to buy tools for our future as journeymen. However, I discovered that it was possible to spend this voucher at Harrison's Record Shop. So, I bought three albums instead: the original Fleetwood Mac's 'Greatest Hits', Van Morrison's 'His Band and Street Choir', and Steely Dan's 'Can't Buy a Thrill'. I was investing in my career, if you think about it, just not one at Shorts. I blagged the tools I needed anyway.

It was a whole new mindset working by myself, though. I was now responsible for my quality of work, meeting deadlines, discussing problems with the charge hand and arranging with inspectors to clear assemblies at certain points in manufacture. Components had to be riveted together before the next stage could begin. If these targets weren't met, we lost our productivity bonus. If you clocked in two minutes late then 15 minutes were docked from your wage packet. I lost pay regularly this way because of late night gigs. On one occasion, I was picked up from Shorts after work and we drove straight to Dublin for a gig. I got back to Belfast just in time to go home, wash, have breakfast and go to work.

I was earning about 40 quid a week. This, plus gig money, meant that I was doing OK. I did overtime too, which topped up my wages even more. I gave my mum housekeeping and started to save for the inevitable wedding with what was left.

My heart wasn't in the job though. I still dreamed of being a professional musician.

One Friday on my way home from work, I met Ferg and a couple of friends for a drink. I had five or six bottles of Piper, a Scottish beer that was popular in Northern Ireland at the time. It was the equivalent of three pints so by the time I got home, I was very drunk. I'm ashamed to say, I was sick in the toilet and had to go to bed to sleep it off. When I woke up, I felt like crap, and worst of all, I'd lost my wage packet, swollen that week with my overtime. It was gone, lost somewhere between the pub and home. I had to tell my mum that I had no housekeeping for her that week. I think I was more gutted than she was.

To be honest, I hated drinking. It's just that everybody did it. I could never take my drink in the competitive pub drinking stakes. I only really started drinking whiskey when I went on the road with Rory. I've made up for lost time, for sure, but it's a love/hate relationship, let's leave it at that.

1973 brought some changes to the political landscape of Northern Ireland. The NICRA campaign for 'one man one vote' bore some fruit. The law was changed to enable everyone over 18 to vote in local elections. As I have already said, I was spending a lot more time in East Belfast and the lines between Nationalism and Loyalism for me were blurred.

I remember 'debating' with my father as to who I should vote for. For him, there was no debate. I should put my X where every other Catholic Nationalist should put theirs and vote against Unionism. In his opinion, that would be for Gerry Fitt of the Social Democratic and Labour Party (SDLP), a coalition established by civil rights activists, Nationalists and some Unionists. Their aim was to unite Ireland by peaceful means. When I suggested to him that there was another point of view, he went mad. He told me in no uncertain terms that if I went against the grain, I was never to come home again.

I didn't fully understand the history of Northern Ireland at that time in my life. I didn't even realise the implications of universal suffrage. I had a vote now and should have made it count. My father's mistake was in not giving me a more balanced argument, informing me of the past that had affected him and his father before him. Instead, I was expected to fall into line without question, and that's something I'm not very good at.

I lived in East Belfast, I worked with Protestants and played in bands with them. I suppose I was naive about the historic and wider situation because of my personal experience at the time. He didn't explain. He ordered. Anyway, in the end, I did as I was told and voted with the Nationalists.

At the end of June, 1972, only days after Gerry and Rod had gone back to London, Raymond Donnan, the keyboard player from M.A.S.H. got in touch. He had been working with The Freshmen for seven months now and he told me that they were looking for a new drummer. He wanted me to come along for an audition at the Floral Hall. They were playing there that evening and trying out some drummers during the day.

The Freshmen were one of the biggest and most respected showbands in the country. They had opened for the Beach Boys on their 1967 Irish Tour and Rory went along to one of the shows. In an interview, Rory recalled that the Freshmen played first and did a medley of Beach Boys' songs so well that when the Beach Boys played the same songs later, they sounded rubbish by comparison.

Billy Brown was a multi-instrumentalist, arranger and musical director. He was the driving force behind the Freshmen's sound and success. They had nine Top 20 hits in Ireland and went on to write a lot of original material. Once again, I spoke to my dad about it. He advised me that I only had three months left of my apprenticeship and why would I throw that away.

I decided to play ball. I didn't go for the audition but who's to say that I would have got the job anyway.

Meanwhile, as Orangemen's Day, July 12th, approached, tensions and emotions ran high. The day celebrates the Battle of the Boyne when the Catholic King James II fought the Protestant King William of Orange on July 1st and was defeated. People prepared themselves for the worst. 1972 had been a horrendous year so far and didn't look like it would be easing up any time soon. Families were leaving in their droves, some temporarily, some permanently.

Gerry's parents moved to east London after his father had been injured in a bomb blast earlier that year. My brothers and sisters were living a day to day existence of fear and intimidation. Riots were frequent and soldiers were nervous. The longer into their tour of duty, the less tolerant they became.

My brother, Emmanuel, 14 at the time, was regularly being stopped and searched. He was pushed around and hit on the backs of his legs. He received a few slaps to the head and was verbally abused. The problem was that, in the riots and when Saracens went by, kids would be throwing stones at them. All kids then became suspects. Those soldiers weren't much more than kids themselves.

One Sunday, on his way to church, wearing his best clothes and heavily polished black shoes that my father insisted upon, he was stopped by a patrol. He was searched and found to have money in his pockets. When asked what it was for, he told them it was for the collection at Mass. One of them tossed the coins into a muddy puddle and ordered my brother to walk through it to retrieve them.

The IRA had begun recruiting in the schools and my sister, Elizabeth, at thirteen, got tangled up in it with some of her friends. She realised that my parents would not have approved of what she was doing but she found the courage to tell them what was going on. My father was livid and made it his business to find out who was in charge locally. He had to meet some heavy, heavy, people in the Provos. He told them that no way was his daughter getting involved. A lesser man wouldn't have had the balls.

Men armed with guns and rifles were now an everyday scene whether they be the Army or the IRA. I would sometimes have to pick my sister, Teresa, up from work, where she made men's suits at McGee's clothing factory. Public transport had stopped running in our areas. Sometimes, I would come out of the house in the mornings to find my car missing. I didn't know if it was the soldiers playing games or the IRA commandeering it. I always found it a few streets away. It got to the point where I would always check underneath it.

One Friday, as I arrived home from work, I was stopped by the Army on the hill just yards from my parents' house. The car was in the middle of the road as I was surrounded by a six-man patrol. They asked me to get out of the car and were particularly abrupt. They brought me around to the passenger side of the car and made me stand with my fingers on the top of the door at a forty five degree angle on tiptoe. They asked me my name, where I lived, and where I had come from.

I told them that I was coming home from work at Shorts. They started to laugh and told me that couldn't be right because Paddies didn't work, that I was a liar, a lazy so-and-so. They were trying to get me to react. They were pissed off for some reason and it was my turn that day to suffer for it. I had to stand like that for 10 minutes or so, which wasn't the worst interrogation known to man, but the whole time I was panicking that my old man would come out and see what was going on. The whole thing would have got very ugly.

They finally let me go and I drove the 20 yards home and parked the car. Luckily, my father and his hot temper weren't at home. For myself, I was learning all the time to keep calm.

My father played the accordion and sang in a couple of drinking clubs in Ballymurphy with a mate of his, who played drums. They called the drummer 'Wee Packy' and I would sometimes repair his drum for him - drum, singular.

One night when they got back to our house from one of the clubs, Packy became very ill. His stomach blew up like a balloon and he was rolling around in pain, in a very bad way. It just happened that a patrol was passing our house so rather than call and wait for an ambulance, my mum asked one of the soldiers if they could help. They did and got him to hospital a lot quicker than we could have and probably saved his life. He was diagnosed with an acute condition, which I don't recall. He died eight months later.

The Evacuation

On the morning of the Twelfth, all sorts of rumours had begun circulating. Stories of impending conflict and bloodbaths were rife. A lot of people from the estates around got together to figure out what to do. It was decided that as many children as possible should be evacuated from these areas in case the worst happened.

My sister, Bernadette, remembers being in the girls' bedroom when my mum called her to the front room and asked her if she would go along to chaperone some of the youngsters to Dublin. Bernadette wasn't yet 17 herself but she agreed to go. My sister, Teresa, didn't want to be left on her own so she volunteered as well.

Bernadette is very strong willed and organised. She and Teresa went to Our Lady of Mercy School for Girls in Ballysillan, where they were taught by the nuns. Bernadette had a tough time there and I think most other girls her age would have buckled under the pressure.

When Bernadette was 15 and preparing for her CSE exams, her teacher at this time was Sister Carmel, who, for some reason, took against Bernadette. That nun never missed an opportunity to humiliate and undermine my sister's confidence. She would wait at the school entrance in the mornings and stop Bernadette before she could get into the corridor and her classroom.

Standing just inside the main door in full view of the other pupils, she would take a 360 degree turn around Bernadette and point with a cane at any imperfections in her school uniform. She would finish by telling her that she was a disgrace to the school.

In class, this woman would verbally abuse and cane Bernadette almost every day for something or other. Bernadette, however, refused to be broken, kept her chin up and had an answer for every occasion. Sister Carmel became more vindictive as the war of wills reached stalemate. Jim Clarke's sister, Marion, who was in the same class, will vouch for the treatment my sister had to endure from this Christian woman.

Bernadette finally told my mum what was going on but my mother found it hard to believe that a nun would do such a thing. Eventually, things got so bad and Sister Carmel so infuriated that she sent a message to my mother to come to the school to discuss Bernadette's 'behaviour'.

My mother went and listened while Sister Carmel ran Bernadette down: she was disruptive, cheeky, rude and would amount to nothing. She said she was sorry that my mother had such a cross to bear. At that point, Elizabeth O'Neill Snr lost it.

My mother told the nun that she was not only a bully but wasn't fit to wear the habit of a Sister of Mercy nor to teach young girls. She added that she was a disgrace to the Catholic Church and threatened to take the matter further. She finished by demanding both her girls' 'cards' as they would not be returning to the school. The school complied but when Bernadette got her card, it said that the reason why she left was that she had been expelled.

When Bernadette left school, she got a job in a cafe. A young guy called Paddy Creed came to our house every Friday night to collect monies that my Mum owed to Bannon and Victor Morris, for general household goods she had bought on tick. He got Bernadette an interview as an office clerk for the company and she got the job. She worked there with Jim Ferguson's sister, Una.

Sister Carmel eventually wrote and apologised. She also said that she had put Bernadette forward for a job as a veterinary assistant. Her act of remorse was ignored.

Teresa was too young to leave school and she went to St Rose's nearby. The class she should have gone to was full so she ended up going to a lower stream and she hated it. At the end of the year, some of her friends were going to McGee's clothing factory for jobs and Teresa went with them. She got a job and went to work the following Monday.

(I'm proud to say that all of my sisters have got college degrees now, despite the interruptions to their schooling that people and circumstances created.)

The three girls: Bernadette, Teresa and Elizabeth got on the coach full of kids going to Dublin, leaving 10 year old Martin at home. I'm sure my mother felt a lot better about Bernadette going with the group. Emmanuel had gone on holiday to Butlins on the North coast with a friend's family. He arrived home the following weekend knowing nothing of what had happened. When the returning family drove through the estate, it was deserted. There were no kids out playing. Nothing.

Anyway, when the three girls arrived in Dublin with the rest of the group, they were brought to an old fever hospital called Clonskeagh that the Irish Government had allocated to those escaping the violence in the North. The wards were converted into dorms and they were to spend their time there until it was safe to go home. Mum, Dad and the two boys joined them at Clonskeagh. A few days later, Emmanuel came back from Butlins and also joined them while I went on holiday with the Russells.

In early August, my parents arrived back from Dublin leaving Bernadette and Teresa to stay at the hospital to deal with the younger kids. When my sisters were due to come home, they rang my mum and told her that they didn't want to come back to Belfast. They had found a flat and jobs and wanted to stay in Dublin. They felt safer there.

Belfast was so restrictive because of the Troubles. Bernadette has just turned 17 and Teresa wasn't yet 16. My mum was afraid for them living in New Barnsley so she agreed and found the 15 pounds that they needed for a deposit on a flat. She went to visit them often, taking Martin with her, leaving Emmanuel and Elisabeth with Dad.

He was meant to be looking after them but, because he drank more when my mother was away, they ended up looking after him. Emmanuel was 14 and Elisabeth, 13. It had a profound effect on them. They must have felt so lonely and neglected. They were too young for the responsibility and vulnerable because of the bleak situation in which they were living.

The trauma of this existence was evident in everyone. I know my mum thought she was doing the right thing trying to mother us all, no matter how far apart we were, but the truth was that the family was fragmenting. In my head, I had been the first to go.

London Beat

Jim planned to spend his annual fortnight's holiday in Blackpool and Brenda and I planned to spend the first week with the family and then head to London to see Gerry for a week. It would be my first trip 'abroad'.

Blackpool was a novelty. The weather was fine and we enjoyed the sights in the first couple of days. We did the amusement arcades and went on the dodgems. The Bed and Breakfast accommodation was a bit dark and dingy and I had to share a room with Brian. By Wednesday, I was doing all I could to get Brenda back there for a bit of hanky-panky while the others did other things.

On the Thursday night, we went to the stage show of 'The Comedians'. The Northern Irish comic, Frank Carson, was on the bill and we saw him in the bar at the interval. He was loud and I wasn't quite sure if I liked him or not. Probably not. By then, Blackpool was beginning to lose whatever charm it had for me and I couldn't wait to get to London.

On Saturday morning, we boarded the train to The Smoke and waved the others goodbye. We changed at Crewe and arrived in London by the afternoon.

The Rory Gallagher Band was really starting to take off and as it happens in these situations, plans changed. The band had to fly off somewhere that day but Gerry organised for their roadie, Gus, to pick us up from the train station and bring us to Rod's house where Gerry rented a room and where we were going to stay for the week.

Gerry must have had a thing about living with drummers. He stayed with me in Belfast. He stayed with Wilgar when he first moved to London to join Rory. It was because Gerry lived with Rod that Rod got the gig with Rory in the first place. When Wilgar got ill and couldn't make some of the shows, Rod depped for him. He eventually got the job full time.

Rod's place was in Knollys Road in Streatham, where he lived with his German girlfriend, Anne-Marie. It was a leafy road with really nice houses on the hill behind the High Road. It was such a breath of fresh air compared to what we had come from and I don't mean Blackpool. Wilgar lived close by and Gerry left me his number to contact him.

Brenda and I spent the first few days trekking around the West End sightseeing. It was so special seeing and being in London and feeling a different city's identity. I felt as if a weight had been lifted from me, just being able to walk about in safety and breathe easily.

We went to a curry house in Streatham, only the second that we had ever been to. We'd been to one in Dublin a couple of years earlier with Gerry and Marty but none of us could eat the food because it was too spicy hot. This first London curry was delicious.

I gave Wilgar a call and he was really welcoming. He was now playing with Mick Abraham's Blodwyn Pig. (Mick had been the guitar player with Jethro Tull.) I went with him to Soho to pick up a kit he was having renovated by Eddie Ryan, probably the best 'drum doctor' in London at the time. His gaff was just behind Shaftesbury Avenue. We went to Rose Morris' music store where Rod bought his Slingerland drum kit. It was reputed to have been played by the great man himself, Buddy Rich.

On Thursday night, one week after we had been to see 'The Comedians' in Blackpool, Wilgar asked us if we would like to go to a jazz gig at the Plough in Stockwell. "There's a great drummer playing there," he said.

Brenda and I met Wilgar and his wife, Irene, on the High Road and took the bus to Stockwell. The Plough was a regular pub - bar in the middle and tables and chairs to the right. To the left was a rectangular room with a stage at the opposite end. The stage was set for a jazz trio so we got some drinks in and sat close to the front.

Right on nine of the clock, the band hit the stage and started to play. My chin hit the floor. The drummer was Phil Seamen, arguably the greatest drummer ever to come out of the British Isles. He was the band leader and he played with such swing, sensitivity and flair. His press rolls were smooth, dynamic and bombastic, all within a few bars. I looked towards Wilgar and he nodded knowingly. He had seen him before.

Phil Seamen was Ginger Baker's hero and now I understood why. He was one of those elite players like Tony Oxley or Bryan Spring, who changed the environment they were in with their great musicality. I looked around the pub in the interval and saw just 10 other people watching this great musician and the entrance was free.

The second set was as impressive as the first. He played with a fag hanging out of his mouth most of the time. For me, he was the height of cool. I feel very privileged to have seen him play because he died just a few months later. His heroin and alcohol abuse caught up with him at the age of just 46.

I left the Plough on a musical high that night. As we left London on Saturday on a flight to Belfast, I knew that I wanted to get back to London as soon as possible to make music.

Back in Belfast, I decided to up my game and take drum lessons. Someone recommended a guy called Tommy - 'Thomas' to me. He was very popular on the jazz and cabaret circuit and he was a founding member of a comedy group called the Club Sound. He was Welsh and had played the drums for The Welsh Guards. I went once a week to his house off the Malone Road, a very posh part of town in the wealthy, leafy south east of Belfast.

We started at the beginning, learning the rudiments. I would have paid the pound for the lesson just to listen to him play those rudiments on a telephone directory, which he often did.

Tommy introduced me to the great jazz drummers, such as Max Roach and Elvin Jones, and I ate it up. We listened to Coltrane and Count Basie. He exposed me to a different form of musical emotion. Not that there was anything wrong with what I was already listening to. I only have to listen to Otis Redding singing 'These Arms of Mine', Joni Mitchell sing 'A Case of You' or John Lennon scream 'Don't Let Me Down' to understand the depth of emotion in a human voice. This was another soundscape, something different that I hadn't heard until then.

Tommy played with the BBC Jazz Orchestra and after I'd been going to him for about six months, he brought me along to one of their rehearsals to play percussion. He said that he would like me to play together with him, permanently, but couldn't promise me anything because of the internal politics at the BBC. (I didn't get the gig but it was still a great buzz to be part of it.)

I also bought myself a Slingerland drum kit on the HP that Jim Russell stood guarantor for. It cost 250 quid new and I still have it.

In November of 1972, CSF played in Dublin at the Eamonn Andrews Studios, and Bernadette and Teresa came along to the gig. It was great to see them and they decided to drive home with us after the show to surprise our parents. It was the first time that they had been back to Belfast since July.

All of Us

For the last two years of my apprenticeship, I had taken a day release course every Wednesday during the day and Thursday evenings. I went to Belfast College of Technology to study a City and Guilds in Aeronautical Engineering. At the end, I got my diploma. More importantly, while I was doing this, I met a saxophone player called Sam Waddell, a really nice guy. We would often talk about putting a band together.

One day, he told me about a friend of his, who was doing just that and was on the lookout for musicians. First off, he introduced me to John McCullough, a young, bass player, in his last year at Grosvenor High School. Sam was a lab technician there, which was how he knew of him.

It was a little strange that Sam was busy finding players for a band that he was never going to be in because they didn't want a sax player. Nevertheless, John and I expressed our interest. Sam's friend was a piano player called John McCormach, who lived on the Donegal Rd. Sam arranged for John McCullough and I to meet them there. Sam didn't turn up but when we arrived, instead there was another guy called Stan Brennan, the would-be singer, with John McCormach.

John and Stan had spent the previous summer in London and had stayed in a massive house with a dozen rooms in Belsize Avenue. It was inhabited by a lot of Irish musicians. Gary Moore and Eric Bell had rooms there, as did Gay and Terry Woods. Phil Lynott was a regular visitor.

Gay and Terry were probably the most established players, at that time, who were living at Belsize. Terry had been with Sweeney's Men, a very influential folk rock group and they were both in the original line up of Steeleye Span. Terry went on to play and write with the Pogues. Back then Gay and Terry were in the throes of putting together their own band, which became the Woods Band.

John and Stan were really taken with the whole scene and Gay and Terry's vocal harmonies, in particular. When they arrived back in Belfast, they wanted to get a band together that combined all of those musical elements from Belsize Avenue that had made such a lasting impression.

Stan was the Rag social secretary at Queen's University and together with Michael Clifford and Roger Armstrong, one of the founders of Ace Records, they formed the Esoteric Music Society - EMS, as it was known. It organised gigs featuring local bands every Sunday night at the McMordie Hall.

Stan had a band of his own called Wee Jimmy and the Wardrobes. The band comprised anyone in the audience who fancied playing that night. It was very Grateful Dead in philosophy, Stan's interpretation of the inclusive San Francisco hippy scene in Belfast. EMS also ran a cinema club showing avant garde films of the era.

EMS began to bring underground bands from England to tour the universities in Ireland, including Queen's in the North, of course. They worked with an agency called Black Hill, based in London. The tour would take in Galway, Cork, University College and Dublin. Bands like Stackridge and the Edgar Broughton Band started to play the Sunday night gig at McMordie Hall, which really upped the ante.

The scene was well established before our new band, All of Us, was born. As the gigs with All of Us were mostly on Sunday nights, they didn't interfere with the CSF gigs.

The McMordie Hall held about 400 to 500 people and All of Us rehearsed in a little room next to it. The first band practice revealed the fifth and final member of the band, Pete Boardman, a guitar player, who was teaching Stan to play bass. He was a Lancashire lad, who moved to Northern Ireland when he was 14. His dad worked for British Road Services and he had relocated to Belfast, where he did the same kind of work.

Pete was a very genuine and honest guy. I liked him from the off. The first time I went to Pete's house, he had 'Abbey Road' on the turntable and we sat and listened to Side A and Side B of that album without saying a word - he was that comfortable to be around.

The whole thing gelled instantly. John and Stan had a list of songs that they wanted to try so we started at the top of the sheet and worked our way down. I hadn't played any of the tunes before so everything was fresh. The songs included one from 'The Rock Machine Turns You On', a budget priced sampler that included such unknowns as Bob Dylan, Moby Grape, Spirit, the United States of America. the Zombies, Peanut Butter Conspiracy, Leonard Cohen, Blood Sweat and Tears, the Byrds, Simon and Garfunkel, Taj Mahal, the Electric Flag (led by the drummer, Buddy Miles, who played with Jimi Hendrix), Roy Harper, Tim Rose, and Elmer Gantry's Velvet Underground. We picked out Spirit's 'Fresh Garbage' for our set list. I wish I still had that album. I played it to death.

The other tracks that we tried were: 'Sinning For You' by Keef Hartley, Neil Young's 'Birds', the Byrds' version of 'It's All Over Baby Blue', which featured on the soundtrack of the movie, Easy Rider, 'Time of the Season' a song by Rod Argent that was a big hit for the Zombies. We did 'Bus Stop' by the Hollies, a folk tune called 'Kitty of Coleraine' and a Fleetwood Mac track, but I can't remember which one now.

Over a few weeks, the students got to know that we were rehearsing there and sometimes up to 30 people would be outside listening. If someone left the room, the music didn't stop. If two or three people left the room, it didn't stop. Once just Pete and I were left and we started to work out odd time signatures. It was the first time that I remember trying to play in that way.

For the next five months or so, we played about a dozen shows at McMordie Hall as the opening act. On one occasion, the headline act couldn't make it and we filled the headline slot.

We opened for bands such as: the Chieftains, who were semi-professional then, Carol Grimes and Uncle Dog, a kind of folk rock band, Quiver, a Scottish band, who had worked with Al Stewart, and Brinsley Schwarz. Both the latter were really impressive and showed a lot of talent. Nick Lowe was playing with the Brinsleys then. The bass player from Quiver, Bruce Thomas, went on to play with Elvis Costello and the Attractions, and to write books, including one on the actor and martial arts star, Bruce Lee.

We opened for the Woods Band, who were superb. Terry Woods asked our bass player, John McCulloch, to join them. Unfortunately for them, the poaching expedition failed because John was in the same predicament as me at the time. He had made plans. He wanted to go to Queen's and get some qualifications before turning pro.

We also opened for John Martyn and Martin Carthy, both London folk players. They asked to play Pete's Les Paul guitar at the sound checks despite them both having acoustic guitars themselves. John Martyn had a gig the day after and no lift so Pete drove him to Coleraine while John chatted the whole way.

One evening in our rehearsal room, the door opened and there were Thin Lizzy: Phil, Eric Bell and Brian Downey.(The first time Lizzy were booked to play for EMS, the posters read Tin Lizzy. Someone had spoken to Phil on the phone and because of his thick Dublin accent, the aitch was lost in translation.)

They came into the room and Phil asked if he could have a go on John's bass. He played with us for a bit. The next time I played with Phil was at the Punchestown Racecourse, when he came and jammed with Rory. The concert was a benefit for Hot Press, an Irish music magazine. U2 were third on the bill. We headlined. There was a reception afterwards and all my family came down. I was talking to someone when this guy came up to me and introduced himself.

"Hello, I'm the Edge," he said, to which I, a tad bemused, replied, "Hello, I'm the drummer."

Our gigs were becoming something to look forward to and we had our own little following on the campus. On one occasion, John and Stan dropped some edible Lebanese Temple Balls before a gig. John started the piano intro to Neil Young's 'Birds' and, when Stan eventually began - and the emphasis is on 'eventually'- he was in the wrong key. When John joined in for the chorus, he chose a different key again. It was a discordant mess but I think the listeners must have thought it was intentional. It sounded nothing like 'Birds', that's for sure.

At the May Ball, we were having a wonderful time doing Grateful Dead's version of 'Turn on your Love Light' and, of course, it was going on and on, as it should. The crowd were really getting into it until some guy with long hair, parted to the side, wearing John Lennon glasses, blue crushed velvet loons and a tie dye t-shirt, started to hurl abuse.

No-one paid him any attention until he decided to throw a bottle. It hit Stan, who ran off the stage after 'Lennon', who was attempting to leg it. Pete and John followed. Pete got to the guy first and started to lay into him. It was a real surprise to all because Pete's the most pacifist person on the planet. Stan tripped on the stairs and cut his hand on the bottle. He had to go to A&E. 'Not John Lennon' had ruined what had been a great gig.

There was a real family feel about those times. Rastus did the sounds. Paul McGuiness did the lights. They looked after us as much as they looked after the headline. We sometimes had two girls, Josey and Joy, sing with us on a few songs. It was a very loose but somehow cohesive and productive time. We were even starting to write some original tunes. The hippy dream came to an end at the end of the university term when we all went in different directions.

All the while, Belfast was burning.

Death Will Find You

By Autumn 1972, Davy Hamilton was getting a lot of offers as a solo artist. He started to make a name for himself on the cabaret scene, working with some of the best names in the business and beginning his ultimately long and successful career.

No sooner had CSF ended when I was offered a gig with a band called Spring, John McCormach on piano and Sam Wadell on sax. At last I was in a band with Sam. Harry Filmer was lead guitar, James Meredith on bass and Dusty Hagan, reputed to have a mighty axe, or so he told us, on vocals. The band rehearsed in a barn in Groomsport out in County Down. The first time we went there, I had to clear it of all sorts of agricultural debris so we could get in and practise.

The band had a lot of potential and we were confident. The repertoire was great. We played tracks such as Chicago's '250624', Santana's 'Samba Pa-Ti', Blood, Sweat and Tears' 'Spinning Wheel', 'Vehicle' by the Ides of March and a track by the Roy Young Band called 'Granny's Got A Painted Leg'. We also did Top 40 tunes such as 'Storm in a Teacup' by the Fortunes.

James would record the Top 20 every Sunday night from the radio and give the band members a copy. We would then decide which new numbers to add to the set. We were a soul band verging on a show band. Add to that, Damien MacIlroy from the Freshmen, the most influential band in the country, was our manager.

We were playing great venues. We did the usual gigs in the North but played a lot more in the South - places such as the Top Hat in Dun Laoghaire, Waterford, Killarney. We also played the TV Club and the Eamonn Andrews Studio in Dublin.

We had a roadie called Raymond, who got the band into a few awkward situations. He was forever pinching tables and chairs from venues. He didn't seem to care that it wasn't his reputation on the line but ours. (He repented later in life when he became a Born Again Christian.)

It must have been a roadie thing back then because Sunshine had two guys that took kleptomania to a different level. James Meredith went to their flat on the Stranmillis Road one time to pick up some amplifiers. He could hardly get through the door for the booty that had been liberated from venues around the country. Yes, there were the usual tables, chairs and pictures but there were also a couple of bears and a full sized wooden carving of an American Indian, which James recognised from a gig in Monaghan.

Sam Wadell and John McCormack were close mates but, as time went on, we all three developed a good friendship. Sam, like most of the guys that I was playing with in those days, was a Protestant and came from the Old Park Road. He met a young girl at a gig, who was from somewhere near Strangford Lough. He fell head over heels for her. The trouble was, she was a Catholic.

Neither of them wanted to mess things by involving either of their families in their new relationship. Brenda and I spent a couple of weekends with them in Portaferry, a fishing village at the mouth of Strangford Lough. We would drive down there on a Saturday afternoon and meet them in a local pub. Sam made his own way there on his Honda 50 earlier in the day. We stayed at a guest house and after breakfast took long walks on the shores of the lough. They were very close.

John McCormack had a car but, John being John, it was no ordinary car. It was an old hearse: one reliable owner, serviced regularly, low mileage. He would sometimes bring it to local gigs and, on one occasion, got a puncture. We searched everywhere in the car for the jack but drew a blank until someone at the venue told us that these vehicles didn't have a manual jack. It wouldn't look good if the funeral director and pall bearers had to change a wheel on the way to the graveyard with the bereaved family looking on. Instead, at the push of a button, a built-in hydraulic leg descended and raised the car sedately so the wheel could be changed as quickly as possible.

James, like me, was holding down a day job at that time and by his own admission, he was asleep there most of the time. We inevitably hit a bump in the road. 'Dusty' Hagan, our singer, was offered a job with a band called Dunno.

Damien McIlroy, our manager, felt we could carry on without him so the lead singing duties fell on James, who did the backing vocals and had a good voice anyway. It was a lot to ask one person to do in such a short space of time. As I had done some lead vocals with Deep Joy and M.A.S.H., I offered my services to share the load. Nerves got the better of me when I made this gesture and James remembers it coming out something like this:"I   c...c...c...ooooould
s...s...s...s...sing   M...m...m...my
B...b...b...b...b..brother
J...J...J...J...Jaaaake."
The other lads did well to keep from laughing in my face.

We did one or two gigs this way but it was clear that the band had lost something. We were to lose a lot more.

Sam had an accident on his Honda 50 and was killed outright. It was the first time in my life that I had lost such a close friend in such a way. He was only 23 or 24 years old, with such a great future. It was a very difficult thing to comprehend or come to terms with because it was so random. People were dying every day in Belfast during the Troubles but this was hard to take in because there was no reason for it. It was simply an accident at a time when we were still young enough to think that we were immortal and invincible.

The funeral procession left his house and headed towards the Old Park Road. There were friends and family, people from outside the music scene as well as musicians - a real cross-section. I was surprised not to see James Meredith and Harry Filmer there.

It turned out that they had driven from Bangor and were running late. When they got to the junction of the Crumlin and Old Park Roads, they tucked in behind a funeral procession that they assumed was Sam's but it wasn't. They followed that second funeral to a different cemetery in completely the wrong direction.

We were all in such shock at the time that no-one thought about his girlfriend or if anyone had contacted her. She was a secret. Only Brenda and I had met her and only a couple of times. We just didn't think. We never found out what happened to her or if she even knew what had happened to Sam.

On a cold winter's night, eight or nine months after Brenda and I had moved to London. I had a call from John McCormach. He was on his way to India and was overnighting in London. I convinced him to come to the East End to see us before he went on his way. He got the train to Forest Gate where I met him at the station. We picked up a couple of bottles of Guinness on the way back to our flat. After a bite to eat, we sat around talking and drinking and he told us that he had spent a couple of months in India and enjoyed it so much that he had to go back. Time slipped away, he missed the last train and stayed over. It was a lovely night and the next morning, we waved him goodbye.

It was the last time we ever saw him.

A month later, he fell down a ravine and was killed. John and Sam died just a couple of years apart. They were great friends and died so young. It still doesn't seem right.

One of the last gigs I did with CSF was on the north coast in a town called Coleraine. One or two of the lads had taken their own cars but most of us were in the van - a blue, long wheelbase Transit with the band name in psychedelic lettering written alongside it. One of our roadies, either Tom or Eamon, was driving.

It was an overcast night making the roads darker than normal. Davy and I were sitting up front and the usual banter after a high energy gig was flying around. Everyone was very relaxed until we saw a checkpoint ahead dimly illuminated by a red light. It was impossible to tell who it was who was stopping us - the Army, the RUC, the UDR or IRA or any number of other paramilitaries.

The driver slammed on the brakes and pulled to the side of the road sending, what we now realised, were Army personnel diving for cover behind their vehicles and into ditches. When the van finally came to a halt, silence descended over the whole scene. We knew full well that any sudden movement and God only knows what would happen. It was bloody terrifying as, slowly, the soldiers came out of hiding, guns at the ready. They checked us over and sent us on our way. It was probably the most frightened I have ever been in my life.

On another occasion, coming across the border towards Newry, Davy, Marian, Brenda and I had a similar experience at another checkpoint. Again, it was dimly lit and hard to see. Davy had to brake hard to avoid ploughing into what was an Army patrol.

The uncertainty of who was setting up and stopping cars at checkpoints was no better illustrated than in 1975, just three years later, when the Miami Showband were stopped near the border, in the early hours, on their way back to Dublin. It was something that was routine for bands going either way, North to South and South to North and both sides of the political divide.

They were stopped at what appeared to be a military blockade but it turned out to be a UVF paramilitary unit dressed in British Army uniforms. The band had been targeted and the subsequent investigation exposed the murky world of the Glenanne Gang, who carried out the attack. The court case revealed that two of them were planting a bomb on the Miami Showband bus and it went off prematurely. The rest of the gang panicked and shot five of the band; three died and two were wounded.

They were one of the most popular bands in the country and the incident exposed the vulnerability of musicians traveling in remote areas at that time.

I was in London by then but it put the shivers up everyone. This was the terror that had been and was around us and it came from every corner and every persuasion. It taught us that there was nowhere to hide. You couldn't lie down anywhere. You just had to get on with it and do what you wanted to do. You lived for the moment.

All Grown Up

A year before we got married, Brenda developed some sort of eating problem. She felt as if she had an obstruction in her throat that made it difficult to swallow. The doctors could find nothing wrong but she began to hide food and sometimes be sick. As a consequence, she lost a lot of weight and we were all concerned for her.

It was the first time I had experienced this part of her. It seemed so out of character. She was a strong and assertive person and this new vulnerability was a shock to me.

Brenda's mother, Maureen, did not show her much sympathy. Not that Maureen was unconcerned but she was old school. She thought that if Brenda didn't pull herself together, or at least make an effort to, she would get worse. It caused a lot of tension in the house and affected their relationship even when Brenda's health eventually improved.

Plans for our wedding were completed by the end of January 1973 and all was set for March 2nd. There were the usual complications: the size of the guest list, which family members and friends to invite. If one partner has a large family and the other a small one, do you invite equal amounts from each side - small wedding - or throw the doors open - large wedding?

In the end, we compromised on 40 guests. My horde was slightly pared down but I was just pleased my Granny Lagan could come. Fergie and Clarkie came, as did Pete Boardman. My sister, Bernadette, was bridesmaid. The service was at St Colmcille's Church in Ballyhackamore. The reception was at the Greenan Lodge Hotel on the Upper Newtownards Road, opposite where Brenda lived. The venues were five minutes apart.

I asked Gerry to be my best man but he couldn't make it because he was on tour in Scotland with Rory. It was Rory's birthday into the bargain so I asked David Hamilton to step in and he agreed immediately.

It was all going well. The service was lovely. The meal was lovely. Jim Russell made a small speech. My dad raised a toast. I said a few words and then it was Davy's turn.

He spoke about how we all met, told a few tales about times we had together, said what a lovely couple we were and concluded by saying that "if Brendan bangs Brenda the way he bangs those drums, they'll have a great life together."

Some of the guests didn't quite grasp what he'd said, some couldn't quite believe what he'd said, the rest burst out laughing. I felt for Jim Russell but I was struggling not to laugh myself. I was on the top table so I kept my head down. Davy was laughing at his own joke. (As I have already said, he did very well in cabaret in later years, which comes as no surprise.)

Brenda and I spent our honeymoon in Dublin, near Stillorgan. On the second day, Brenda rang her mother to tell her that we were safe and sound and everything was OK. Half way through the conversation, Maureen asked Brenda straight out: "Has he done it yet?"

Brenda, not usually at a loss for words, was speechless. She could have replied, "He has been doing it for quite a while," but it didn't seem wise.

When we got back from our honeymoon, the family agreed that we would live at the Russell's house. Brenda's brother, Brian, had started going out with a very pretty, quiet young girl called Elizabeth Rogers. Their new relationship was a sweet addition to the family but there were still tensions in the home between Brenda and her mother. Trivial things such as the making of packed lunches caused difficulties. Maureen expected Brenda to make mine for me like a good wife.

It all got too much and we decided to move on and get a place of our own. We found a flat before we told Jim and Maureen of our decision and, almost immediately, relations between us all improved.

It was a furnished flat in a massive converted Victorian house at 124, Upper Newtownards Rd. Ours was Number 2 with a monthly rental of 26 pounds. The flat had a kitchen, a private bathroom and toilet and a massive bedroom/lounge. We moved in on the first of June, 1973. Brian and Liz were regular visitors and I had room to store both of my drum kits. Mum and Dad came to visit too. All of a sudden, we felt very grown up.

I started a residency at the Celebrity Club in Royal Avenue with Terry Holland, Paul Bennett and Phil Turner every Saturday. It was a quiet, low key gig but good nonetheless because I hadn't played with Paul since Angelo Stone days. Davy Hamilton, meanwhile, was doing a residency at the Imperial in Bangor with a band called Sparkle. I'd sometimes go down to see them. Pete Boardman was playing guitar and there was a young bass player called Trevor Boyce, and Billy Bell on drums. I depped for Billy for a couple of weeks.

My friend, John McCollough, was now at North East London Polytechnic and, before he went back after the summer break that year, he did a gig in Belmont with an innovative band called Swift. John Mason was the piano player and Robin Lavery played drums. They had a sax player too, whose name I can't recall. John Mason, just twenty, was a very accomplished musician for his age, with both jazz and classical influences in his playing.

Swift played a style of music that was completely different to any other I had heard in Belfast. Their music was sometimes deceptively simple in arrangement while, at other times, very complex. They combined tunes such as Soft Machine's 'Chloe and the Pirates' and 'Out-bloody-rageous' with Stevie Wonder songs sung by the drummer, Robin. They played songs by Chick Corea and also included Cannonball Adderley's 'Mercy, Mercy', written by his piano player, Joe Zawinul, who would become a big influence on us all with his band, Weather Report.

After the Swift gig, John introduced me to the others and I exchanged numbers with John Mason. It seemed to me that John was the musical driver in the band and, possibly, the one who put it all together.

Davy Hamilton, meanwhile, had another new band called Chaser with a great line up: Billy McCoy and Billy Brown, who had played together with Just Five on guitar and bass, Billy Bell on drums. As I wasn't doing many gigs at that time, I'd go and watch Chaser in Bangor and I'd meet up with Pete Boardman and the Boyce brothers, Trevor and Terry, who played drums at the weekends.

Later that year, John Mason got in touch to say that Robin Lavery had left to rejoin his old band, Chips, and asked if I would do some rehearsals with them. That's all it was but it was a great learning experience for me: playing in odd time signatures and so forth. When John McCollough went back to college in London, they had no bass player. I suggested Trevor Boyce and, happily, he got the job.

Gerry got back home on one of his, by now, less frequent trips. Rory's schedule was full on by that time. Ferg, Gerry, Brenda came to the Celebrity Club for my gig and afterwards we let our hair down. The craic was mighty as we downed more than a few pints. Come closing time, we decided to head back to our flat, play a few sounds and get messed up some more.

As many people did back then, I was about to drive while under the influence of alcohol. Gerry was learning to drive at this time and Brenda and Ferg kept going on about letting him have a go. About half way home, for some incomprehensible reason, possibly because my judgment was alcohol impaired, I agreed.

Things were going pretty well until someone announced that they had the munchies and wanted to get something to eat from a petrol station. It was almost opposite the flat.

The correct procedure would have been to drive past the petrol station and turn into where it said 'Entrance'. Some sage in the car said, "Don't worry about that!" while another said, "Go past!". This debate lasted for a few seconds at most, but it was enough to confuse our Gerry, who missed both 'Entrance' and 'Exit', crashing into a high kerb and stopping the car dead.

I got out and went round the driver's side to move the car off the road but it wouldn't start. We all got out of the car and when I looked underneath my precious little Mini, there was oil everywhere. The sump was cracked. We had to push the car into the forecourt of the house and the next day, I got a mechanic over to assess the damage. Not only was the sump cracked but the impact had pushed the sub frame back. The car was a write off.

I told Gerry and, good man, he immediately offered me what the car was worth - 120 quid. Gerry was travelling back to London with Ferg so he suggested Ferg would bring the money back for me on his return. Unfortunately, Ferg spent the money on God knows what. It took me about three months to get just eighty pounds of it back.

It was an early lesson to me that the middle men always get a percentage, if not the whole fee.

The Real McCoy

Back at Shorts, I had been moved from the production line in the main factory to work on the prototype of the SD3-30 passenger aircraft. It was being built in a hangar close to the fibreglass shops and the runways.

Much of the time was spent waiting for decisions to be made by management, designers and draughtsmen. The process was slow and boring. You had to make yourself look busy without actually doing anything, which, as any fool knows, is actually harder than working. I missed the banter and buzz of the main factory and I would sometimes go walkabout to the main factory pretending to be picking up drawings or the like, when really I was looking for company.

The fibreglass and paint shops were kept very busy at lunchtimes. If, as was often the case back then, someone had an old car with a rusted wing or sill, it would be driven to the rear and, within the 40 minute lunch break, the old wing would have a skin of fibreglass applied to it. The next day it would be filled and rubbed down to smooth perfection and, on the third day, the car would go to the rear of the paint shop for the new fibreglass to be sprayed.

Sometimes, a whole car would be resprayed with aircraft paint, which is polyurethane based and looks very different to car paint. These cool cars cruised down the Belfast streets like miniature jets.

I had a call from my old friend, Raymond Donnan, who was now playing with the Real McCoy show band. They were unhappy with their drummer and would I come in for an audition. The band had just reformed and were based in Dublin so it wasn't easy to set one up. I saw this as my opportunity to move on, leave Shorts, and turn professional.

Swift were rehearsing for their one and only gig they did with me in the lineup at Queen's University, Belfast. The Real McCoy happened to be playing nearby in Bangor so they came to check me out.

They turned up at about five on a cold Saturday evening looking very different to us - stage ready, well groomed and sharp. They stood at the back of the room and listened to a few numbers. They were all very friendly and, after a quick chat they left for their own show. I wasn't sure how the audition had gone, to be honest. I wasn't even sure if the music was to their taste but Raymond called a few days later to tell me I had the job.

I was naturally very excited but also a little uncertain about making the big decision to give up my job at Shorts. The other guys had an equal stake in the profits of the band but they wanted to put me on a wage - 30 quid a week. My wage at Shorts was 40. They said that if things went well, I'd get more. It was a significant drop in pay but, for me, the gamble had to be worth it. I just had to sell this, plus the fact that I would be away from home four or five nights a week, to Brenda. She took a bit of convincing but went along with it in the end.

I handed my notice in at Shorts, had a few drinks with the lads and on Monday, March, 4th, 1974, I headed to Dublin with Raymond Donnan for my first rehearsal as a professional musician.

The rehearsal was called for one in the afternoon at the Gate Theatre, which is on the one-way system at the opposite end of O'Connell Street from the River Liffey. We arrived bang on time to find no-one else had, and nor had the equipment. Eugene, the roadie, a Derry man with a thick accent, turned up in the band's VW van at about three with the gear. The rest of the band turned up at around four. I wasn't used to this and it put a seed of doubt in my mind.

Mike O'Brien was the lead vocalist, Barry Woods was the pianist/multi-instrumentalist, Gay Brazel, played pedal steel guitar, Raymond, was keyboards/multi-instrumentalist, Alan Holland, was on bass and now, me on drums. This phase of the band had been going for just six months.

The original line-up was formed in 1968 and only Mike remained. They had been associated with some of the top names on the Irish music circuit at that time. Eddie Campbell, the guitar player, had also played with the top crooner of the day, Englebert Humperdinck. Keith Donald, the sax player, went on to play with Moving Hearts and the guitar player, Tiger Taylor.

To call the Real McCoy a show band wasn't an accurate description. They were more pop. Like a lot of Irish bands at the time, they recorded songs that had been big hits in the UK and/or US. Their first three singles all reached the top ten in Ireland. Their version of 'Quick Joey Small' reached Number One. They were doing great business all over the country and Mike O'Brien surprised everyone when he left the band in 1972. He joined Billy Brown, ex the Freshmen, to form the Brown O'Brien Band and moved to Canada for a while to take up a residency at the Toronto Ballroom.

Mike's place was filled by a girl called Tina Reynolds, who carried on the success of the band with more Top Ten hits. Unfortunately, the band was involved in a head-on collision in the summer of 1973. Tina and Keith Donald were both badly injured and that was it for them and for the band. Mike O'Brien came back from Canada to reform them.

The quality of the musicians in the Real McCoy was undeniable. Barry was a fantastic player. I stayed with him and his family when in Dublin and he would practise up to six hours a day. Gay Brazel was also a wonderful player. Raymond could play anything and had a great voice and Mike O'Brien was a great front man. Louis Walsh - yes, that one - was our manager.

We did three days' rehearsal which, quite honestly, could have been condensed into two. On Friday, we headed to Tuam in County Galway for the first gig. Driving from Dublin today would take about two and a quarter hours but back then it took four.

I just wasn't prepared for the reception the band received. The dance hall was just outside the town and big enough to hold about 2000 people and it was packed for the two hour show. They must have come from miles around. The female attention the boys in the band enjoyed was astonishing. This was rural Ireland but sexual favours were, apparently, very much on the menu.

We played Saturday and Sunday in the west and Raymond and I drove home after the Sunday night show, arriving in Belfast in the early hours of the morning. I was on a high, I felt liberated, a bit reckless. It was by no means my perfect musical dream but it was music and it wasn't Shorts. Come Thursday, and we were off again. It was like this for the first two or three months.

It wasn't ideal living with Barry, who was a family man with kids, so I started to travel to the shows early with Eugene. It meant I could practise before the others showed up. I travelled back to Dublin with the band just because it was quicker. I would sometimes drive because I didn't drink. Mike O'Brian sometimes brought his Ford Capri and I got a buzz driving that. You only had to stretch your big toe over its accelerator pedal and it upped the speed by 20 miles per hour. I drove down Naas Road like I was Steve McQueen in *Bullitt* until the others woke up - probably because of the G forces - and freaked out.

On stage, Mike wore really cool, bootcut Levis from Canada. When they needed replacing, there was only one shop in Dublin that sold American Levis. They only had straight legs but Mike nevertheless bought them even though they were too long. His sister turned them up for him.

Unfortunately, she got the measurements wrong and the left leg was cut six inches shorter than the right. She sewed them back together hoping he wouldn't notice but he did and he wasn't very happy. Mike was always immaculately dressed, you see, except for one occasion when the Garde came across him and a girl in the back of his car and neither of them were dressed at all.

(Gay Brazel was the opposite. He was engaged and didn't believe in sex before marriage. He took a lot of stick because of this but a nicer, more principled person, you would never hope to meet.)

My sisters, Bernadette and Teresa, suggested that I stay with them while I was in Dublin. This made things easier for Brenda because she would sometimes come with me and stay at the girls' flat. On one of these weekends, the band had a rare night off so the girls and I went out for a drink. That night when we got back, I was very ill, almost passing out in the toilet with the pain.

Brenda and my sisters were shocked when they saw me but just thought I had had too much to drink and put me to bed. I eventually fell asleep and by the morning, I was OK. A couple of years later, when I was living in London, it happened again. I went to see our local doctor. He sent me for a barium meal test. When the results came through, I was called in and told that I had been very lucky, they had found the scar of an ulcer on my duodenal tract. The ulcer had perforated but fortunately the acid hadn't leaked into the rest of my body. Good news all round but I have to tell you that evacuating barium is, basically, shitting a white brick.

By the middle of May, it was clear that things weren't going well for the band. For all the great musicians it had, and Louis Walsh himself, things didn't seem to gel. It felt like we were trying to recreate something that had long gone. It just didn't feel right. The band just couldn't recapture the spark that the previous line ups had had. Some weeks I was earning more than the others on a fixed retainer, which was terrible for morale.

Someone, probably Louis, came up with a rock 'n roll theme for us along the lines of Mud, then at the height of their career. So, we went to a tailor in Dublin and got measured up for gaudy suits and creepers. The resulting effect was a bastard blend of Elvis and Liberace. There were photos taken, which I haven't seen since 1974. If they are out there and anyone finds them, please rip those threads to shreds. Anyway, we went the whole hog. I sang lead vocals on Ringo's big hit of that year, 'Sweet Sixteen'. Every cheesy straw was clutched at but things went from bad to worse. This inglorious incarnation of the band didn't last long.

Mike was the first to throw the head up and refused to wear the suit. We were doing a show in Culdaff in County Donegal. There had been a Guinness strike for six weeks. Murphys and Beamish flooded the market but when you want a Guinness, that's what you want and it didn't improve anyone's mood that there wasn't any. We had a few sour games of darts before the show which I won. Mike called me 'Lucky' with much bitter sarcasm. It was a meant to be a joke but with the way things were going, me on a retainer, the gigs not bringing in money, the stupid suits, the strike AND me winning at darts, I felt it was a dig.

Death Spiral

In early July, Gerry breezed through Dublin on his way to Cork with his new girlfriend, a blonde called Gill Fitzgibbon. (She was a student at the time and is now a professor in Cardiff.)

Brenda and I met them at their hotel for a few drinks. I hadn't seen him since he crashed the car. He looked great. He'd just come off tour and had money in his pocket. It was a good night and a real lift to the spirits but Gerry was quite surprised that I could now match him pint for pint. I told him about the Real McCoy and that it wouldn't last much longer. I said that I'd like to move to London eventually. A few days later, we found out that Brenda was pregnant. It wasn't planned but we felt pretty good about it.

Everything was moving fast. A few days later, Barry Woods left the band, leaving a very big hole to fill. Mike found a guitar player - Mick Carras - from Dublin, who had just returned from London. He was a wonderful musician much influenced by John McLaughlin's Mahavishnu Orchestra and the like. He wasn't really show band material but he needed the gig. Paul Farrell, who was also from Dublin, came in on sax, when Gay Brazel decided he had had enough. Fact was the Real McCoy was in a death spiral. The band wasn't rehearsing and its playing quickly became sloppy.

Mick and Paul were travelling with Eugene in the van most of the time and one night after a show in Derry city, Eugene told them that he knew a shortcut out of town. The two Dublin lads didn't question him on this as it was his hometown but Derry, at this time, was a very divided city and just as dangerous as Belfast. As they drove through an area with no street lights, they were confronted by an army checkpoint.

Eugene panicked, possibly because he had two Southerners with him, and attempted to drive through it. Mick screamed at him to stop, slapping him around the head to make him come to his senses. He eventually did stop and, after a routine search, they were on their way.

It's hard now to fully explain how fragile the situation was back then. One stupid decision like Eugene's could have cost them their lives. We were all - the people and the soldiers - living on the edge.

Soon after, Alan Holland, the bass player left, and once again I suggested my old friend, Trevor Boyce, as a replacement. Trevor came into The Real McCoy for the last five or six weeks of its existence. Eugene had worn out one van and was working hard on killing the second. It came as no real surprise when Mike informed us that, at the end of August, he was calling it a day.

He made the announcement after a ropey gig at the Revolution Club. To be fair to everyone, the Real McCoy were suffering what all the show bands generally were having to accept. The Dublin scene was crackling with new bands such as The Boomtown Rats and the showband scene looked and felt old fashioned.

Brenda and I talked about our options. I could try to get my old job back at Shorts, look for another showband job - which I did, briefly - or head to London, which was really what I wanted to do. I had itchy feet because I saw what life could be like when I visited Dublin and imagined how it had to be so much better in London.

I remember Gerry talking about a London flat that Rory's piano player, Lou Martin, rented it but had never lived in it. I think it was going to be his groupie pad. He thought the gals would be lining up but, in fact, it was rarely used and he had mothballed it. (Lou actually lived with his parents in a fine, big old house in Plumstead.) The flat actually belonged to an Irish builder for whom Gerry's Dad looked after the accounts. I rang Gerry and he said he would ask Lou if he needed that flat. A week or so later, Gerry got back to us saying it was ours if we wanted it.

The decision was quickly made. My family were glad that I was getting out of Belfast. I did the last couple of weeks with the Real McCoy on autopilot. Nothing went right. Eugene got us horrendously lost on the way back from the west to Dublin, so we arrived at eight in the morning instead of four.

After another long overnight drive back to Belfast, the sun was just coming up on a lovely summer's morning, Raymond and I were stopped at a remote border crossing by the Garde. One of them took our details and went to check us out on the car radio. He seemed to be gone for a long time. We were nervous but his partner, embarrassed by the delay, apologised to us. By way of mediation, he opened his packed lunch and offered us a sandwich. This, while a few miles up the road, people were being slaughtered. Neither of us had the stomach for it.

Ray, a dapper and suave man, knew he had to make some money while he figured out what to do next, musically. He decided to help his father out at the coal merchants so he asked me if I would help him out for a bit delivering coal. It was worth a few quid, so I agreed.

After our last gig with the Real McCoy, Ray and I went straight to Newtownards and loaded up the lorry for the Monday coal delivery. It was back breaking. I'm strong but not a big man and the bags were as big as me. I was meant to do the Tuesday but Ray rang later that day and cancelled. I don't know why - I think he or his dad must have lost confidence in my physical abilities - but I was relieved. Another job for the glorious O'Neill CV: coalman for a day.

The next couple of weeks, Brenda and I spent saying our goodbyes and packing. I had to ship my drums over and all that sort of thing. The plan was that I should go two weeks ahead, get organised and get a job.

The night before I left, we had a drink in Ballyhackamore with Brian and Liz, Davy Hamilton and Billy McCoy. Billy tried to persuade me to stay. I didn't have a job but he said he'd get me one. My mind was made up though and, on lucky Friday, September, 13th, 1974, Davy Hamilton drove me to the airport and I left for London.

LONDON

The Band with No Name

Gerry was waiting for me when I came through Arrivals at Heathrow's Terminal One late in the afternoon. He had organised a cab to take us to Forest Gate in the East End but we had time for a pint. We were walking up the stairs to the bar when Gerry saw someone he knew. Noel Redding, bass for the Jimi Hendrix Experience, was in a rush to catch a flight but he took the time to chat for a minute. I was impressed. Cabs and rock heroes. What next?

We turned up at St Anthony's Catholic Working Man's Club in Upton Park, east London at around nine in the evening. It was a popular place with people from every walk of life: doctors, lawyers, teachers, builders. Gerry and his dad were members. The beer was cheap and the conversation colourful and I was to spend quite a bit of time there over the next few weeks. Gerry's parents put me up at their flat in Canning Town and he and I ended up sharing a room and a bed yet again. Some things don't change.

On Monday, we went to see Lou's old flat at 96 Pevensey Road in Forest Gate. It was a one-bedroom place next to a railway line that carried cars from Ford's factory in Dagenham to the rest of the country. I could see Gerry's dad's office from my windows at the back of the house. It made me feel right at home, which was just as well as it would be for the next 11 years.

The first train came past each morning at half past six carrying its freight, sometimes, cylinder-shaped oil and gas containers. The train clanked by slowly and the weight of it shook the house for the four or five minutes that it took to pass.

On Wednesday night, Gerry and I went to the Bridge House. This was its early incarnation as a pub in Canning Town before it became a legendary music venue. We saw a local guitar player there called Terry Newman, who had been involved with the Small Faces in their early days.

At the weekend, we went to a pub just off Clapham Common to see Rod De'ath and Lou Martin jam with Ramrod, the band that they'd played in before joining Rory. (The name Ramrod they had nicked from a beer available at the time.) I got to play a few numbers with them. So ended my first week in London and it had been a blast. The second week came with a reality check. I had to get a job.

Gerry's dad, Sean, kindly offered to drive me to the Ford factory to apply for one. Gerry came with us and, as we drove through the front gates, I truly felt like a prisoner on the run being returned to jail. The buildings looked dark and imposing as we went in to pick up the application forms. I didn't want to seem ungrateful but this was the last place that I wanted to be. I couldn't wait to get far, far away from there.

A few days later, Gerry had a call from Rory to go and rehearse. Before he went, he left me Jackie Lynton's number. Jackie was a blues and rock and roll singer, who had been with Savoy Brown for a couple of years and co-wrote some of Status Quo's hits - 'Again and Again' being one of them.

He was a renowned lyricist. He'd take old cockney songs and customise them for a laugh. My personal favourite was his transformation of 'Underneath the Arches' into 'Underneath Me Arsehole, Two Bollocks Hangin' Dahn'.

Jackie had just released his first solo album, The Jackie Lynton Album, and Rory had guested on it. Gerry told me that Jackie needed a drummer and I should give him a call. After Gerry had gone, it took all my courage to pick up that phone. Jackie answered almost immediately. His strong, London accent was upbeat and friendly but, as soon as I started to speak, my brain felt as if that early morning freight train was rumbling through it. Gerry's name came out eventually and I said something about Rory. I think I said 'drummer', twice.

Jackie said, "Who the fuck is this?" and I made another attempt at selling myself, with little added coherence. In the end, he said, "Someone's having a fuckin' laugh," and put the phone down on me.

He never heard from me again.

I felt dead in the water but that weekend I met a bass player called Tony Ciniglio at St Anthony's Club. He was playing with a function band that hadn't been named yet. They played anywhere they could get a gig - British Legion halls, Irish Circuit parties, you name it. They needed a drummer. It wasn't what I had in mind nor what I had hoped for the previous week when I phoned Jackie, but it was a start.

Brenda arrived in early October just under a month later, and Gerry and I went to the airport to meet her. On her first night in London, Gerry brought us to the Speakeasy in the West End.

The Speakeasy was one of the coolest places in London and had been since the mid-Sixties. Unknown bands would play for next to nothing because the industry would be there. It hosted some of the biggest names in the business: Hendrix, Pink Floyd, Zappa, and the Wailers. The Beatles, the Stones, their entourage and roadies would go there for late night drinks. Sadly, it closed in the late Seventies but that night it was in its pomp. We both felt like we had landed on another planet.

The following weekend, Tony Ciniglio asked me to do a couple of gigs. He picked me up in a little VW van, the back of which smelt like a slaughterhouse. It was a company vehicle that he used to deliver meat.

Tony started work really early but he wasn't one for going to bed before midnight. The result was that he would sometimes nod off at the wheel. He would startle himself awake and brake really hard, throwing his arm across the cab to stop whoever was in the passenger seat from going through the windscreen. He'd apologise and nod off again. And so it went.

He was a nice guy and I liked him but the other two guys were always on his case. Pat Curley played guitar and sang. He ran a newsagents in north London and was an amateur heavyweight boxer. His temper matched his division but he never did seem to win any fights. Battered to hell, he would look at me and say, "I didn't realise they made men with 32 inch chests." Barry Fitzgerald also played guitar and sang. He fancied himself as a ladies' man but he was just a wide boy from Essex. I gigged with the band with no name for a couple of months.

We were meant to play a gig in Notting Hill, which turned out to be double-booked. By the time we arrived, the other band had already set up. Pat was livid and we went across the road for a pint. As we walked through the double doors of the pub, I heard music that just blew me away. On the small, cramped stage were three West Indian guys playing reggae. I hadn't ever heard live reggae before and, man, did it sound good. The groove and rhythm were so seductive that I didn't want to leave.

Gigs we had but I had to get a job, any job, so I went and got one cutting PVC sheeting in Silvertown next to the old Tate and Lyle factory. It was as awful as it sounds - the pay, the conditions and the way the workers were treated. I left after three days.

I was in a bit of a bind because I was afraid to commit to a proper job, one that I couldn't walk away from. The next week I got a job as an inspector with an engineering firm in Barkingside. It made car components - spark plugs etc. I had to check the dimensions of parts coming off the lathes. If they didn't comply with the standard, I told the machinist and they had to adjust the machines.

One of the machine operators, a guy called, Duggie, was a very belligerent little man altogether. If I flagged a problem, he simply told me to "Fuck off".

As luck would have it, he had been a drummer and his nephew, John Rich, was also a drummer, who played with a local band called RDB. After we found we had this in common, we got on well. He continued to ignore my instructions at work in the same way, however.

A fellow inspector there sometimes gave me a lift home in his three-wheeled, Robin Reliant. If it was windy, it would undulate like a pedalo on the high seas. One time, in heavy rain, he lost control of it and we ended up facing the direction we'd come from. Having survived the turmoil of Northern Ireland, the irony of dying in a clapped out Robin Reliant on the Barking Road was not lost on me.

John McCullough lived 15 minutes away from us in student accommodation near West Ham tube. He introduced me to a friend of his from Northern Ireland, a guitar player called Larry Dundass. He lived on the other side of London, in Wandsworth, south of the river, in a top floor flat with a mixture of students and budding musicians.

The top floor at 92A Merton Road, Wandsworth, could have been a template for 'The Young Ones' comedy sitcom but they'd have had to clean it up a bit. Two of the guys went to Chelsea College of Art: Twig, the thinnest person you've ever seen, who wasn't actually dying, and Trevor Davis, a bass player from Northern Ireland. A drummer called Norris Adair had a room there, too. Larry's brother, Geoff, often came to stay and many others passed through when they were in town.

Larry had set up a music system in the 'communal' area where you could always find an album cover that had been used for joint construction. Empty cider cans were tipped behind furniture. The toilet cistern overflow poured down the back wall.

The kitchen was a health hazard but it did have a fire escape down to the back garden. The mouse population of the area would hang out with us. One in particular was held dear by all until Trevor Davies attacked it with a penknife.

John McCollough once put a Fray Bentos pie into the oven to heat through. Ovens in Northern Ireland in those days were all electric and he didn't realise this one was gas when he turned it on and left it. When informed of his error, he opened the oven door to light the gas. The subsequent explosion was powerful enough to singe the threads of his jeans.

I rented a little van to transport my drum kit and Brenda, by now eight months pregnant, to Larry's. We set off to Wandsworth, armed with a London A to Z. It was murder. We had a Chevy Chase moment from 'European Vacation' at the roundabout of The Elephant and Castle when we just couldn't see our way to get off it. Round and round we went like hamsters on a wheel.

It was the music Larry played that made the squalor and the stress of getting there worth it. It was so varied and wonderful. We started to practice and rehearse in Larry's bedroom, which ended up being covered floor to ceiling with egg boxes for sound insulation and the windows were blocked out with heavy curtains. It didn't work. We pissed the neighbours off on a regular basis.

Swift

Brenda's pregnancy went well but she was admitted to the old Forest Gate Maternity Hospital early in February for observation. I went straight to the hospital from work and Brenda had already gone into labour. The attitude towards husbands attending the birth of their child was very different back then. They let me see her for a few minutes and then I was ushered into a waiting room. I would have liked to have stayed but I just had to wear out the carpet next door while they got on with it. I could hear everything and it sounded horrendous. What the eye can't see, the mind will exaggerate and I was imagining the worst. Eventually, there was calm and quiet and the nurse arrived to tell me I had a baby girl and she took me in to see them both.

Brenda was exhausted but happy and there she was, the first of my four wonderful children, a beautiful baby, Gillian Frances O'Neill.

The staff weren't too keen on me hanging around so I said my goodnights and went to make the phone calls. I called Jim and Maureen first and, when I heard their familiar voices, I became very emotional. I felt a long way from home for the first time since I'd come to London. I spoke to my mum and dad and then I called the trusty Mr McAvoy. We went together to St Anthony's Club to wet the baby's head.

Jim and Maureen arrived a few days later to help out. Jim stayed for a week and Maureen, for a month.

Meanwhile, Tony Ciniglio wanted to stretch out and do something more creative musically. He asked me along to a couple of jam sessions with him. The session was in the back of a typical Camden pub with a front bar and a stage to the right. When we got up to play, a guitarist Tony knew got up with us.

It turned out to be Mark Knopfler. It was just before he formed the band Cafe Racers. Even then, he stood out from the other players. We passed comments to each other back and forth but I didn't pay him that much attention. Neither did Terry Murphy when Cafe Racers played the Bridge House a year or so later. How wrong we can be sometimes.

John, Larry, and I were really enjoying playing together and wanted to develop what we were doing. The music we were listening to at Merton Road varied from the Mahavishnu Orchestra, Chick Corea, Weather Report and Miles Davis all the way to Little Feat and James Brown, with a heavy dollop of Frank Zappa. Larry was really into Zappa.

We needed a piano player so we put an ad in *Melody Maker*. Through a friend at 92A, we got some free time in a rehearsal studio in Lots Road for the auditions. We couldn't make up our minds out of the few players who turned up. One of them, Hugh John, phoned Larry a few days after to see if we had made a decision. Larry replied in his unhurried manner, "Not yet," and put the phone down on him. We eventually did decide on Hugh, mainly because Larry and John were very impressed that he had a Fender Rhodes electric piano.

We couldn't have made a better choice. The three of us had been working on a few original tunes but Hugh brought a new musical thought process to the table. We all soon agreed that a saxophone would complete the sound. Hugh was working at the GPO - the nationalised General Post Office - at that time and through a work friend of his, Neil Gibbons, we were introduced to John Sanderson.

John was from Derbyshire, a very strong trade union man and a few years older than us. He was working in London as a supply teacher while trying to move his musical career forward. He came from a more straight ahead jazz background than the rest of us. He was really into Weather Report and a London band called Major Surgery, featuring Don Weller on saxophone and a blues guitar player called Jimmy Roach. I ended up doing a lot of gigs with Jimmy in the Eighties. Hugh listened to a lot of classical music and avant-garde jazz; Everything from Bartok to Cecil Taylor, Sly Stone to the Brecker Brothers, was on the agenda.

We called ourselves Swift.

The London music scene was very diverse in 1975/6. You could take your pick. In every other pub in the city, music ranging from rock, jazz, blues, reggae and soul was on offer. In the East End, the gnarly old pubs still had old 'Joannas' for the old sing song. Terry Murphy took over the Bridge House in Canning Town and forged it into the best live music venue in London.

One night after dinner, while Maureen was there, I thought about what John, Larry and I were doing and I made up my mind to go to the Bridge House and get us a gig. I took the bus and Tube to Canning Town, found my voice and asked the landlord, John Murphy - brother of Terry, who made the place what most people remember it as - to book us. To my surprise, he did. I only had enough fare to get me back to Upton Park. I had to walk the last few miles home but I didn't care, I was ecstatic.

When he took another pub, the Royal Oak, on the Barking Road in Canning Town, he booked us again. Sadly, poor John died in rather sinister circumstances a couple of years later.

I was made redundant from my job as an inspector after about five months and the local Jobcentre sent me for an interview at Hammond and Champness, a lift manufacturer on the Blackhorse Road in Walthamstow. I got a job measuring, cutting and drilling great big RSJs for the construction of lift shafts, which were assembled on site to very accurate measurements before they left the factory.

Working there was the first time in my life that my face really didn't fit. The only person who communicated with me was the charge hand, who delegated the workload. My name was 'Paddy', which I hated, mainly because it is not my name. Nevertheless, I kept my head down and got on with the job.

It was at about this time that the IRA began a campaign of leaving incendiary devices in retail stores overnight. I was made to feel that simply being Irish, a 'Paddy', put me in the frame. Remarks made daily about Northern Ireland were so skewed that I tried to explain the reasons for the Troubles: civil rights, injustice, and so on. I realised that no matter what I said, they just didn't get it. They thought that if you were British, you had the same rights as everyone else and somehow the violence was all about religion. They had not experienced what I had. My reality was not their reality. They were looking at the immediate outcome of something. They did not understand the motives behind the violence. For me and the families of Northern Ireland, it had been a long time in the making.

I was on a hiding to nothing. In the 18 months that I worked there, I befriended one guy. He was from Newcastle and wasn't really fitting in either. One Friday, he asked me if I fancied a pint at lunchtime and at half past 12 we drove off to a pub by St James Road Station in Walthamstow. When we walked through the door, the place was packed. It was a strippers' bar. The girls were lovely and the bar was doing a roaring trade. The East End had quite a few bars like that. My friend was a regular at this one. Me, I was an innocent abroad.

Jazz Fusion

The legendary summer of 1976 was one of the driest, sunniest, and warmest of the last century in the UK. Week after week, the temperature was above 30C. The highest temperature recorded was 35.6C. It was glorious. London felt like Southern Italy. The pubs were empty but the pavements and beer gardens were full. Our windows were flung open and we had picnics nearby on Wanstead Flats. The grass on the Flats was bleached yellow and its ponds and lakes dried up.

In early summer, my mum and dad and brother Martin came for a couple of weeks. We did all the usual tourist stuff including the Tower of London. (The old man was very impressed by the size of Henry the Eighth's codpiece.) Brian and Liz came in August.

Week in, week out, the Bridge House was the main attraction. It was beginning to get up and coming bands, not only from all over the capital, but the whole country and beyond. Local bands such as RDB (Remus Down Boulevard) and Slowbone, a really, good band that did well in Japan, got the chance to play there.

Over the next few years, bands as diverse as Chas and Dave, The Blues Band, Depeche Mode, who signed their record deal there, Tom Robinson, and Dire Straits performed. U2 and the Stray Cats are said to have played their first UK gigs there. Singer/songwriter, Chris Thompson, who joined Manfred Mann's Earth Band in 1976, had a weekly residency. The volume he played at would flatten your trousers. Terry would 'guest' stars from many other bands each week, including Steve Marriott and Ronnie Lane, two of my childhood heroes.

When Gerry was home, we would sometimes nip round there mid-week and, with his reputation as RG's bass player, we were welcomed with open arms. There was never any rush to leave. It was too hard to. I think Brenda, with good grounds, began to resent these nights out. Without a babysitter, someone had to stay home to mind Gillian. She did, occasionally, come when we could find one but the onus was on her. That's how it was then.

One night in early December, I saw a TV interview on the news with a young band who were destined to turn the music industry on its head. Bill Grundy's altercation with the Sex Pistols on television really did seem shocking at the time. Using 'fuck' on TV now barely registers but then it made the papers. Not that it never happened. The theatre critic, Kenneth Tynan, had outraged the country by saying it in 1965. In 1973, the journalist, Sir Peregrine Worsthorne, did likewise. Glen Matlock and Steve Jones took it to a whole new level.

The journalist, Bill Grundy, goaded them to 'say something outrageous' and they obliged, and so made a direct connection with every disgruntled teenager in the country. As for Bill Grundy, he was toast.

Whether punk was a fashion, musical, or political statement or all three is still, for me, debatable. I get the fashion part that was driven by Vivienne Westwood and Malcom McClaren with his involvement with the New York Dolls. He used shock tactics to get attention but I doubt his politics were really for the benefit of anyone else. With bands like The Clash, I felt it was a genuine political tool.

By its nature, Punk had to have a short shelf life. As a musical force, I believe it was one dimensional, and after the Sex Pistols' one and only magnificent album, 'Never Mind The Bollocks, Here's The Sex Pistols' defined it, there was no more to be said. I never understood going to gigs to spit at people and heaven forbid that anyone would spit at me, but out of the embers of punk came Elvis Costello and the Attractions, Ian Dury and the Blockheads, the Police and the Pretenders. They had a punk attitude but included other great musical traditions.

I started going to see free jazz musicians such as drummer John Stevens, who founded the Spontaneous Music Ensemble. The name says it all. Up to eight musicians would begin to improvise with a series of short sounds or a drum beat randomly creating soundscapes and walls of energy that would last up to 40 minutes. The listener could make their own mind up how to interpret the sound that they were hearing. I found this approach to music exhilarating.

There are three generally accepted ingredients to create music: rhythm, harmony and melody. The guys influenced by free jazz artists such as Ornette Coleman, Albert Ayler and John Coltrane were discarding these rules to create something unpredictable, chaotic, minimalistic and, sometimes, very aggressive - it was the rhythm of life as I had experienced it.

John Stevens and players such as Trevor Watts, Evan Parker, Paul Rutherford and Derek Bailey, were following a long, jazz, tradition of pushing boundaries.

Not all free jazz was completely random. Composers such as Ornette Coleman and Cecil Taylor created angular and abstract music. There was no 4/4 to it.

Ornette was much respected by Rory. Once, with Taste, they shared a hotel and Rory ended up in the next room to Ornette. He said that Ornette practised all day long before going out to the show that night. Taste's 'On the Boards' album is strongly jazz influenced and features Rory on the alto sax. I believe it was Ornette who inspired Rory to pick up the instrument.

Since I first heard the Buddy Rich Big Band, jazz has enthralled me. My drum teacher, Tommy Thomas, introduced me to Coltrane, Art Blakey, Max Roache and Elvin Jones.I love the idea of breaking down musical barriers and I love the atmosphere created on the Miles Davis albums, 'Milestones' and 'Kind of Blue'. The latter became a landmark album not just because of the great musicians who played on it, but because of Miles' fascination with modal scales, the scales entrenched in ancient music. He used them for improvisation rather than using complex chord progressions as a harmonic framework, as used for example in bebop.

Piano player Bill Evans, like Miles, listened to classical composers, Ravel and Rachmaninoff, in particular. Their use of the Dorian modal scale is similar to, and has been adapted for, blues music. John Coltrane took this approach with his great quartet of the 1960s. During the last 10 years of Coltrane's life, his music was constantly changing, as was that of Miles. Innovative musicians like these will always have my total respect. They never rested on their laurels. They were always looking for something new to embrace. Looking back was not an option for them.

It was against this jazz background that Swift developed. We were light years away from these musicians in skill and innovation, but we were inspired by them and learned so much from them. A band like the Spontaneous Music Ensemble had more empathy with the DIY aspect of punk than arena rock and the pop music business. Swift, in its way, was steadily developing a jazz fusion sound and every stage in between. We drew on the profusion of new sounds and musical genres all around us. It was all up for grabs.

Upstairs at Ronnie Scott's was becoming a regular gig for us. Playing there gave us free entry to the main club after our set. (One of the waiters there was a musician called Paul Bowen from Northern Ireland and, as we got to know him, he came to Merton Road to hang out with us. He'd walked out of a degree course at Queen's University, came to uni in London and walked from that, too. He had chart success a few years later with his band, the Star Jets.)

The atmosphere in Ronnie Scott's was great. It was the upmarket jazz club in London then, as now. Ronnie had a very droll delivery when introducing the main acts. He would tell some strange jokes that I never really understood - I was too unsophisticated - and his quartet would play between the sets of the main attraction.

We saw Betty Davis, Miles' wife, sing there. She was a total funk queen, pre-Grace Jones. We also saw Elvin Jones, the great jazz drummer. It was mind blowing. Over the next couple of years, we saw the greatest international acts of the day including Buddy Rich, Nina Simone, George Adams and Don Pullen, who both played with Charles Mingus.

The house band always had great British players. Two great drummers, John Marshall and Martin Drew, were regulars. Martin Drew went on to play with Oscar Peterson and John Marshall with Soft Machine. Louis Stewart, a superb, Irish guitar player, performed there and ended up playing everywhere with everyone. Ronnie's was a real source of inspiration for young bands.

I kept in touch with blues and rock through Gerry, and the weird and wonderful avant-garde through Swift. The debauched Sixties and Seventies passed us by in that respect. We were into music first and foremost and the parties that happened, happened after.

Our residency at the King's Head lasted about six months. As the band improved and gained in confidence, our reputation grew. Hugh's compositions were getting stronger. We were an instrumental group so titles for songs couldn't come from a lyric. Hugh had to draw from what he thought was important to him or what interested him. We ended up with titles such as 'Put it on the Red, John'.

There was a double meaning to this one. John Sanderson was a Leftie and John McCullough liked a bet. 'Left and Left Again' was another, as was 'Mizpah'. The latter is a Hebrew word mentioned in the Bible. It means 'watchtower' and came to represent an agreement that is only witnessed by God. "Viva Frelimo" was a song that got its title from the guerilla freedom fighters in Mozambique.

In 1977, the Greater London Arts Association ran a competition to find the Young Jazz Musicians of the Year. The winners would be paid 50 quid per show on top of the venue fee wherever they played, promoting jazz, in the UK. The only stipulation was the average age of the band had to be under 27 years of age. We averaged 25 so we applied and got accepted. There were no heats, just one day at the Shaw Theatre on the Euston Road.

The Shaw was a cold and soulless place compared to the hot, steamy clubs that we were used to playing in. Our slot was in the afternoon and we played a couple of our pieces with easy confidence. At the end of the day, the GLAA judges felt that two acts deserved the sponsorship, which would last for two years. Swift and a band called Lighthouse got the gig.

It meant so much to us. Part of winning the competition was that we actually got to play at the prestigious Ronnie Scott's. The GLAA sponsored a night there to introduce us to the jazz scene. It was a nerve-wracking experience but one hell of a buzz.

Chris Jenkins had been acting as our manager but after we won the competition, he said that he didn't have the time to commit to us fully. We asked our number one fan, Roy Patterson, if he would take the job and he agreed.

Roy abandoned his last year of college where he was studying computers and IT. He was later quoted in Melody Maker saying: "It was my last year of study for my degree, but, having read Carlos Casteneda about Don Juan and the Yaqui way of knowledge, I decided to take the cubic meter of chance and drop my studies and manage the band."

I don't remember him saying this to us at all but, if he did, it would have gone right over my head.

Roy soon put his organisational skills to good use and the gig list grew. That summer we played the elitist Bracknell Jazz Festival headlined by Archie Shepp. Just as the sun was setting, Welsh jazz supremo Stan Tracey's Octet, with the great Brian Spring on drums, played the main stage.

With the silhouette of Octet in the background, Kryssie, standing on the side stage, took a picture of my daughter, Gillian, with her 'I am Two' birthday badge that she had worn since February. I had seen Brian Spring warming up outside talking to some girls. It struck me that we were now in this jazz family of musicians and it felt so good.

An old mate from Belfast, Gerry McIlduff, who was now playing with the Pretenders, came to our show. He told us that there was as much of a buzz at our gig as there had been at any other he had seen all day. For me, it was just amazing to be there.

.

Swift On Tour

Swift was asked to play the soundtrack for a low budget, suburban, north London wildlife documentary. At first, we thought the idea was a bit twee and not quite befitting of our status as jazz rock pioneers. When we found out that they wanted it all improvised, we changed our attitude.

It was to be recorded in Hornsey College of Art, Crouch End, in a wonderful big room there. The college was well known for its experimental approach to art. As a silent film was shown, we were asked to simply interpret what we saw on the screen - birds, cats, foxes etc. It would then be edited down.

While we were waiting for things to be set up, Hugh and I wandered down the corridors looking at all the art exhibits. We came across a rectangular box set into the wall, quite low down almost to the floor, and behind glass. The box contained an electric cable with a plug attached to it suspended from the top end of the longest side. Three or four inches below the plug and clearly out of reach was an electrical socket. The art critic in me stirred. I turned to Hugh and said, "That's pretty stupid." His answer was, "Brendan, you need a university degree to understand that. It represents the meaning of life. No-one reaches their ultimate goal."

The only thing that prevented me from punching him in his smug, educated face was my deep and abiding fondness for him. As for the film, I have no idea what happened to the strange fruit of that surreal afternoon.

Our next trip was to Amsterdam. In typical Swift fashion, two gigs became one. It was at the Melkweg - the Milky Way - and we were excited at the prospect. A)it was Amsterdam, B)it was the Milk Veg, which was where it was at in the European hippyverse since it opened in 1970. It was a former dairy farm, located at Lijnbaansgracht, near Leidseplein, a happening part of the city. It was, and still is, a non-profit-making cultural centre and had various differing capacity rooms for concerts, dance and theatre.

We started off early in the morning, arriving in Amsterdam in the afternoon and going straight to the venue. The place reeked of marijuana. The stage was low, maybe three feet off the ground, and around the edges of the room people lounged on large cushions at low tables, chatting and sipping coffee. We got our equipment in and began the sound check. Those who were there seemed to enjoy what we were doing, which gave us confidence for later.

The show itself was a bit of a let down. We had a great crowd, who seemed to listen respectfully but, after each number, the applause was indifferent. Fact was, everyone was stoned out of their minds. We could smell and taste the dope as we played. A couple of policemen wandered through the venue but were not moved to make any arrests. It was all very new to us Brits. In the UK in those days, you could get two years for possessing a roach. Afterwards, people told us how good they thought it was and we began to think more positively, telling ourselves that the dope had just numbed the crowd's hands.

After the gig, like typical tourists, we went to the infamous red light district to check it out. It was a very strange thing to see women for sale standing in the windows. It actually made me sad. When I was playing with Rory, a group of us went to the Eros Centre in Hamburg in 1982. Rory, of course, absented himself. The place was an underground mall and totally different. It wasn't like in Amsterdam, a street of shops where everyone went by gawking. When you went into the Eros Centre, you entered their world and the girls were in control.

Anyway, we didn't hang around in Amsterdam's soul destroying red light district. We made our way to a coffee shop where we bought ganja and blissed out.

The next day, on our way home, as we approached the Belgium border, a couple of the lads decided it would be a good time to confide in us that they had some hash left. Every border back then involved a search. If you were a band, it was a certainty.

Some bright spark came up with the idea that we should eat it. I was a marijuana virgin but the devil in me awoke and I went along with the plan. We went through the Belgian and French borders without a hitch. After that the gear started to kick in. I lost control of my thoughts and every stupid thing that came into my head, my tongue happily articulated.

I went on and on about the wondrous beauty of the sunset until an exasperated Hugh, the arty one with the university degree, told me it was "just the sun going down". I passed out and felt nothing until I was propped up, semi-comatose, against the door of my flat in London. Someone rang the bell and was back in the van and off before Brenda got downstairs. To make matters worse, Brenda's parents were staying with us. God knows what they thought. Brenda explained that I was "overtired".

In 1978, Swift did at least 150 gigs while John McCullough and I were playing in covers bands to supplement our income. The schedule didn't leave much time for relationships but those we had were a real cultural mix. Larry had a steady girl, Linda, John had been with Hazel, a part Mauritian, part English girl, a long while, Hugh and Angela, a Jewish girl, were married. John Sanderson's marriage that had been on the rocks for a while, broke down. He eventually started going out with Annie, a beautiful, tall, full of life black girl, who was a friend of Larry's.

We were intrigued as to how John of all people could have managed to form a steady relationship with this fabulous woman. How can I put this? Great as John was, and kind hearted, He was a dour Derbyshireman, a schoolteacher - he may well have taught geography - very left wing in thought and demeanour. Annie was a bit more rock and roll.

One night, as John was giving me a lift home, I broached the subject of the miracle of this relationship. He replied, measuredly, "It takes me a long time to come me load. They seem to like this."

Returning Heroes

My job at Hammond and Champness came to an abrupt end when the company had to scale back and make redundancies. As I was one of the last employees taken on by the firm, I was the first to go. I wasn't sorry. It meant I could spend more time practising and making music.

The Swift calendar was filling up and we were playing more gigs out of town. The extra money from the GLAA was invested in transport and a PA system but we could just about get by with gig money. I was awarded an extra fiver a week by my socially minded band mates because I was the only one with a family.

We were booked to play three shows in May in Northern Ireland, then on to Scotland with a couple of gigs in Northern England on the way home. It was our first little tour and a heroes' return for Larry, John and I in the 'wee North', or so we hoped.

Unfortunately, nothing had changed back home. The gig at Queen's University was cancelled because of a Loyalist strike. The stewards had apparently withdrawn their labour as a result of intimidation. I don't know what we expected. We knew it was a risk but when you are not in the eye of the storm, you get complacent. You forget how bad it can be. It was the first time I'd played in Northern Ireland for three years. It was good to be back but, to be honest, I felt a bit divorced from the problems of the Province.

John Sanderson very nearly didn't make the trip because he was so concerned about security. It didn't help that Hugh wound him up by telling him that, if a bullet went up the bell of his sax, it would smash his teeth and he would never play the sax again. The only sax disaster that actually happened was that the roadie, Geoff, misplaced it while packing up in the dark and left it on a hedge. Fortunately, some kindly hedge botherer handed it to the police and he got it back.

The other gig in the Pound Club, Belfast, went ahead and another added, to make up for Queen's. The reception the crowd gave us was great. The third gig was in Wilmar House, Newcastle, County Down.

John McCullough did an interview with Gloria Hunniford, a local radio host in those days, on Downtown Radio. Harry Filmer, my old guitar friend from Spring, thought John was full of himself. I think it was just John's way of playing the situation. It's called 'promotion', I believe.

John was good friends with Taste's John 'Wilsie' Wilson's young brother, Rab. Through him, we invited Wilsie along to the sound check at the Pound. He was very flattered that we had a tune dedicated to his old band, Stud. He jammed with the band for a while and showed that he hadn't lost any of his flair. We got on great and he invited me to his house the next day where he had a kit set up in his garage.

We chewed the fat and listened to music all afternoon. We were both big fans of Tony Williams, Miles Davies' drummer in the Sixties. As we listened to his records, I said that I would love to get a wooden snare drum for that warm tone that Tony had on his recordings.

Later, John drove me back to Brenda's parents' house where I was staying and when we pulled up, he handed me a Hayman wooden snare drum. "This is for you," he said. I was overwhelmed.

After the Friday night gig, Jim Ferguson invited us all to his flat in Dundonald in the suburbs of Belfast. In typical Ferg fashion, it got very mucky. He plied everyone with drink, that we were very receptive to, and the lot of us were a total mess the next day. Someone was inevitably sick inside their sleeping bag. It was either me or Hugh but I reckon it was Hugh.

The rest of the tour was a lot less convivial but the venues were a lot better. As a band, we wanted to cross boundaries and not just play to the converted in jazz clubs. We played in a mixture of polytechnics, colleges, jazz clubs and arts centres. At the Glasgow college gig, the venue was packed and had to turn away nearly two hundred people.

Chris Welch of *Melody Maker* saw a few of our gigs. He had taken an interest in the band from as early as July 1976. He devoted a full page to us in *MM* after the tour and railed at the unfairness of the music industry at that time.

He was, as always, complimentary and encouraging about us as a band and as individual musicians but, in this piece, he was scathing too about the punk scene and the money lavished on undeserving prog rock combos and new wavers by the labels. The real talent, he said, could barely make a living. He highlighted the obstacles we faced playing our sort of music, not from the people who heard us, but from the industry. It was flattering to read that he thought Swift was one of the best new bands on the jazz rock scene. With the publicity we got from *MM* and elsewhere being so very positive, the gigs kept coming.

The truth was, the reaction to our music was mixed, depending on the venue, of course. One time, I overheard a veteran jazz musician in a club in south London say that he hadn't heard anything so fresh in years. However, another night in a college in Wrexham, North Wales, we made less of an impact. As we performed to a packed student union's hall, I closed my eyes at one very deep and meaningful part of the set. When I opened them again, six young men were 'mooning' at us and receiving far more attention than we were. It was a Friday night and the kids really just wanted to hear 'Brown Sugar'. Pearls before swine.

Sometimes, it really did click. There was one memorable night in a little arts centre in Chester. It wasn't full but there was a good crowd. The people knew where we were going and what we were about and came with us. John McCollough said after the show that we had created a kind of musical synergy, something much bigger and better and more expressive than we ever thought we could achieve.

Unfortunately, we were going nowhere. We recorded some demos but I don't ever remember them being sent out to anyone. I don't know why. Perhaps, at heart, we didn't believe in ourselves.

Rory

Rory's seventh album 'Against the Grain', released by his new record label, Chrysalis, in 1975, was his most successful to date. He and the band did an extensive US tour to promote it and played to their biggest audiences, headlining, often at 7000 seat venues. On their return, they embarked on a pretty lengthy UK tour that climaxed at the Royal Albert Hall. Gerry invited Brenda and I along. I got a real buzz seeing my old childhood friend up on stage playing there, I can tell you.

Lonnie Donegan introduced Rory and the band. He was one of Rory's childhood heroes and the stage was set for a great night. Another Irish musician, Fiddler Joe O'Donnell, who had played with East of Eden, opened with his band. When RG hit the stage though, it was like the whole Albert Hall got a shot of pure adrenalin. The band was tight and on it. I got goosebumps listening to it. The first five or six numbers were just fantastic but slowly, inevitably, the sound started to deteriorate.

Like many rock and roll bands who play the Albert Hall discover, if they get too loud, the acoustics suffer. The place wasn't designed for music that makes your ears bleed. I saw Them Crooked Vultures there a few years ago and they fell into the same trap.

With Nine Below Zero, we opened there for Eric Clapton on one of his twelve night runs. His onstage sound level was set very low. It made it possible to get a great sound out front through the PA system. It was a great shame for RG back then because by the end of the night, the sound was, frankly, a bit of a mush.

In the New Year, when things were quieter for the RG band, Rod De'Ath threw a party at his house in Knollys Road. Once again, Brenda and I were invited. Rory and his inner circle were there as well as Rod's family and friends. As the night progressed, I had imbibed enough liquid courage to sidle over to Rory.

The only other time I had got to talk to him was back in Dublin in 1973. They were playing a couple of shows there and staying at the Ashling Hotel along the quay, past the Ha'penny Bridge. I had arranged to meet Gerry there at noon. Brenda and I arrived a bit early and there was no-one to be seen. After 10 minutes or so, Rory appeared. He had missed breakfast and was looking for something to eat. He was on great form and he talked about the gig the previous evening and the tour. He was so relaxed, jovial even.

Gerry eventually showed up closely followed by Rod. There was nothing to eat at the hotel so we all piled into my little Ford Anglia 105E and headed towards O'Connell Street to find some bacon and eggs. Three quarters of the Rory Gallagher Band were on my back seat.

On the night of Rod's party, I tried to engage Rory in an earnest conversation about jazz but he wasn't in the mood. He was there to relax and have a good time. He gave me the swerve.

Rory's next album release was 'Calling Card' in 1976, recorded at Musicland Studios in Munich and produced by Roger Glover of Deep Purple. I remember Gerry bringing a copy to the flat just before its release. I thought it had a great selection of songs: the title track, 'Moonchild', the funk influenced 'Do You Read Me?', 'Secret Agent' and the beautiful ballad, 'I'll Admit You're Gone'.

For some reason, this was the first of his solo albums not to make gold. In hindsight, Rory was probably suffering at the top end exactly what Swift was suffering at the bottom: the arrival of punk and new wave. Nevertheless, the band set off on a global tour to promote the new album.

Rory's next project was to be recorded in San Francisco, USA, with Elliot Mazer producing. Mazer had worked with well respected artists such as Neil Young and The Band. Rory's label, Chrysalis, wanted a big push for this record. They were constantly trying to get him to release singles but Rory refused to comply. It was alien to how he saw his career developing and Rory was a bit mule-like in that regard.

The recording sessions at His Master's Wheels Studio were fraught with tension as to how the music should be recorded and/or interpreted. Mazer was influenced by where he came from and was trying to mellow out Rory. Rory wasn't about mellow. He was about angst. Mazer actually brought in a Mexican mariachi band with horns to play on 'Brute Force and Ignorance'. There was a definite culture and personality clash, to say the very least.

Everyone spent too much time in each other's company: Mazer with Rory, Rod with Rory, Gerry with Rod. I heard all this from Gerry at the time. After the backing tracks were recorded, the band were hanging around for six weeks in case they were needed for an overdub or change. Too much time was spent in the bar with too little to do.

In the end, Rory, quite literally, binned the lot at great expense to himself and the label. He didn't feel it was right and wouldn't be persuaded. Apparently, Rory had been to see the Sex Pistols in San Francisco at some point during the recordings. He was very impressed by the sheer energy of their performance. That was what Rory felt he was about.

When he and the band returned to London, Rory made some major changes. He let Rod and Lou go. It must have been a tough decision having worked together for five years or more. Gerry was kept on and Rory went about looking for a new drummer to replace Rod. Gerry asked me if I would like to audition.

I told him that I was very happy playing with Swift and I didn't want to change direction at that time. I did say that I would love to play one time with Rory, if for no other reason than to say that I had. I went to the Points Studios a couple of Saturdays later.

It was a great buzz to play with the man but it was obvious that my style of playing at that time didn't suit him. Typically, Rory was very pleasant, polite, and complimentary. Gerry told me after that he was impressed but I was too jazzy in style. I already knew that and had never expected to get the gig. I truly hadn't wanted it anyway because I was so into what I was doing with Swift, but, hey, you know, I'd played with Rory Gallagher.

The next time I saw him was at a rehearsal after Ted McKenna joined the band. Ted was really much more suited to what Rory required. I went with Gerry, said "hello" to everyone and went off for a few hours to do something else. When I got back, they'd finished and we all went out for a drink.

Swift opened for Osibisa, Ian Gillan and John Mclaughlin at the Rainbow but, as good as things were going for the band, personalities were beginning to clash. The relationship between John Sanderson and Larry had become very fraught. Neither could see each other's point of view on anything. John didn't like certain attitudes on life that Larry held. Larry, in turn, thought John was a hypocrite, who failed to practise what he preached. John had also become too critical of Larry's guitar playing. Hugh, too, was beginning to find discussions with John, infuriating.

One night as we were heading towards Exeter, we hit a road that was full of potholes and craters. John moaned so much that Larry threatened to stop the van, drag him out and beat the crap out of him.

Around this time, we began to meet some musicians who had gone to Leeds College of Music. All of these players knew of us because of the GLAA sponsorship and wanted to know what we were about. Guitarist, Steve Topping, and drummer, Gary Husband, were both very accomplished. Gary sat in with Swift a few times and, already, at just 21, was a very impressive drummer.

Both had an aura about them. They were destined to do well. Steve is now involved with many top West End shows as an arranger and guitarist. Gary has performed with the top jazz musicians in the world, including playing piano with John McLaughlin's band. Mark Ramsden was a tenor sax player who came to see us a lot and lived with Hugh for a while. He moved to Germany in the Eighties to play with many top jazz players there.

When John Sanderson eventually left the band, we placed an ad in the trusty *Melody Maker* and recruited Pete Thomas, tenor sax and flute. He was really into Latin music at that time and one of his favourite sax players was an Argentine free jazz, tenor sax player, Leandor 'Gato' Barbieri.

Pete's upbeat and outgoing personality gave us a new start. He had a strong sense of rhythm and his original tunes brought a fresh sound to the band. His approach was very different to ours. He was a schooled musician and would sometimes question our reasons for playing in certain time signatures or arrangements. We felt that the unorthodox way we did things was what drew attention to us in the first place. With his influence, we occasionally added percussion to the line-up, either John Cuthbert or our old friend, Terry Boyce.

Later in his career, Pete worked with artists such as Fats Domino, Elton John, Joe Jackson, REM, and PJ Harvey. A producer and arranger, he became Head of Jazz and Pop Performance at the University of Southampton.

We were booked to play some shows in Ireland in November 1978: two in Dublin, one in Belfast, book-ending the week. Leading up to our departure, we did a run of gigs up North culminating back in London at the Plough in Stockwell.

One gig was at the Phoenix in Cavendish Square in central London. It was a great jazz venue at the time and we drew a good crowd and the atmosphere was great. After the gig, I noticed Brian Spring, Stan Tracy's wonderful drummer, conversing with some people in the audience. I couldn't miss the opportunity to introduce myself.

We talked and, eventually, I asked
him if he would give me some lessons. He
linked his thumbs together and said,
"Keep practicing and you'll fly like a
bird", with that, he flapped his hands
like wings. It wasn't really what I
wanted to hear then even though, looking
back, he was just telling me that I was
on track.

I strongly felt that I needed help
in all aspects of my playing. I wanted to
learn so much. I saw the great Tony Oxley
one night in Ronnie Scott's and asked him
about lessons. He gave me his number but
I didn't have the money to follow it up.

Wheels

Anyone who has been around musicians will tell you that the major subjects of conversation, in this order, are: music, women and wheels, with a smattering of football banter. Wheels, any wheels, are a serious business and the lack thereof can nip a promising band's career in the bud.

Roy had bought himself a World War Two fire engine for transport and I managed to get myself a Mini Estate to carry my equipment. A couple of years later, I drove into a petrol station on the Romford Road and as I opened the door, a strong gust of wind ripped the door off its hinges. I had to drive home looking like a partially opened sardine can.

Our band van was temperamental about starting due to the lacklustre distributor and points, but Larry managed to keep us going. After the Plough gig, we went to Roy and Kryssie's flat, the idea being to travel overnight and catch the morning ferry to Dublin.

The van played up and we sat around gloomily for a couple of hours while Larry and Geoff tried to get it going. We eventually set off but thirty miles from the ferry port, in the pitch dark and lashing rain, the inconsiderate pile of junk seized up. Larry and Geoff got soaked trying to coax the engine to life and they eventually got it going. Three miles later, the van breathed its last.

There we were, at the break of dawn, stuck by the side of the road, again: cold, damp and down in the mouth. Larry tried his best but it was over. Whatever happened, we were going to miss the first gig in Dublin at Trinity College. Ironically, we were meant to play with a band called the Rich Kids (featuring Midge Ure and the Sex Pistols' original bass player, Glen Matlock).

Everyone was ready to call the AA and head back to London but I couldn't see why, having come this far, we should turn back. I made a dramatic call to arms, urging the band to get to the ferry somehow and do the gigs no matter what. My stammer took a hike as I channelled Henry Vth.

I haven't a clue how we got to the ferry but we did. We diverted our journey to Northern Ireland.

Geoff waited for the AA to get the van back to London while Roy rescheduled the Trinity gig for the following Saturday afternoon but we played UCD that night.

Larry's and Geoff's cousin, Peter Law, used to be a regular DJ at the Wilmar in Newcastle, and a great friend of the owner, Turlough O' Hare. Peter had got us a gig there. He organised for his friend, Conor Gribben, to give us a lift to Dublin in his van.

Conor met us off the ferry and helped us with the few instruments we were able to carry. I had a set of cymbals and sticks. Conor also helped us borrow equipment for the Belfast Fringe Festival show at the Museum, next to Queen's University. It was an all-seated affair and we went down well. My father-in-law, Jim Russell, came along. He had always had his doubts as to what I was doing but he was pleasantly surprised.

Conor made that tour. Without him, we would have been up shit creek. He got us to Dublin on the following Saturday for the two gigs. In return for all his help, we were to bring a motorbike back for him from Belfast to London. Geoff arrived in Dublin in a great big bus with all of our equipment and Roy and Kryssie in tow.

By this time, Hugh was using a Hammond B6 organ with Leslie speaker cabinet, a big square job, shaped like a water tower with a revolving propellor-like contraption inside that made the sound. It was a brute to carry but it sounded so cool. The Beatles used one to get that trippy sound on their guitars. At the end of the Small Faces single 'Itchycoo Park', the dying sound was a Hammond and Leslie being switched off.

Despite the drama, the gigs went well. We crashed at my parents, who were now living on the outskirts of Dublin in a place called Tallaght. The family had left Belfast in 1976 to join Bernadette and Teresa when the situation in Belfast got too extreme for them. They weren't alone. Quite a few Catholic families went to the south at that time. My Dad got a job easily enough, the HGV instructor's job, I mentioned earlier - the one he lost through 'celebrating' with his students when they passed.

The next day, we got our bedraggled selves onto the ferry home with a bottle of Paddy whiskey and a few pints of Guinness to keep us company.

Back at Pevensey Road, Gilly was now three and growing up fast. She spoke with a Belfast accent. Being around us, Gerry and grandparents, she'd picked it up first. As soon as she went to nursery though, she lost it for a Cockney twang. Brenda and I decided to try for another baby to complete our family. Connaire Padraig O'Neill was born in October, 1978.

I know, you couldn't get a more Irish name but we were feeling more conscious of our Irishness. When you move somewhere new, you want to hold on to something from home. I didn't feel so Irish in Northern Ireland. In London, I felt it and it made me want to remember what it was like to belong. It's interesting how a long view of something, like your homeland, makes you want to understand it a lot more. It's not nostalgia or nationalism, it surpasses that. It's about roots and what they make you as an individual.

I started to take an interest in traditional Irish music and found singers, groups and music that I just wasn't aware of in Northern Ireland. Brenda had been reading a novel called *Trinity*, by Leon Uris, an American Jewish writer. It was about two families of hill farmers from Donegal: the Larkins and the O'Neills. The hero and central character was called Conor Larkin. I think Brenda fancied the character and the name. We also happened to have a book of Christian names and found an older, Gaelic, version of Conor, which was Connaire. That was how my son got his name.

Pevensey Road had a few characters of its own. Our next door neighbour Rose wore a big, black backcombed bouffant and the shortest skirt you ever did see. Her and her old man, whose name I forget, had lots of kids, I'm not sure exactly how many. They kept their animals in the back garden: chickens, geese, a couple of dogs and, for a short while, a horse. Everything had to go through the front door into the handkerchief garden out the back. We had suspicions that they were really travellers who had settled down.

Billy and his wife lived on the corner and the outside of their house was done up like the OK Corral. Another guy opposite always had two or three cars he was working on out on the street. When we needed a new engine for the Swift van, I asked him if he could get a reconditioned one and fit it for us. He said, "Sure," but he would need the money up front. We agreed on a good price.

We got the van to him, he took the engine out and there the gutless van stood parked up for two weeks. When I asked him when it would be ready. He replied, "Soon." It was nearly a month later when we got the van back. Special Branch paid me a visit a few days later.

The number on the 'new' engine in our van matched one that had been taken out of a Transit in the dead of night, a week before, in north London. Very reluctantly, I became a witness for the prosecution and had to attend the infamous Snaresbrook Crown Court to point the finger at my laconic neighbour. It wasn't his first offence so he duly got banged up for a few months. Meanwhile, we were down an engine and the money.

Like I said, a band without wheels is a band going nowhere. Transport is as key to a band's success as their instruments. Fortunately, Hugh's father-in-law found a new van and negotiated a very keen price for us. Top man.

Small Time Crooks, Small Time Gigs

We were offered a support slot with John McLaughlin's One Truth band at the Rainbow Theatre. The success of that gig - despite a 350 quid 'buy on' fee - spurred Roy on to chase other supports with high profile artists such as Billy Cobham. He contacted John Peel and Janet Street Porter for radio slots and got one for BBC Radio London. He approached various record companies but our music just wasn't accessible enough for the mainstream.

In the past, some of the opening slots we did were just wrong. For example, we opened for the Pink Fairies, a really popular grunge band before the description was invented. It was a wall of noise. The punk scene was on its way. Somewhere, we had missed a beat.

We did some gigs for a jazz promoter that Hugh knew, called Johnny Edgcombe. Johnny was from Antigua and had a colourful past having been involved with Christine Keeler in the Sixties. He was her lover when she was working as a nightclub hostess. When he moved into her flat, he realised that she was involved with a number of men. She told Johnny that 'Lucky' Gordon, a West Indian friend of his, had threatened to tip off the police about a drinking den that Johnny ran. She added that Lucky had assaulted her and held her captive. Johnny went at luckless Lucky with a big knife that left his face requiring 17 stitches.

Christine denied to the police even knowing Johnny or that she had said anything to him. When Johnny found out about this, he went looking for her with a gun and pumped umpteen bullets into the door of the place where she was staying. He served time for all that but the murky case led to the discovery of the 'other men' in Christine's life including, of course, John Profumo, the then UK Secretary of State for War.

Johnny got into the jazz scene when he left prison. Man, was he hard-nosed. When he found out about the GLAA Award, he withheld our gig money. I mean, we shouldn't expect to get paid twice, should we? Greedy bastards. Naturally, we didn't feel like arguing the toss with him. Ultimately though, Johnny was a small time crook getting us small time gigs. He died in 2010 of cancer.

The band's bank account was always in the black but money was tight. We restricted our wages and poured everything into the band. We hired the Hammond organ out on occasions. Rory's old drummer, Rod De'Ath, was a customer.

On New Year's Eve, 1978, John McCullough and I did a cabaret gig with saxophone player, Mark Ramsden, and a piano player friend of his from west London. It was a typical gig of the time with bingo and a star turn doing a guest spot. When it was over, the piano player said a mate of his was having a party and he lived close by. He said it would be cool for us to call in.

It was a ground floor flat with a dozen or more people there. As we arrived, one girl was breastfeeding her baby. We were introduced to the host, a blonde guy in a checked shirt and brown leather pants. This piano player had worked with the guy in Germany with an experimental composer, Eberard Schoerner. The blonde guy's name was Gordon Sumner, better known as Sting. His first wife, the Belfast actress, Frances Tomelty, was there too.

I knew nothing of the Police at the time apart from seeing the name on a poster at a club where they had played the night before Swift. Years later, Nine Below Zero signed to Sting's record label, Pangea, and we toured Spain and Scandinavia with him for a month on the release of his album 'The Ten Summers Tales'.

Our old friend, John Mason, was now living in Mundania Road in a large bedsit situated next to Peckham Rye Common. It had once been the posh side of the area but this place was now divided into bedsits. Slowly, the house was occupied by John's friends and the extended Swift family. Norris Adair, John Cuthbertson and John McCullough and his girlfriend moved in. It was a new location for us to hang out, do a bit of recording and party.

Since John Mason had left Frupp, he had dedicated most of his time to practising - up to eight hours a day - while listening to his hero, the jazz piano player, Keith Jarrett. He met a Danish girl called Charlottie while he was in Scandinavia, fell in lust and brought her back to London.

Charlottie was very open minded and had no inhibitions with regards to her sexuality. I went to John's flat one day about something or other and there on the bedside table was a recently used vibrator, fresh with pubic hairs. She got a job as an escort and one of her clients was Telly Savalas aka Kojak, the lollipop sucking cop, who was very popular on TV at the time. John didn't seem to mind. Mundania Road didn't have the crazy notoriety that Larry's flat had but it was a fun place to be.

Gerry continued doing jam nights at the Bridge House in Canning Town. Chris Thompson, of Manfred Mann, did a similar thing, which he called Filthy McNasty - no connection with the late, infamous music pub in the Angel. The line ups changed depending on who was available. To capture the essence of these packed shows, Terry Murphy, decided to record one of Gerry's jams, which became side two of one of Gerry's solo albums, 'Bassics'.

Gerry asked me to play percussion alongside Ted McKenna on drums. The great Steve Waller was guitar and vocals, Lou Martin on keys, Little Stevie Smith on harmonica, Mick Eve on sax, and Ron Cartney on trumpet, with, of course, Gerry on bass. Playing 'percs' was a new experience for me. Not one that I wanted to make a permanent experience, although it was great to be part of that ensemble.

A great jazz and blues package came
through London and we felt we were owed a
band treat. It was at the Victoria
Theatre and the line up was the McCoy
Tyner Quartet, Sonny Rollins, John Lee
Hooker, Buddy Guy and 'Junior' Wells, in
that order. I'm sure they rotated it but
that's how it was when we saw it. It was
an amazing bill. On the face of it, it
shouldn't have worked but it did. These
guys were some of the best exponents of
black musical culture from the Fifties
and Sixties, from 12 bar blues to modal
improvisation. I felt both sides in equal
measures.

Not Waving, Drowning

I gave up eating meat. It wasn't a sudden thing. Hugh and John Sanderson were vegetarian and I became more interested in so-called 'healthier' eating. Brenda and I shared cooking duties and I always cooked veggie.

Me being a vegetarian was never a problem at home in London, but it was when we went to stay with Jim and Maureen in Belfast. It was a culinary culture shock for them and no mistake.

Maureen was preparing a big roast dinner when I mentioned that I would prepare my own meat-free meal. She got very upset with me for interfering with her routine. The whole process of cooking together was most uncomfortable. Maureen was a very kind, big hearted woman but a little volatile, shall we say.

We were about to sit down to eat when she lost her patience with me. She stood at the table, opposite me, and waved the carving knife, while she gave me a piece of her mind. "Why did I have to be different?" "Why couldn't I be normal?" "Why couldn't I just join in?"

It was awkward to say the least. Everyone just sat there dumbfounded as she let rip. I don't even remember if we ate the meal but, afterwards, Brian, Elisabeth, Brenda, myself and the kids spent the afternoon wandering the grounds of Stormont in shock.

Of course, it wasn't just about the food. This was a rock and roll step too far in her eyes. My lifestyle and my goals in life were alien to her. She couldn't understand me. I don't know if Brenda had confided to her mother about our situation or whether Maureen was just airing her opinion. She thought that I was leading my family into a dead end street and she had to say something.

I gave up meat for four years but my 'healthy' eating regime came to a halt on the first French tour with Rory. I couldn't get the energy nor the vitamins I needed for those gigs from the food available on tour. I was permanently exhausted. The lack of Vitamin B, in particular, was making me anxious. Phil McDonnell, the tour manager, called a doctor, who thought we were just a rock and roll band looking for uppers. He gave me tablets the size of horse pills that were pure caffeine when it was liver and fresh red meat that I needed.

Not only had I changed my diet but I was moving slowly towards a complete lifestyle change. I bought a couple of books on yoga and meditation and I started jogging around the Wanstead Flats, a large piece of grassland common near Pevensey Road.

It was all very gradual and tentative at first. Every Friday afternoon, when I didn't have a gig, I'd go to the Atherton steam baths and sauna on the Romford Road. There was an area in there that was perfect for some yoga stretching.

All sorts frequented the pool but on a Friday afternoon, the sauna was dominated by three main groups: gays, West Indians and Irish builders. They all tolerated each other. I, on the other hand, being a fresh faced Belfast lad, was a wee bit wary.

The first time I walked into the wooden cabin with my towel covering my manhood, there was just one vacant space on the top bench, next to the gay guys. There's always one dominant character in any group and the main man in this one was a very tall, slim, bald, loud, East End bloke. The space was next to him.

He decided to have some fun. With just a few inches between us all, he shuffled as close as he could to me. I could feel the hairs of his arms. When I tried to grab an inch of space the other way, he sidled up a bit closer. I sat there poker-faced while he and his mates had a chuckle at my expense.

The only thing I could do to relax was put my meditation into practice. I began to breathe slowly and to focus. Unfortunately, what came into focus was the biggest penis I'd seen in my life. The owner was Charlie, a middle aged West Indian. I swear his schlong was between eight and 10 inches long, at rest. It dangled downwards towards the bench below like a thick knotted rope hanging off the side of a ship.

When I got showered and dressed to head for home, I saw a flamboyant figure standing in the foyer. He wore a bright blue Afro wig, stacked high heels, white boots, flowered shirt, black leather pants and a fringed shoulder bag. It was my mate from the sauna. Turned out he was a gay club DJ.

Our flat in Pevensey Road only had one bedroom so when Connaire got a little older, we gave the kids our bedroom and made the front room our bedroom/living room. It was cramped for us but at least Gillian and Connaire had their own room.

Gilly was coming up to primary school age and Connaire was a little boy with a lot of energy. Together with my constant practicing, our place was a bit of a hub.

The flat beneath us in Pevensey Road had been vacant for a while before it was taken by a guy called Chris Bray from somewhere in north London. He was a chef and we eventually got to know him. He would come to us for a drink and sometimes we would go to him. I think he had just come out of a long relationship. He seemed like a pleasant, interesting guy and he soon became one of our circle of friends. Gerry had a new girlfriend, Linda Campbell, and they were often at our place. Linda was a really nice girl with strong political views. They weren't the same as mine, which led to some lively debates.

My relationship with Brenda wasn't right though. She was distant. She finally told me she didn't want any more kids. We discussed it and decided that we had our family now so I agreed to have a vasectomy.

The positives were obvious but the negative was that after a five year period, it would be almost impossible to have it reversed. Apparently, your body builds up antibodies that kill off the sperm. I didn't foresee me ever wanting to reverse it. Life isn't predictable though, is it?

The vasectomy didn't hurt. I took the bus home after. That said, my sacrifice didn't have the desired effect for me. Things between Brenda and myself didn't improve.

(I did decide to have it reversed before the five years were up. What a bastard. It's three hours of microsurgery and a horror show after.)

I used the vasectomy as an excuse not to do a couple of Swift gigs. Things in the Swift camp weren't going too well so it wasn't as much of a problem as it could have been. Pete Thomas then announced that he was leaving the band. He wanted to do other things but said he'd stay until we found a replacement. It wasn't our only problem though. At that point, we rehearsed at Larry's flat and the van was kept there. He and Geoff humped the gear into the van before and after the shows. The fact that he fixed and maintained the van put extra pressure on him and I think he felt used.

Our problems were compounded by the fact that we had fewer gigs and were all claiming unemployment benefits, while declaring our earnings from the band. The dole was a young musicians lifeline back then. Hugh and Larry eventually got summoned to the dole office and questioned about their finances. The result was their dole was cut and this put even more pressure on the band because they had to find work.

Our sponsorship from the GLAA was coming to an end. Our bank account at the end of 1978 was in the black by £270.84. We weren't going to survive long on that.

Our guitar player friend, Steve Topping, had been coming to a few gigs of late and was complimentary about some of our new compositions. When we played in his hometown, Liverpool, in December 1978, he came along and got up to play with us. He was impressive and, together with Hugh, there was a lot of musical empathy.

John McCullough, Hugh and I deliberated for a long time about how to move forward. We had a real bond with Larry and we'd been through so much together and, in a way, achieved so much. We couldn't bear to think how it would affect Larry if we replaced him. We took the easy way out and let Swift fizzle out before we began working with Steve on a new band: Drowning Not Waving.

I Rock

As Swift was dying, I did another rehearsal for one of Gerry's jams at the Bridge House playing percs. When we took a short break, I couldn't resist sitting behind Ted's kit. The guitar player, Dave Edwards, started to play some chords of a song we were working on and I played along. Ted's drums were big sizes and tuned for a big sound. When Gerry came back, he was surprised. At that moment, I sounded like a rock drummer.

Ted wasn't always into these side projects so Gerry asked me to sit in for some demos in North London, playing drums. From there on, we played some gigs together. It became the Gerry McAvoy Band. Robbie McIntosh played guitar just before he joined the Pretenders and went on to play with Paul McCartney, Norah Jones and John Meyer, to name but a few - a wonderful guitar player.

For my part, this was the first time that I had been in a real recording studio with a real rock band. I realised that I would have to take a different approach to playing this style of music when at a jam session a certain guitar player, Dennis Stratton who played with Iron Maiden for a short while, told me to put down my 'brushes' and pick up some 'sticks'.

Hugh, John McCullough, Steve Topping and I started to rehearse every Friday in a church hall in Peckham. We worked on compositions written by Hugh and Steve but sometimes we would just jam, record it and see where that took us. It was a new experience for us all but one that I relished. The musical ambitions of the band were born out of jazz rock but with a big input from 20th century classical music, which was a huge part of both Hugh's and Steve's background.

We worked like this for a few months then decided that we would extend the sonic possibilities and add colour and texture. To this end, we advertised for a sax player and found Lyn Dobson, who played sax and flute. In fact, he played the flute solo on Manfred Mann's 'Pretty Flamingo' and, in the Sixties, he had played with Georgie Fame and the Blue Flames. Lyn went on to play with Soft Machine and Keef Hartley. He also recorded with Nick Drake and John Martyn. Lyn was an interesting character, really into Indian classical music, as was Steve.

Hugh was the one making the calls about gigs and Roy Patterson helped with his contacts. I only remember us doing a few gigs, and one stands out for all the wrong reasons.

It was in an arts venue in the North East and, at this stage, we had no band transport so we had to rent a van to get us there. Hugh and I shared the driving. When it came to show time, there was a good crowd in, getting close to full, so we took to the stage with confidence. It was short lived.

After the second tune, Lyn decided that he didn't want to play the remainder of the rehearsed set. He discarded the music charts and launched into an improvisation leaving us with no alternative but to join in. We were all in favour of improv but felt this was neither the time nor the place. We had come to perform the pieces that we had been working on for months and to improvise only where planned.

The hippy in Lyn was fully released when he took off his shoes and sat down on stage cross-legged like an Indian yogi. Unbelievably, the crowd liked it but the whole thing was a let down for us. It just wasn't what we had set out to achieve. As I drove back to London, I felt a bit numb.

It turned out to be the last gig we ever played together. Lyn was questioning John's role in the band and was keen to try someone new. It was a difficult situation. I had known John from Belfast and had wonderful times with him over the years, as we all had. He and I came from different sides of the divide in Northern Ireland. People mistook us for brothers. I was, and still am, very fond of him but things were changing musically within the band and our ideas about the future, as individuals, were changing too.

John was working with the British Council and I think he was looking for a new career. No sooner had John decided to leave than Lyn got involved with a punk band from Coventry called the Flies and he left.

Hugh, Steve and I soldiered on and recruited a double bass player called Paul Rogers, a friend of Hugh's from Wales. Paul was, and still is, playing free jazz. He is a very well respected player, one of the best in his field. He has played and recorded with some of the leading names of the genre. He spent time in New York and now lives in France.

That line up of the band didn't perform any gigs but the rehearsals and jam sessions were something that I really looked forward to.

Steve later said in his biography, released to coincide with his debut album, 'Early Promise - Late Flower', that it was a shame the band was never properly recorded and praised Hugh highly for his compositions and improvisational approach. That said, by the middle of 1980, the band had all but fizzled out.

There are still a few cassette recordings of 'Drowning Not Waving' floating around. Had we just been trying everything that we could after the demise of Swift to keep live that creativity and freedom we'd possessed? It was, for us, all about music.

The truth was we hadn't thought about the audience and weren't able to tailor our sound to communicate effectively to one large enough. Experimentation and the beauty of complex sound is all well and good but you have to communicate something else, be it a narrative or an emotion. It wasn't that we weren't good enough as musicians, we were probably just not generous enough.

I found myself doing all sorts of gigs to earn some money. The north London Irish circuit, working men's clubs, blues gigs, whatever came. I played in the Rolls Royce Working Men's Club twice: opening for Lonnie Donegan and Ted '3-2-1' Rogers. Years later when touring Germany with Rory, we met Lonnie Donegan in Hamburg or Frankfurt. When I mentioned the Rolls Royce Club to him, he completely blanked me. I saw him later in a bierkeller cornered by three frauleins - him, with his heart trouble and all.

At that time, my dreams and aspirations had all but evaporated. I wasn't playing music I was passionate about and I was on the dole queue once again. Meanwhile, Gilly and Connaire were full of life and energy, Connaire keeping us entertained with his toddler mischief. To our friends, everything probably looked normal but Brenda and I were bickering and arguing over our prospects.

Both my parents had worked but Brenda came from a traditional background where her dad was the sole breadwinner and her mum looked after the home. The situation may have been frustrating and disappointing for her but she was reluctant to help our financial situation, even if it was only working part-time. The onus was on me to find a way forward. After all, it was my dream and desire to make a living and a life from making music that had found us in a one-bedroomed flat in east London.

I almost gave up. I suggested to Brenda that we head back to Belfast. I could try to get my old job back and play at the weekends. It could also have been very lucrative but Brenda really didn't like that idea. There was a reason, of course, one that I was blind to at the time.

Chris Bray was spending more and more time with us. When I would leave for a gig on Saturday, he would be there. When I got home from a gig, she would be at his place, the kids upstairs. I didn't like that. I was jealous too but chose not to dwell on it too much. I didn't feel, under the circumstances, that I could object to her having a friend. She hadn't really made many new local friends - she only ever met up with people she knew from Northern Ireland.

About this time, I was introduced to a recording engineer from Northern Ireland called Davey Smythe and his wife, Valerie, who had just moved to Bean, a hamlet, in Kent. Davey had converted their large garage into a studio and named it Wizard Sound Studios. He had a small network of musicians from Northern Ireland that he knew and would ask to come along to work in the studio to iron out the initial problems. Through a friend of a friend, I was asked to go down there.

Gerry had been wanting to do a solo album for a while. He wanted side one to be a studio recording and side two, the live recordings from the Bridge House. Gerry was able to do what he wanted on his downtime from Rory's band. In fact, Rory came along to some of the Bridge House gigs.

I suggested Wizard Studios to Gerry and we both went along to meet Davey for Gerry to have a look-see at the equipment there. Davey had a Studer 24-track recording machine and a pretty good mixing console. He had built both a vocal booth and a drum booth and, even though it was all new, it had a good feel.

The local pub was walking distance and we all went there for a pint and an evening meal. This sort of 'facility' is vital for keeping bands happy with a recording studio. The Northern Irish banter, which we call 'humour', helped clinch the deal. Despite Davey calling him 'Geraldine', Gerry decided to record there.

Gerry asked Dave Edwards to play, while Davey and I recommended Lawrence Thompson, another great guitar player from Northern Ireland. Davey played some saxophone and, despite the occasional hiccup with the equipment, things went well.

Every night after recording, Gerry and I liked to unwind with a pint so I came back late. Brenda was OK with it because it was Gerry and, as such, counted as a lads' night out. I was home a lot more anyway. Even so, things were building up between us. We were short of money and still short of time together.

RORY

From Zero to Hero

It came to this. I was broke and living in a one-bedroom flat by a railway track in east London with my unhappy wife and two energetic young children. My musical career that I had come to London for with such hope was in the doldrums. Fate then intervened and gave *me* a reason to stay.

Like a bolt from the blue, Ted Mckenna, the drummer for The Rory Gallagher Band, handed in his notice to the man. Who knows why but Ted wanted to move on. He would be playing his last gig with Rory's multi-million selling band at The Palais des Sport in Paris on 20th February, 1981. For me, Ted's departure was a second chance.

I had auditioned for Rory before in London when I was with the band, Swift. Unbelievably, I couldn't have cared less then whether I got the gig or not. My head and heart were with Swift and what we were doing but now the band was no more.

I gave my old friend, Rory's bass player, Gerry McAvoy, a call and asked if he would put my name forward to be considered for an audition. A few evenings later at around six, the phone rang.

"Hello, Brendan, it's Rory here".

Cool as, without the bloody stammer that had plagued me all my life, I replied, "Hello Rory, what can I do for you?" He thought this was pretty funny and that put me at ease right away. I was to come along to Nomis rehearsal rooms behind Olympia. He gave me the date and time.

I arrived early on the day. Rory's right-hand man, Tom Driscoll, was already there and helped me with my drums.

Tom was a Teddy Boy when he first heard Rory and it changed everything for him. From that moment he was a massive fan. He started working as a roadie for Rory in the early '70s and was a permanent fixture by the time I arrived. Calling him a roadie is a severe understatement. He was, like I said, Rory's right-hand man, confidante and his most reliable and faithful friend.

Even so, when it came to playing and rehearsing, no-one was allowed in the room but the band, not Tom, not even Donal, Rory's brother and manager. It was strictly music time.

During the first day's rehearsal, we played a little, chatted a little, and played some more. Rory gave me no direction at all. He just wanted to play, see what my instincts were.

I was uptight. I needed to impress so much that I couldn't relax at all. After a couple of hours, I packed up, shook hands with the lads and went home. By Rory's standards, as I would find out later, it had been quite tame. Nevertheless, what Rory was about had become much clearer to me that day than at my first try out with him when I was with Swift. Just with his guitar, Rory was the piano player, the sax player and the guitar player all rolled into one. He filled the sound completely and nothing compared with Rory in terms of energy and intensity. Nothing.

I can't say I enjoyed the audition. It was, frankly, torture. My wife asked the obvious questions of me but I couldn't tell her that I had done well. Rory had other players lined up and I didn't think much of my chances. Gerry and I spoke but he was non-committal. He just didn't know, only Rory did.

I was amazed to get the call back to Nomis. This time, the playing was harder, more intense, and much longer. It was extremely physical. There was less chit chat. We also played more of Rory's tunes this time around. I was more confident and played with more urgency and determination. Afterwards, Rory thanked me for coming and Tom helped me pack my drums into the car.

I wasn't sure what to make of this matter-of-fact dismissal. I couldn't read Rory then. It was like having a go at Braille for the first time. I thought that I had done a better job but, in truth, I was no surer about my prospects than after the first audition.

I got a third call.

This time round, we had a much more fluid rehearsal and started to feel a lot more together. Rory's rehearsals were just like a gig, only longer. The average gig would be three-plus hours. The rehearsals were four plus. Compared to what I had been doing, it was very, very physical. I had to learn to enjoy that.

When we finished, I was drenched in sweat. I changed and, as I packed my drums down, Rory asked if I fancied a pint. We went to an old pub, the name escapes me, in a road behind Nomis, where, over the years to come, we bumped into a few musos including the likes of Motorhead's Lemmy and Slade's Noddy Holder. The pub was packed and, after a couple of drinks, Rory suggested that the three of us, him, Gerry and me, have a bite at an Italian restaurant close by.

Half-way across the road, Rory turned to Gerry, pointed at me and said, "Meet Mr Sticks".

He must have thought that I had left my tongue on the bar in the pub. I just didn't know what to say. Gerry was chuffed and shook my hand. We went for the meal and talked but my mind was racing with the consequences of what had just happened. This guy was an international superstar and I had just hitched a ride.

Uncoupling

When I got the call from Rory for a second chance at auditioning with him after Ted resigned, I had never wanted anything so badly in my life. When I actually got the gig, when I became his Mr Sticks, I went home full of it and myself. Brenda's low-key reaction confused me. I wasn't sure how pleased she was, if at all. I didn't get it. It was everything that I had wanted. Everything we had wanted, so I thought. Was it everything she wanted? I wasn't sure what she wanted anymore.

I thought that this was the beginning of the end of our problems. To be in such a successful band, with Rory Gallagher himself, to have a regular income - £4000 for the next album and put on an initial wage of £200 a week for the tour. Back then, certainly for me, for us, it was more than good. It was like all my birthdays had come at once.

The next day, I phoned my mum and dad, Brian, everybody, to tell them the good news. They were all delighted. My dad hated the music, hated loud music full stop, but he was very happy for me.

Rory went home to his mother's place in Ireland to work on material for the next album, which would be the next project for the band. He always worked alone when he was writing. Almost immediately, however, I was included in all the events related to The Rory Gallagher Band.

Rory's younger and only brother and his manager, Donal, was good friends with *Blue Peter* host, Peter Duncan. Peter, along with his friend, the actor, Phil Davis, who was famous at the time for his role in *Quadrophenia*, wanted to record a single. Donal arranged for Gerry and I to play on it. When Peter had a housewarming party in Chelsea, Gerry and Linda, Brenda, the kids and I were all invited. Anita Dobson - 'Angie' from *Eastenders* - a big star then, and, of course, future wife of Queen's Brian May, was also there.

We went for drinks in Finch's Bar in the Fulham Road, which Rory frequented regularly as did the team who ran Rory's office in Redcliffe Gardens around the corner. They included: Diane Worthy, his trusted secretary, Peter Collins, the tour manager, who seemed to be forever on the slot machines, and Tom Driscoll. There was a guy, John Arnison, a booking agent, who shared the office. He went on to manage Marillion.

One evening after the office had closed, Gerry and I met them all in Finch's and Donal came along. The conversation turned to Rory's live shows, how intense and how long they were. John Arnison looked at me and said, "I hope you're ready for this. Rory eats drummers."

I did know what Rory's shows were about. I had seen enough of them. Ted McKenna was a big man but he told me on a number of occasions that the effort required for an RG show had played havoc with his back. I was about to reply but Donal gave John a look that said everything and the conversation moved on quickly.

Rory set a date to start rehearsals before setting off to Germany to record the new album, 'Jinx'. We were heading to Dieter Dierk's studio in a small village near Cologne. Jinx would be the third album Rory had recorded there. He felt comfortable in that environment.

About a week before the first rehearsal, Gerry asked me to go with him to pick up the master tapes for his own album 'Bassics' from Kent. It marked the end of one project, making way for the new. I was on a high. I felt that all the years of hard work and hardship were beginning to pay off.

I got home just after 11 at night. Brenda was already in bed, which was unusual. I was just about to go to bed myself when she said that she needed to talk to me. Without any hesitation, or much emotion, she told me straight out that she was having an affair with Chris Bray and wanted a divorce.

I was stunned. Call me naive, but I never believed that such a thing could happen to us. I was from Belfast. I'd never known <u>anyone</u> who had got a divorce.

A massive feeling of rejection rocked me. It quickly turned to rage. There was a book on the table that I had just bought her. I grabbed it, ran to the kitchen, fell to my knees and tore the thing to pieces. I was in agony.

I'm not sure how long it took but somehow I regained enough composure to go back and ask her why and why now. Things were turning a corner. The future was ours. All she could say to me was that it was over and this was what she wanted. She wanted to be with him.

I didn't think of him at all at this point. It was the thought of losing my precious family that was whirling around my head. The next morning, after a sleepless night, the harsh reality of my situation hit me. I had to think fast. I didn't want to start rehearsals with Rory, go to Germany for what would turn out to be a month and leave Gillian and Connaire with Chris Bray. I just couldn't stand the thought of it.

I rang Gerry and told him I was coming over to see him. He was living at Linda's place then and, when I got there, I told him everything that had happened and everything I wanted to do. I didn't have the money for the flights so I asked Gerry to lend it to me and he said he would without hesitation. He was livid. He had known Brenda as long as I had. He agreed to help me in any way he could.

I rang my parents and told them that I was coming to see them for a few days with the kids. They were so excited about it. I felt terrible because I had to keep a stiff upper lip until I got there and could tell them face to face. For some strange reason, maybe to keep things as normal as possible for Gillian and Connaire, we all went to Linda and Gerry's for a drink that night. Gerry picked us up but, however much any of us tried, if at all, it was a tense, unsociable, night. When we got back, I told Brenda that I intended to take the kids to my parents while I was away. She agreed. The next day, I took the children and went to Dublin.

The family were overjoyed to see us all but my mum had to go out for a meeting or something she had planned to do. My Dad was getting ready to go to work as a night watchman, so I was there with the rest of the family that evening. I didn't say anything to them. After I got the kids settled in bed, I asked Bernadette if she would drop me off at where my Dad worked. It was then she asked if everything was OK. I said it was but she knew something was very wrong.

I picked up a bottle of whiskey on the way and my Dad knew, as soon as he saw me, that all was not as it should be. I told him the story as I worked my way through the bottle. He was shocked to see me drinking like that and wouldn't drink with me. I stayed the night with him and the more we talked and I drank, the more angry and helpless I began to feel.

The next morning, I told my mum and asked if they could look after the kids while I was in Germany for May and June. She was dismayed. Being a fine, upstanding Catholic, she'd never imagined such a dreadful thing as divorce would happen to anyone in her family but, of course, she said, "Yes."

I stayed a couple of days and got back to London, two days before the first rehearsal. I was punch drunk and hungover. I didn't drink the day before the rehearsal but, emotionally, I was done and it was obvious from the first notes we played in the studio. Rory must have been thinking that this wasn't the guy he had played with a few weeks back and he was right. It was a struggle from the start. I wanted to do it. I wanted to be there. I just didn't have the heart. It was terrible.

When we were packing up, Rory left the room briefly and Gerry told me I had to talk to him. It was something I already knew I had to do. When Rory came back, Gerry discreetly left the room. Standing on the low stage together, I apologised and explained as best I could what was going on. He just listened and let me talk. The way I played that day, he could easily have let me go, saved himself potentially a lot of trouble and found another player, but he didn't. There were no ultimatums, nothing. He gave me a chance and when I asked for an advance on the album fee, he agreed to that as well. That says everything about the man.

Jinx

Over the next week, distracted by the music, I recovered myself. It was time for me to head to Germany. It was going to be a lot of hard work and a challenge but one I was determined to embrace. I badly needed something positive in my life at that time. At first, my mind was in two places at once but slowly I was able to focus and put London out of my mind.

Most of Rory's drummers had an association with the Paiste Cymbal Co. Donal suggested that on route to Germany, he and I make a small detour to their factory in Nottwil in Switzerland to pick some up.

It was my first experience of how doors will open when you play with a successful band. In the artist room, the Paiste rep let me hear a whole range of cymbals and told me I could have my pick. These were the most expensive cymbals in the world and they were wonderful, full of colour, character, and personality. When I'd finished trying them out, I wondered how much I could reasonably carry. In the end, I took six or seven. From that day, I have always played Paiste cymbals.

Another flight and we arrived at Dieter Dierks by the evening. No buses, no Tubes, no dodgy vans and near death experiences, no cheap seats. This was the big time. A sleek car picked us up from the airport.

Rory, Gerry and Tom were already at Dieter's with the engineer, Jurgen Kramer. Rory had worked with Jurgen before and liked what he did. The studio was residential so there was never a reason to be late. We all had our own private rooms, which I was glad of.

The next day, we went about trying to find the best sounding part of the room for the drums, and the best part of the next two days finding the right sounds for the instruments before a recording button was pushed. From the control room window was an overview of the large recording studio that had vocal and drum booths along one side. Rory didn't want drums in a booth for this album. He wanted us all in the same space for a 'live' feel.

The first few days of recording didn't go as well as Rory would have liked and I could feel his frustration. It was down to me and my lack of experience. I had to do better. I couldn't let it get personal, just get on the case and fix it. Slowly, things improved and we began to get a few tracks down.

We wanted for nothing. The fridge was always full of beer and you never went hungry. After each evening's recording, they set out a big spread of cheeses and hams and that was after the breakfasts and lunches. Some nights, Rory liked to go to the local bar in Stommel for a change of scene. It was a typical country pub, full of farmers who liked fart jokes.

Peter was the proprietor and knew the lads from the previous times when the band had been at Dierks. It must have been quite something for Peter and the locals to have the RG Band drinking in their pub; Rory was a huge star in Germany at the time.

They had a dartboard there and we always had a couple of games. Eventually, we were competing against the locals. I'm pretty good at darts and what I find is, the more I drink, the better I get. A healthy rivalry developed until we were challenged to play against a pub team from a neighbouring village in Pohlheim.

We needed a six man team so RG, Gerry, Tom, Jurgen, Peter, the landlord, and myself, became the Kamikaze Darts Team representing Stommel. We even had team sweatshirts made up with our names emblazoned across our chests. Despite our fearsome appearance and reputation, I think we were soundly beaten but I can't be sure. I do remember Rory, Gerry and I playing table tennis very badly back at Dieter's place at about six in the morning. When Tom was next in the pub, Peter's wife asked what we all talked about all night since Peter couldn't speak a word of English and we couldn't speak a word of German. Tom was at a loss to explain to her satisfaction.

Rory had to go back to London for a couple of days, leaving the rest of us at the studio. Everything came to a halt so we had time on our hands. One night we went to see the Grandmothers of Invention, who were playing nearby. Tom was a massive Zappa fan and wanted to go. Mostly, while Rory was away, we just chilled. One day, I went shopping and bought a pair of white overalls, Lowell George style. I didn't have the courage to wear them until the last day in the studio. When I did, no-one said a word.

Dieter managed the Scorpions, a very successful rock band, probably Germany's most successful band at the time. While Rory was away, a couple of the guys turned up at the studio after a tour. One guy's wife met up with him there and they stayed a day. They had the room next to mine.

I woke about ten-ish to the sound of their lovemaking. It went on and on. After a while, I couldn't take any more and went for a walk. I swear that every time I went back to my room, they were still at it. There's no other way to put this: they literally fucked all day long. I saw him a couple of times walking through with some sandwiches to take back to the room. I never saw the girl. It was the talk of the studios. We were all sick with jealousy.

Throughout the whole recording process, there was only ever the band and Jurgen, with Tom at hand to help out when needed. The title track of the album was 'Jinxed'. It has a kind of a rumba feel to it. To get the desired effect, I played the snare drum with the snares off for the verses and choruses. (For those who don't know, the snares are the thin wires that touch the skin to give that tight, military, sound.) Rory wanted them on for the guitar solo. There wasn't enough time for me to flick them on so Tom sat next to me for the whole recording and flicked them on and off like a bike mechanic in the Tour de France. He'd never done it before but he was pretty good at it.

When we had recorded all the tracks, Rory asked us to listen to and review them. He mentioned a lovely ballad, 'Easy Come, Easy Go', in particular, and asked if we could do it any better. Gerry thought it would be hard to improve on it and Rory eventually agreed.

On the last day, dressed to kill in my white overalls, I talked to Tom about my drums and I overheard Rory say to Gerry, "I think he's getting into it now." I was obviously looking, feeling and, more importantly, sounding more confident. It was so good to hear that from the man. The next day, Gerry and I flew back to London leaving Rory to work on overdubs.

While I was in Germany, I regularly called my folks and the kids. I'd arranged to meet Brenda in Belfast and bring the kids to her. The day after I arrived in London, I flew to Dublin.

It had been almost six weeks since I had seen Gillian and Connaire. They seemed so much more grown up to me. Gillian was six and Connaire was two and a half. I was glad to see how well they had fitted into family life with my parents. Gilly was helping my mum in the kitchen and my dad was teaching Connaire nursery rhymes. I still have a tape of them singing 'Baa Baa Black Sheep' together. Connaire did everything, even singing and talking, at 100 miles an hour. At first, I thought he was just tripping over himself, anxious to say things but it was becoming obvious that he was developing a stammer.

On the second day I was home, my dad was talking to Connaire and each time he tried to answer, he got stuck. My Dad would get him to stop and try again. I listened to this for a few minutes and all those years of people telling me just that - the prompting, the turning away, the giggling - came flooding back. I couldn't stop myself shouting, "Stop it. Don't do that to him."

Dad just looked at me in astonishment and said, "It's just what your mum and I think's best." My father did think he was doing the right thing but I knew from experience, it just causes more anxiety. The whole thing was over as quickly as it started but Dad did take on board what I had said. It was the first time in my life that I had raised my voice to him.

I was very grateful to my parents for what they did at that time. At the drop of a hat, they came to the rescue; a selfless act on their part because their lives had to be put on hold and change for a while.

Gillian, Connaire and I took the train to Belfast to the Russell house. The kids didn't seem to notice that anything was wrong. For them, it was a happy reunion. The atmosphere was strained but there was no animosity. Brenda wanted to stay in Belfast for a while for things to settle down and think things through. I stayed with them for a couple of days before heading back to Dublin but while I was there, I found time to talk to Maureen. She told me that Jim and her were very upset about what had happened and that Jim had expressed his thoughts on the matter very strongly to Brenda.

Aftermath

I thought that hanging around in Belfast was a waste of time and, in any case, would aggravate the situation. I wasn't at all interested in hearing any more about what had happened between Brenda and Chris or why.

Gerry thought it would be good for me to get away and have some fun. He asked me to go with him to the Lisdoonvarna Festival in County Clare in the west of Ireland. The added bonus was our old mate, Dave Edwards, would be playing there with his band.

The Lisdoonvarna Festival originated in the mid-18th century and, ironically, was famous for match making, a long tradition in old Ireland. The practice started in Lisdoonvarna when the landed gentry went there to take the waters, which were famous for their mineral content and health giving properties. While the toffs were there, they would try to find partners for their offspring. Over the years, it developed into a traditional music festival and, by the 1970s, it was a full blown rock affair.

Dave's band had the last slot on Saturday night - Sunday morning, to be precise. Either Diane or Pete from RG's office found us a B&B - nothing short of a miracle given the thousands who were going. We rented a car from Dublin airport and headed west, leaving my worries behind and arriving in Lisdoonvarna at lunchtime.

The whole town was buzzing. A massive tent city had evolved at the edge of town, populated by students, hippies and bikers. Traditional musicians played in the streets and most of the pubs had music. The bill in the big tent that year included: Lindisfarne, John Sebastien, De Danann, one of Rory's favourite Irish bands, Stockton's Wing, Chris de Burgh, Moving Hearts and Country Joe McDonald (without The Fish). We got ourselves settled and hit the pubs where we drank Guinness steadily throughout the day.

At some late hour, Gerry and I made our way backstage where we bumped into Paddy Maloney, the wonderful uilleann piper and founder of the Chieftains. He was, at least as, if not more, drunk than we were. He informed us that he was playing at a Mass at nine in the morning the next day and wanted Gerry and I to go play with him. He tried very hard to coax us into it but we respectfully declined. The last time we saw him was around 2am still holding court and looking for a rhythm section.

By the time the Dave Edwards Band took to the stage it was way past their 1.15am slot. By now, what was left of the audience was drunk, stoned, or both, and incapable of giving Dave and the lads, who were probably the only sober people there, their due.

Gerry found this unacceptable. Indeed, he took the crowd's general apathy as a personal insult. Having learned nothing from our teenage experiences of the pointlessness of goading a crowd and fortified by a twelve hour Guinness binge, he took centre stage. He grabbed the mike and bellowed at the crowd to raise their game for this wonderful band from London. The crowd remained resolutely indifferent and Gerry eventually staggered off the stage, grumbling to himself.

I spent my time more usefully. I had struck up a conversation with a very pretty girl. When she left, I followed her. She introduced me to some of her friends, who were rolling joints and passing them around. I soon found myself succumbing to the weed and unable to speak. Unfortunately, the pretty girl left me and no match was made. I can't remember much else.

After the Festival, we spent a 'quiet' day or two in County Kerry before heading back to London.

Back home, Jim Clarke called me from Belfast to say he had heard what had happened and that he had met up with Brenda. He couldn't understand why she was insisting on a divorce. He told her that she could have had the affair in secret and maybe it would have run its course.

Jim is a pragmatic person, which is why he is good at his job. Emotions don't come into his decision making. He advised me to do everything I could to keep the family together. I told him that I was determined to try.

It was very strange being back in London in the flat on my own. I felt hollow and weightless. I avoided Chris in the downstairs flat because I didn't want any confrontations that might make me feel better but make matters worse. For his part, he said nothing to me.

Fortunately, depression stayed away. Things were moving on in my life so fast that it couldn't settle and wrap its tentacles around me. I needed to keep focused on the future. Rory was planning shows for late August/September and there would be rehearsals. I had to keep going.

I was in constant contact with Brenda and the kids while they were in Belfast and, as the weeks went by, I detected a change in Brenda's mood. She was having second thoughts. Eventually, she said she wanted to come back and give things another try.

I wondered what had brought on this change of heart: was it pressure from her parents, what Clarkie had said, maybe her brother Brian had encouraged her or did she genuinely want to be back with me? I felt vulnerable to false hope but so happy at the thought of being united with my family again. Their return and Rory's rehearsals coincided and I was determined to make it all work.

I went to Heathrow Terminal One on a Sunday night and got caught in heavy weekend traffic. Brenda and the kids had been waiting for over half an hour when I arrived. She told me she thought that I had changed my mind and decided not to come.

As if. I had already gone to an estate agents in Forest Gate. I thought that with my future earnings, I could buy a house and give my wife and kids a proper family home. I had to make this work and, thanks to Rory, I felt that I at least had a chance.

Rock on the Tyne

The first festival booked for the band was Rock on the Tyne at the Gateshead National Stadium and Rory wanted to do a warm-up show beforehand. Someone, possibly Gerry, suggested the Bridge House in Canning Town. It was a great idea and the date was set for an impromptu gig on August 27th. I believe Terry Murphy was given only two days to advertise it but it sold out mostly by word of mouth.

The rehearsals with Rory went well. We did the soundcheck and Rory suggested going somewhere quiet for a drink. We drove to a pub we knew called the Golden Fleece in Manor Park, overlooking the Wanstead Flats. I sat there with the lads feeling full of anticipation, excitement, and fear. The fear's always there.

When we got back to the Bridge House, a queue was snaking around the corner and down the road. I was stunned. Around 700 people had turned up. The Bridge House, I'm guessing, held 500. There were no Health and Safety regulations then. (To give you an example, my figures are there or thereabouts, the Marquee was sometimes rammed with 800 people but, after H&S legislation, they were permitted just 350.)

It was a warm, humid, summer's night and inside, the Bridge House was like a cauldron. There was no discernible airflow. The pub had a large square lower floor, which, at its far end, had some stairs up to a bar and a raised area where the stage was set against the back wall. Later, for capacity and convenience, Terry moved the stage downstairs along the side so people from the top at the bar could see down and more people could see the band downstairs.

It was quite a high stage - about four feet up - and people were rammed right up against it. I was tucked in at the back. Rory wasn't jumping around and whipping the crowd up like he normally did because his aim was just to play and routine the set. Nevertheless, it was a Rory gig and that always meant high energy. This was my first ever with Rory and I gave it my all.

As time went on, the sweaty, pressure cooker, atmosphere overwhelmed me. There was no air, only a soaking, stifling humidity. I could barely breathe and three quarters of the way through the two hour plus set, my strength just ebbed away. I heaved myself up and staggered away from the kit to open the doors behind me to the dressing room in an effort to get some air. Tom Driscoll came over immediately to see if I was OK.

"Tom," I said," I don't think I'm going to make it."

He looked me dead in the eyes and said, "You will."

I took a few big gulps of air and went back to work. Tom was right. I did make it. I didn't die but I was done.

You had to be very fit to play with Rory. When we played the 'Rory at Midnight' gig on January 5th, 1984 in the Ulster Hall, Belfast, we opened with 'Follow Me', probably the top end of the energy level for a Rory song. The crowd went crazy and, from that point, the show didn't slow down for two and a half hours. I had to be on top of the beat the whole time. It sapped you. At the end of a show like that, I'd be drenched in sweat and completely exhausted. So much for "money for nothing and your chicks for free".

After the ordeal at the Bridge House, I was certainly more confident about our next gig, my second, the Rock on the Tyne Festival, in Gateshead.

The festival was groundbreaking for the North of England, which had been starved of major outdoor events for most of the '70s. Gateshead City Council approved the use of its new international sports stadium for the rock event over the August Bank Holiday weekend. It would feature both new wave and old school blues rock acts.

The last, but certainly not least, member of Rory's team I was to meet was Phil McDonnell, Rory's sound engineer and future tour manager. Phil had worked with the original Fleetwood Mac and too many others to list. He was a tough tour manager with a dry sense of humour. In the years that followed, he got me into all sorts of scrapes on the road, leaving me to get myself out of them. But, Phil also proved to be caring and sensitive. He was a family man and a great guy.

On the morning of August 29th, our whole entourage took the train north to Gateshead for the show. We never toured with family, friends or girlfriends. This was work. That was Rory's mentality.

The band was augmented for the next few shows by two saxophone players and top blokes: Dick Parry, who played with Pink Floyd - he did the solo on 'Money' - and Ray Beavis, a Bristolean, from the Graham Parker Band. Throughout that journey, I had my headphones on to familiarise myself with the whole set that I had recorded on tape. I wanted no mistakes. This was it, the real deal, and I was nervous.

We went to the festival site in the evening to catch the Saturday night headliners: Elvis Costello and Ian Dury, but we missed Ireland's latest rock and roll stars, U2, who had played earlier in the day. The Sunday line up, which we headlined, included Dr Feelgood, Ginger (Baker)'s Nutters and Geordie favourites, Lindisfarne.

They say about 15,000 people attended the festival, which made it the largest ever held in the North East of England. The pressure was on. Backstage, I could sense the stage crew willing me on. (Tom had told them that it was my first every gig with the band.)

It was massive for Rory. Punk had happened. New Wave had happened. He had basically been ignored by the press for a couple of years. It made the vast crowd's reaction to Rory when we came on stage so amazing.

As for me, I was used to more intimate, packed gigs where you could see the whites of the crowd's eyes. This crowd spread out like a single organism, deep and wide, the people just small details and very far away. When Rory appeared, there was a great roar as the crowd surged forward. They sounded like 40,000 never mind 15. If it hadn't done so before, it now dawned on me that this was an entirely new level of the game.

In an interview with Carol Clerk, Rory admitted to being jumpy at playing his first major show with his new line-up. If he was, I didn't notice. In fact, Rory was always a bit nervous before any show. He'd walk back and forth wringing his hands such was his desire to make it great, to be great.

In her review of the show, Clerk said that he needn't have worried. Rory had pulled a far bigger crowd than Costello or Dury and got a more tumultuous reception than those two artists put together. She said the crowd started a 'Rory' chant before Dr Feelgood had even left the stage and the reaction to Gallagher swept the site in great waves of emotion that intensified as the set neared its conclusion. I felt that onstage. It was an experience unlike anything I had ever known.

I had been in the eye of the storm for sure that night. But ask me how I felt it had gone? I don't remember. Other people gave me a better understanding of what had just happened. Rory didn't say much and I was to learn that Rory was never one for post mortems. For him, it was always, that's done: onwards and upwards.

In just over a week's time, we were due to leave for Athens to play at the New Philadelphia Stadium, and two days later at Thessaloniki. It would be the farthest from home I had ever been, mentally and physically.

When I got back to London I was exhilarated. I felt like a hunter bringing back the loot and full of stories to relate. Brenda's response was depressingly low key. The big downer was to follow.

After a few days, she told me she had to see Chris one more time to dissolve their union, face to face. I took it at face value, sort of. It was another part of the domestic drama that was being played out. She went to see him one evening and when she got back late that night, I didn't question her. The next morning, she told me that she couldn't live a lie and that she and Chris were getting a flat together, for them and for the children.

It didn't shock me this time. I didn't fall to my knees and tear up any books. The gig had both drained me and showed me what I really needed to be fulfilled. I had risked everything to get to this point. The past four months had been tough but I had to think clearly.

I thought about the conversation with Jim Clarke but it wasn't for me, not even to keep the family together. I decided that it was self preservation time. I might be losing my wife but I wasn't about to lose everything that I had worked so hard for my whole life, and near enough got myself killed trying to achieve. I had to think about myself, otherwise I would crumble to nothing and not be able to give my kids a thing. What truly mattered now was getting my head straight for the band's tour of Greece. By the time I got back, Brenda and my kids would be gone.

ATHENS 1981

Rebels Without A Cause

The Rory Gallagher Band arrived in Athens in the early evening of September 7th, 1981. The entourage included Donal, Peter Collins, Phil McDonnell, and saxophonists Ray Beavis and John 'Irish' Earle - the latter replacing Dick Parry.

Irish was a wonderful character, who spoke with a posh Dublin accent and had a great walrus moustache. He had worked with the Boomtown Rats and played the sax solo on Thin Lizzy's 'Dancing in the Moonlight (Caught Me in the Spotlight)'. His wife had advised him that, while he was in Greece, he should drink ouzo. "It's like wine," she said, "not too heavy." On the day off between Athens and Thessaloniki, he bought himself a bottle, sat on a beach in the baking sun and drank the lot. He was off his face by tea time.

I was 29 years old and the furthest away from home that I had ever been. The rest of these guys, including Gerry, had been around the block, more than once. When the plane door opened for us to disembark, I felt a sense of childlike excitement. Walking onto the steps, the warm Mediterranean air wrapped itself around me like an embrace. There was a smell of sea and pine in the air.

When we got through to the arrivals area, three beautiful young Phillipino girls presented us with large bouquets of flowers. I don't remember going through customs, perhaps that had been taken care of by Donal or Pete.

Outside the terminal building, we got into a limo and drove towards the city. We left the sparkling Aegean sea behind as we drove past the first Olympic stadium and on to the Caravelle Hotel, which would be our base for the next five days.

Athens was like nowhere else I had ever seen. The sun shining on the white buildings was so intense. My first glimpse of the ancient Acropolis with the temple of the Parthenon brought home to me the great antiquity of the city. I felt the history of the place. I was standing somewhere that looked both to the Eastern world and the West.

The hotel itself was modern and beautiful, one of the best in the city. It reeked of luxury and money. The first day or two, we didn't have much to do so Gerry and I asked if there were any live music clubs to go to. We were told about a club called Tiffany's, which was in the picturesque Plaka district near the Acropolis, and had blues bands playing most nights.

Nothing happens early in Athens so around 11 in the evening on the second day, Gerry and I went along to the club and were very pleasantly surprised to find a young Greek band with a guitar player called Dimitri 'Jimmy' Vatikotis. When the band had a break, the owner, who knew we were coming along, introduced us. Jimmy asked us if we would jam with them, which we did. He turned out to be one hell of a character. Takis Liarmakopoulos was their regular drummer, a really terrific guy and a good player. We became friends and I keep in touch with both of them to this day.

The next day, Phil Mac went to the football stadium where we would be performing to check the progress of the stage building et cetera. He was very disappointed that things weren't as far along as he would have liked. With typical Greek charm, he was assured that all would be well by the next day - "avrio, avrio". This did nothing to reassure him, needless to say. Tom Driscoll was having similar problems getting our equipment into the country. No-one knew anything. No-one was in a hurry.

That night we were invited to go to the ballet at the amphitheatre at the Acropolis. Rudolf Nureyev was performing in 'Swan Lake'. Rory wasn't in to it but Gerry, Donal, Phil Mac and I wanted to go for the experience. As we waited at the bar to be picked up, someone mentioned that Bo Derek, who starred in the hit film 10 with Dudley Moore, was at the other end of the foyer with her husband, John. The toilets were at the other end of the foyer and some of us suddenly got caught short, me included. Star struck, we all had a good look at her as we walked past. She was a stunningly beautiful woman.

With a capacity audience of 5000, the atmosphere in the amphitheatre was spectacular. The evening was warm and balmy and the semi-circle of ancient stone seats reached up to the sky. We were unable to all have seats together so Donal and I had seats on a lower level while Gerry and Phil - who, as a kid, used to cry about his sisters getting to go to ballet classes and not him - sat higher up. I don't know what the craic was up there but I'm sure I heard them giggling in the quieter passages. For my part, the performance blew me away. It was a thrill being able to glimpse the great Nureyev off stage, still dancing to keep warmed up.

Later that night, Gerry and I took Rory to Tiffany's for a change of scene. People took photographs of us with Rory. Once again, Gerry and I got up for a jam. It was a great night. Rory loved it because there was no pressure on him. He had a couple of beers and watched the band play.

Day Three and the stage and PA still weren't ready. There was a press conference scheduled to be held at the Hilton Hotel and Rory was to do an interview on national TV. The organisers were keen to get as much coverage for the show as possible.

The government-controlled TV station was not all that keen. It was election time and the situation was tense. It looked like the Greeks socialist PASOK party was going to sweep away the old conservative order and give Greece a left-wing government for the first time in its history. They'd had Fascism, nearly had Communism, they'd had the Junta, they'd had Conservatives and now the Socialists wanted a go.

The TV journalist knew it was a big deal to interview Rory at this time but others had to be convinced. The job went to Iosef Avramoglou, a 23 year old music journalist and promoter, from the Happening music store, who had gone to England to persuade Rory - no small feat - to play Greece. Iosef had previously arranged for Ian Gillian to play in Athens at the Sports Hall, a basketball stadium, where the Police also played.

Iosef told me that in order to arrange the TV interview he had to get many 'permissions'. They were expensive, which is one reason that he had gone to Coca Cola to sponsor the shows. For some left wing Greeks, that was unacceptable.

"The amount of money we needed was big - work permit, state permit, many permits. We had censorship then - logocrissia - you had to give the lyrics of the songs to the Ministry of Press Information, the Department involved with journalists."

"As for the television interview, I had to use a politician for that. It was a huge success to have an interview with this journalist. We had two channels in those days and this was the main channel of state television."

There was also a press conference held in a large conference room in the Hilton hotel. We sat behind a long table. Rory sat in the middle with Gerry and I flanking him left and right. The place was packed. The journalists' questions were the normal music ones you'd get asked. Rory did all the talking.

Out of the blue, the nature of the questioning changed. It became forthright, controversial and political. They asked Rory if he supported, funded or sympathised with the IRA. We were stunned. It was the first hint that this gig was going to be very, very different.

Rory was seen as a rebel, who bucked the system and went against the grain. The Greeks assumed that because he was Irish and because of the Troubles in Northern Ireland that he was a political rebel as well as a musical one. In Greece, hardcore punks, rock fans, blues fans and hippies alike thought of Rory as a people's hero. Rumours were circulating about him. One ridiculous rumour was that Rory had been a pallbearer at the funeral of Bobby Sands, dressed in full uniform with IRA insignia, bearing the rank of Major.

Another problem was that the country really didn't have any experience in putting on stadium events such as this. For many years, there had been a military dictatorship, referred to as 'the Junta' or 'the Colonels'. There wasn't much rock music, if any, on the airwaves - only martial or traditional music was played on the State radio. Live rock and roll was certainly not permitted.

The last live rock band to play in Athens was the Rolling Stones at the Panathinaikos AC stadium in 1967, a few days before the military coup. It was the last show of the Stones' troubled European tour in what had been a troubled year for them. They'd been busted for drugs in the UK, they were travelling under Interpol warrants and were harassed by customs at every border and by the authorities at every turn.

Their third from last concert in Zurich in April 1967 was a semi-riot. Mick was grabbed by a fan who'd got onstage and Tom "Mr Get-It-Together" Keylock, the band's chauffeur and 'fixer', broke his arm trying to fight the guy off. The Stones played Athens from the centre of the football pitch surrounded by fans, who were separated from the stage and bullied by a cordon of armed police.

At that gig, a few songs in, Mick gave poor old Tom Keylock carnations to throw into the crowd. Tom tripped, the police grabbed him and started manhandling him, at which point the band came to his rescue and got stuck in. The authorities pulled the plug on the concert and the incensed Greek rock fans rioted.

On April 18th, 1967, the Stones and their entourage, all bar Bill Wyman and his girlfriend, left the country. Two days later, Wyman heard gunfire. There were tanks in the streets, the Greek Royal Family had been deposed and the Colonels had taken over.

The Stones' gig is always referred to by the Greeks as the Concert of the Carnations. No foreign band was ever allowed to play in Greece again until the Police in 1980. The Rory Gallagher Band would be the first football stadium-sized gig, this time at AEK's New Philadelphia stadium. Messages about the gig had been daubed on school and college walls and everyone was talking about it.

Iosef remembers what a big deal it had been to get the New Philadelphia, home of one of Greece's top football teams, AEK.

"The club didn't want to provide the venue even with the money we were willing to pay because they were afraid that what did happen, would happen."

"We used Achilleas, the brother of the old Prime Minister and former President, Konstantinos Karamanlis. Achilleas was the Minister of Sport and he called AEK to ask them to provide the venue. We made an upfront down payment as guarantee for the damages - a 250,000 drachmas. Then, one dollar was worth almost 60 drachmas. Connections. It was all about connections."

There is a photograph of the three of us at the Hilton press conference. Gerry and I have blank 'oh fuck me' faces. We weren't even supposed to be there. Rory had just asked us along for a bit of company. His head is at an angle as he looks out at the press corps. You can almost see the cogs of his brain whirring as he calmly answered the questions.

No Ordinary Gig

The shows in Athens and Thessaloniki had been sanctioned by everyone of importance. The gig was seen as a symbol of Greece opening up. The socialists, PASOK, had given it the nod but not officially because of the sponsorship by Coca Cola.

The sponsorship had been needed to cover the Happening's many costs. However, Coca Cola was considered a reprehensible American capitalist organisation by the Greek Far Left. Iosef has spent a lot of time then, and since, explaining to people, who want to talk about the gig, why he needed such a sponsor to realise the whole project.

To make things worse, Iosef had to get the police to handle security because there were no security firms around in those days. It meant high tension in the city and, unfortunately, it had repercussions.

The night of the press conference, Donal organised drinks and a kind of party for the band and the journalists, at the hotel's disco. Phil Mac was on great form and after a couple of drinks, he and I had a heart-to-heart about the recent events in my life. He could see how upset I was about the whole thing. He did impart some words of wisdom to me, something I will always remember. He said that no matter what happens, your kids will still be your kids. It made me feel better.

A young girl was hanging around and eventually joined our company. She was very pretty and wore a beaded headband and loose flowing clothes. She wasn't the kind of girl that I would normally be attracted to but, after a while, we struck up a conversation. I hadn't been talking to her long when she told me she was an Arabian princess and wanted to go to bed with me. I do remember thinking to myself, this really is a different world.

Day Four, the day of the show, and the stadium still wasn't prepared. The sound check was called for early afternoon but the stage still wasn't ready. There were two towers with the sponsor's flags flying from them. The fierce afternoon wind the Greeks call 'meltemi' nearly brought the towers down.

The stage was erected next to the goal posts and, with our back to it, we faced two tiers of seats with a large standing area in between. It was a big old arena, for sure.

There were different accounts of the presale tickets being bandied about. I heard a figure of 14,000 sold with 3000 held back for a walk-up, making the capacity of the show 17000. The ticket price was 500 drachmas, which seems dirt cheap but back then Greece had very high unemployment and low wages.

A security barrier of plywood or some such material was set up two metres from the stage. Tom was as stressed as hell trying to chivvy the Greek workmen along. Things weren't moving fast enough for him. We did the sound check late between four and five and it went OK.

There was some talk of the band being brought to Nea Philadelphia by helicopter, maybe because of the traffic in Athens at that time of night but it was decided against. We went back to the hotel, had some late lunch and a rest, then met in the foyer later as we would for any other gig.

People with tickets had been arriving at the venue and it was slowly starting to fill up. The organisers hadn't employed any proper security on the door but instead, for free tickets, they got members of a local band called the Magic De Spell, who had released a single with the Happening label. They were told to sit at the double doors and take ticket stubs and extra cash. When everyone was inside, they were to come to the dressing room and lead us onto the stage.

Long before this though, people had been arriving at the gate and asking to be let in for free. They were told no way but they refused to leave and a bottleneck formed outside the gate.

What no-one could have foreseen was the number of people who would turn up either with or without tickets. There were thousands trying to get in for the show. It got to a point when the Magic De Spell, correctly judged the situation to be getting dangerous. It was well above their pay grade and they abandoned their post. The gates were flung open and the crowds surged in. Estimates on the number of people that got in is between 30 or 40 thousand.

Inside the ground, Lynyrd Skynyrd's live album was pumping out. All four sides of it were on repeat. A local poet and political activist jumped onto the stage and grabbed a microphone. He pleaded with the crowd for money to get some of his fellow activists released from jail. The audience was unmoved and booed him off.

Our drive to the stadium was uneventful. We arrived an hour before we were due on stage and the tension had already started to build. No-one knew how many people were inside the ground at this point but it was humming with excitement. We could see those around us were jumpy, too. We, ourselves, were a little anxious at the lack of normal protocol. Things were barely under control.

Donal asked where the security for the band was. The answer was there wasn't any. At that point, the organisers panicked and contacted the police. As we did our pre-show rituals to warm up, about a dozen officers in full riot gear arrived in the tunnel outside our dressing room to escort us on stage.

Phil Mac made his way to the sound tower with Kostas, a guy from the local PA company. It was so hot that Kostas took off his jeans and put on a pair of shorts ready for work at the desk with Phil. What we couldn't see, but Phil could from his vantage point overlooking the ground, was that there were a lot more anti-riot police gathering behind the stage.

The people couldn't see them because the police were at ground level. When they did see them, they made it plain that they didn't like it.

At nine, Donal and Rory made the decision to lead the band onto the stage.

Endaxi

We proceeded to the stage flanked on either side by fully armed 'Specials', primed for action. People were everywhere, even by the side of the stage. They weren't rough but they were effusive. We had to move through the heaving audience and I'd never done that before.

Dressed in a white tee with 'The Happening' on the front and shorts, Iosef made the introduction to the crowd and, as soon as he was done, we ran on stage, as Rory always did. The crowd surge demolished the security barrier. People were now crushed up against the stage and even leaning up and over it, a really dangerous situation, not only for us but the fans.

Once on stage, Rory asked someone how to say 'thank you' in Greek. He couldn't quite get his tongue around 'efharisto' so they told him to try 'endaxi', instead.

The atmosphere was fully charged and we didn't hold back. After the first number, Rory said his new Greek word, "endaxi" assuming that it meant 'thank you'. It actually means "all right" or "okay". It was like pouring fuel on a bonfire. People up on the stands jumped about so much that the whole structure bowed. It looked like it would collapse at any time.

The emotion and passion coming from the Greeks was incredible. Seventy five percent of that audience were young males under 25 years old and they fully expressed themselves. Rory yelled 'endaxi' after every track, which pumped them up even more. Guys kept attempting to get on stage - not to do us harm but out of pure 'kefi', as the Greeks say - and Iosef and the guys from the Happening were running about trying to keep control.

Eventually, they were overwhelmed.

People threw their arms around Rory as he played. He carried on regardless. Rory was used to people invading the stage. One time at another memorable gig, there were so many people on stage that Tom Driscoll put his massive arms around a whole lot of them and threw them off stage, Rory and all.

One review of that gig said, "It was one of the few times that the crowd and the band became one happy entity floating slightly above the ground. It was one huge party."

The Athens gig was the usual two and a half hours and, as it drew to its close, people just lost their heads. Some climbed the PA towers on either side of the stage. It was mayhem. The situation felt like a balloon overinflating and about to go 'bang'.

The incident that actually 'ignited' the show was when someone literally set a fire under the stage. This was later blamed on groups of left wing anarchists, who were in the audience seeking to avenge themselves against the 'provocation' of bringing Coca Cola to the party. I wasn't aware of it but there was an attempt then to try to get us off the stage to safety.

The police came to life and began firing gas canisters indiscriminately into the crowd. The chaos turned to panic and, finally, anger.

Rory saw more than I did, stuck at the back as I was. In an interview for Hot Press magazine in 1997, Rory described the very real danger we found ourselves in.

"A short while into the show, I started to see all these flames, way at the back of the stadium. They were burning down restaurants and shops on the streets outside the gig. I think they wouldn't let enough people into the stadium or else they let too many in but, anyway, the police arrived and started to fire CS gas at us. It was the most frightening gig I've ever done. That CS gas is dangerous stuff. It messes up your eyes and you can't see where you're going or anything."

The show was now well and truly over and we had to get out of there. It was every man for himself.

Such was the weight of numbers on stage, it was hard to tell who was who. The platform felt like it could be submerged at any minute. I'd stopped playing but I was stuck on the rostrum at the back of the stage and, in the rush to get the band to safety, I was left behind in a seething, roaring crowd.

Smoke and gas drifted across the stadium and the stage. With no help coming, I dropped the few feet down off the rostrum into the melee. The crowd consumed me. The last time I had felt that threatened was back in Belfast when that poor soldier was shot behind my car. Pumped with adrenaline from the gig, I fought my way out.

I caught up with the others in less than a minute. Rory had been led off stage by a policeman. The guys from the Happening surged around us and took us back to the dressing room. Meanwhile, Tom and his roadies were securing the gear. All that I lost that night were a couple of bass drum pedals.

Once inside the dressing room though, John Earle realised he'd left his sax onstage and ran back for it. When he returned, he had his precious sax but he had been hit on the leg by a tear gas canister and the fumes contaminated the dressing room.

(For a few gigs after, John felt ill after playing. What he hadn't realised was that some gas had got into the bell of the sax. The instrument had to be completely dismantled and cleaned professionally.)

Like me, Phil Mac and Kostas had been trapped. They had tried to run through the crowd to get backstage but the gas got to them. They had to take a leg each of Kostas's jeans to wrap around their faces as they pushed through the crowd. People were running every which way to escape the stadium.

Our transport was already inside ready to go, but we were forced to wait for the all clear. We were then directed via a different route to get away from the stadium.

It all felt very familiar to me. There was an eerie silence outside. Cars had been set on fire, windows had been smashed and there were bricks and stones lying everywhere. It was like Belfast after a riot.

In that same *Hot Press* Magazine interview, Rory recalled: "When we eventually got backstage, there was so much confusion that we couldn't be sure who was going to protect us and who might attack us. There were those semi-militia guys walking around and they looked very threatening. So we jumped into a car and got out of there....it was a nightmare. We were soaking wet and our eyes were watering and we were all literally trembling. The gig itself had been great, by the way. But it was very frightening. I just didn't want to die on a football pitch in Greece, not even knowing what was happening."

The band was taken straight to a restaurant up in the pine-covered Lycabettus Hill, where a booking had already been made for after the gig. It was a beautiful spot with spectacular views over the city. It should have been relaxing. Instead, we all sat dumbly and tried to take in what had just happened. We weren't so much exhausted as wired. Rory was quiet. You could see he was thinking and thinking about what had gone down

Iosef eventually turned up and was mightily relieved to see us. He had been trying to account for everyone. He'd seen Rory had been escorted downstairs by a cop and was OK. Unfortunately, Iosef was a wanted man. Not only were the police looking for him for organising this crazy show but the anarchists were out for revenge.

He'd got himself safely out of the stadium by taking off his tee shirt, which identified him as an organiser, and running for his life. Eventually, he saw someone letting himself into an apartment block. Iosef sneaked in with him and hid there for three quarters of an hour before taking a cab as far from where he was as he could.

Only he and Donal were really talking. They were contemplating the aftermath and who would be held responsible. Apart from the destruction of property, 300 people had been hurt. Mercifully, no-one had died. The next day, Donal heard rumours that there were warrants out for our arrest but they were just that, rumours.

We had a good drink to steady our shattered nerves and had some more when we got back to the hotel. Donal and Phil were pretty well oiled and decided to carry on after the rest of us had wisely retired. They went to Phil's room on the eighth floor.

Donal bought a bottle of Metaxa, and Phil a bottle of scotch. By the time they had finished the scotch, it was six in the morning and Donal suggested opening the Metaxa. Phil declined. "I'm not drinking that shit," he said, so Donal, eager not to offend, opened the window and let the bottle drop the eight floors to the ground.

They were still going when there was a knock on the door. It was Peter Collins, the tour manager, explaining that a bottle had shattered the windscreen of the hotel chef's car and the police had arrived. The police were suggesting that the missile had come from Phil's room. Phil claimed that he had been asleep for hours and knew nothing about the incident. Donal was hiding unseen in a corner of the room and said nothing. Pete went away and they heard no more about it.

The show had not gone as planned, to say the least, but Iosef was thrilled.

"I'd been dreaming about this concert for four or five years. I was sure it would be a smash," he said.

(Donal was convinced that the start of the all-night music marathon Rockpalast had led to the Greek gigs, but Iosef said he had never seen them because of the strictly censored broadcasting in Greece.)

The Greeks were Rory fans through and through. They bought the band's records and a guy called Ioannis Patridis, the A&R Manager for Polygram, played him constantly on the radio.

So, Iosef, had gone to meet Rory and Donal in London just on the strength of hearing his music on vinyl and on the radio.

"I had no idea how he was live," he said.

Well, he knew now.

Thessaloniki

We were to fly to Thessaloniki that morning because we had been booked to play at an indoor sports arena in Thessaloniki on the 14th, the next day.

The Athens gig had been widely reported and made the television news in New York and London. Of course, it had also made the Greek national papers and not in a good way. There was talk of calling the next gig off because of what had happened. The negative publicity in the Greek national papers put a lot of pressure on us, more than was necessary. We were still worried about being arrested.

Years later, Iosef told me that there was no way we would have been.

"For what reason? No. No. Donal had a feeling - someone told him that this could happen, that's all. It could have happened with the Rolling Stones at the time of the Junta, yes. In 1981 - we had had seven years of democracy. If there was any chance of that, we wouldn't do this type of business. I was more afraid of what bands could be carrying at the airport. I was always well organised. I do remember someone threw a bottle from a window and smashed a Mercedes window below. The police made enquiries about that."

Iosef had a lovely little hotel booked all to ourselves by the beach, outside the city of Thessaloniki. (This is where John Earle had his wonderful first face melting experience with a bottle of ouzo, you may remember.) After the events of the last couple of days, everyone wanted an easy, chilled night so we went to a little bar next to the hotel. During the evening, I stepped outside for some fresh air.

After a couple of minutes, I heard angry shouting coming from inside and ran back in. In an absurd act of macho cruelty, a guy had thrown a kitten at a dog to impress us. Everyone in the bar started on him, including Rory. We quickly called it a night and left. I slept well but the next day, everyone involved in the upcoming show was on edge.

It was sold out but the build up was nowhere near as intense as Athens. People were ticketed and it was inside, so there was not as much to go wrong as in Nea Philadelphia. Takis, my new friend, had driven all day from Athens to be at the gig.

We started the performance tentatively, wary of what might kick off, but very quickly the show was in full swing. There was a police presence but it wasn't an obvious one, no riot police that I can remember. It went great. The crowd loved it and we enjoyed ourselves. It just seemed so damned normal after what we had been through.

As soon as we finished playing, soaked in sweat, we were bundled into a car to be taken back to the hotel. We were on a real high after the show and it took a few minutes for us to realise what was going on and at what speed.

The driver, a well-built young man, was driving like a getaway driver after a bank heist. Not only that, he had a girl on his lap and she wasn't just sitting there. It was like a scene from a Balkan Bonnie and Clyde.

We thought it was quite amusing, at first, but the man was crazy. He drove through red lights, screeching and braking hard around the bends, being fondled all the while by his girl. In the end, we all yelled at him to slow the fuck down. We just weren't in the mood.

We sat in silence as we drove through the countryside. About a quarter of a mile from the hotel, the lights of which we could see winking in the distance, the car came to a stuttering halt. It had run out of petrol. The driver just sat there, humiliated, while Donal vented at him.

We were literally dripping in sweat in that car. After a couple of minutes, we opened the doors, left Sonny Boy and his muse behind and legged it to the hotel. Rory didn't say a word but he was fuming. After a quick shower, a drink was badly needed. The next day we headed back to Athens and the Caravelle Hotel.

It was over.

Rory and the rest of the lads got the next plane out of Greece. Rory was never to return.

Gerry and I went back to Athens where Gerry's girlfriend, Linda, met us. They had planned a holiday on the island of Mykonos and they invited me along. I accepted. After all, what had I to go home for?

The three of us that stayed behind met up with Jimmy at Tiffany's. It was good just to chill out. It was the first time we had got to speak to Jimmy about the gig. He thought it was absolutely fantastic, the chaos, the lot. It was clearly the most spectacular event short of a revolution to have happened in Greece for years.

(The Greeks absolutely loved it and they have never forgotten it. Even now, you mention that gig in that country and people sigh and smile.)

When the evening ended and it was time to go back to the hotel, Jimmy invited me to his place for a glass of wine. It was about two or three in the morning, not late by Greek, or Irish, standards, so I agreed.

He lived near the port of Piraeus and when we arrived, his very attractive girlfriend was there waiting. She was an English air hostess based in Athens. We sat around drinking, talking about music and travel and as the sun came up, Jimmy suggested that I stay. I didn't really mind where I slept at this stage so I said, "Yes."

They both withdrew into the kitchen and, as I sat in their living room overlooking the sea, I could just hear their muffled, urgent conversation. What roused me from my meditation was Jimmy saying "Just take him to the beach and fuck him."

I was, naturally, quite startled. A few minutes later, the door opened, they came back in and nothing more was said. Her answer had clearly been "No."

All I can say by way of explanation is that I was witness to a complete clash of cultures. This was Jimmy's ultimate gift to me: his girlfriend. Neither she nor I really understood.

Later that morning, after a few hours sleep, hungover, and with no crash helmet, Jimmy took me on the back of his Honda 50 to the Caravelle Hotel through the busy streets of Athens. It was the same route that we had driven just nine days before but I suddenly felt, after a long, long time, that I hadn't a care in the world.

All You Need is Love

My return to London was bitter sweet. I should have come home on a high. I had survived Rory's baptism of fire and tear gas. I should have been celebrating with my family, but the flat was empty. Brenda, Gillian, Connaire, and Chris Bray had moved into a rented house in Ilford. For the first time in a long while, I had no-one.

I made any excuse to go round theirs during the day. It wasn't a good idea. The lines had been drawn. I saw Gilly and Connaire regularly but I needed to find other ways to fill my time and that usually meant the Bridge House or drinking with Hugh at his place.

Rory spent that time finishing 'Jinx' and, in November/December, we did a UK tour dubbed 'University Challenge'. We hit nearly every campus in the country.

1982 began with band rehearsals and a month-long French tour. Nine days back in London and then a five week tour of Germany. We did the summer festivals including the headline slot for the prestigious Loreley Festival on the banks of the Rhine. Not for nothing was Rory known as the hardest working rock musician around.

I was exhausted most of the time. I was living on nervous energy but that's band life. At least I had no time to feel sorry for myself.

In late August, we began a three and a half month 'shed' - indoor - tour of the States opening for Rush. We sold out all the big venues including two nights at Madison Square Gardens. It was the biggest grossing US tour of 1982.

In a break in that tour, we did a run of club dates - 12 shows in 10 days plus one 'travel' day to get from San Francisco to the East Coast. In two of the clubs, we did double shows. In the last club, My Father's Place, in Long Island, we were on stage for four hours and 25 minutes for the two sets. The sheer intensity of it was the best tonic I could have had.

Directly after that show, at four in the morning, we drove on to Detroit to pick up the Rush tour. I sat up front with the driver and, as dawn broke, autumn announced itself in all its colours. It was beautiful and I was content.

Once back home, I started to go to Dublin more often to see my folks. I learned to see and understand them from an adult's point of view. It was more than 10 years since I had lived with them and I now realised the hardship entailed in bringing up a family and keeping one together.

I loved going to the pub with my dad and my brothers and sisters. My mother would never come no matter how much we pleaded with her. She had the soup and stew ready for our return and the singsong would start. Everybody did a turn.

I remember once, Brian, my brother-in-law, and Elisabeth doing the dirty rugby version of 'Swing Low, Sweet Chariot' with all the visuals. We were all laughing but, thankfully, I don't think my ma got the gist of it - or she made out that she didn't. Never mind, there we were following tradition, history was repeating itself.

In late 1983, I happened to be in a pub in Loughton, Essex, called the Wheatsheaf. Gerry used to go there and drink.

I was there with a drummer friend of mine from Belfast, Peter McKinney, and his girlfriend, Frankie, when I noticed a slim, blonde girl in high heels walk up to the bar. She stood on the brass foot rail and bent over the bar to speak to someone. I couldn't take my eyes off her bum. It was a peach. She was very, very pretty. Sadly, as quickly as she had arrived, she left.

On New Year's Eve, I invited Brenda, Gilly, Connaire and Chris Bray to my flat in an effort to keep some sort of connection with the kids. (I know, I'm a saint.) Gerry was drinking at our local, the Holly Tree, and he said he might call in after the pub closed. I didn't expect him to but, just after half midnight, he turned up with a few folks from the pub, bless him. Among them was that fabulous girl from the Wheatsheaf.

The chaos Gerry and his inebriated chums brought to the awkward evening was a welcome relief. I fixed drinks for one and all and saw the girl was inspecting my record collection. We struck up a conversation.

Maggie O'Malley is of English, Irish and German heritage, all wrapped up in pure Essex. I felt a connection between us almost immediately. Brenda commented that the tall, skinny blonde 'has her eye on you' and I thought 'from your lips to God's ear'. Maggie isn't that tall, actually. She does love a high heel though.

It so happened that Gerry was seeing Maggie's friend, Caroline Morgan, and he'd meet them on a Monday night after their dance class at the Golden Fleece on Capel Road bordering the Wanstead Flats. I started to turn up at these rendezvous and all four of us started regularly going out together. The girls began coming to the gigs that Gerry and I did around London when we weren't on the road with Rory.

After one such gig at the Cartoon in Croydon, we all went for a meal and Maggie told me that she was going on holiday for a week. When I dropped her home that night. I told her that I was falling in love with her. She didn't say much then but when she came back from Greece, she came straight to my flat with her luggage and never left.

We were married in January 1986 and are still together. We have two wonderful girls, Jennifer and Katherine, who are all grown up and making music of their own in their own band.

In September 1997, I got a call from my mother. She had had to call an ambulance for my father in the early hours of the morning. His health had been deteriorating for years. I was worried but I was on tour and it didn't seem that urgent.

A couple of weeks after he went into hospital, I was in Ireland on tour with Nine Below Zero and after a gig in Baltimore, West Cork, we had a day off. Billy Miskimmin, our harmonica player, was still living in Belfast and was going to drive home. I decided to drive overnight with him and Billy dropped me off at the hospital in Dublin en route to Belfast. It was 5.30am.

I stood at the double doors at one end of the hospital ward and about half way down on the left hand side, I spotted my dad sitting up in bed. He was surprised but very pleased to see me. I was shocked at how diminished he was. He looked so white and frail, a mere shadow of the formidable man that I remembered.

We chatted about this and that as the nurses came and attended to him. I told him that Jennifer and Katherine were learning to play the piano. It brought a smile to his face. Before I left, I held his hand and told him that I would be in touch real soon. Just as I reached the double doors, I turned to look back at him one more time. He had a look of total loss and helplessness on his face. He had tears in his eyes. It dawned on me that it had dawned on him that we would most probably never see each other again.

Back in London, a week later, I phoned the ward to see if Jennifer could play the piano over the phone to her grandad. My brother, Emmanuel, was there and it was not good news. Charlie was now in a side ward and not really aware enough for Jen to play for him. A week later, he passed away. He had incurable bowel disease.

Since moving to London, in 1974, my parents and I had developed a telephone relationship. I would ring them frequently. If my mum answered, we would natter about this and that, family gossip, you name it. If my father answered, it would be a quick "hello" and "how's it going?" before he said, "I'll git your mammy for ye."

He wasn't one for small talk so when my mother died of stomach cancer 12 years later, losing her had more of an impact on me. Sometimes I would go to answer the phone expecting to hear her voice at the other end of the line. It took me a while to come to terms with it. With the passage of time, I began to miss my father just as much.

I would love to be able to go to his local pub with him again because, when all is said and done, that's where he shone most. The singing, the banter, the story telling, the endless ribbing and laughter. For all the turbulent times created by too much booze, the frustration at the lack of money, the pressures of the environment we grew up in, so often on the edge of friction. I like to remember him most with a big smile on his face singing an Al Jolson song with a pint in his hand. We should always remember the good times.

In the years touring and recording with Rory Gallagher, I met the most incredible musicians. I shared the bill with the likes of Frank Zappa, James Brown and Jethro Tull. I also had the good fortune to jam and play with Albert Collins and Jack Bruce.

For all of this, the truth is that Rory's adoring fans were just as important to me as the experience of being with and playing with these great musicians.

Once, in Belfast in the late Eighties, we played the Ulster Hall and, before we could play a note, the audience gave him a standing ovation. It lasted just a few minutes but it seemed like an eternity. They cheered and clapped. It was a very emotional moment. The crowd was full of love for the man, who had never let them down and had come through the worst with them.

I experienced so much with Rory but, if you asked me which tops the lot, it would have to be Athens. Nothing will ever exceed the drama and thrill of that explosive few hours on stage in the New Philadelphia Stadium on the evening of September 12th, 1981. I have been told many, many times by many Greeks, who were there or who just heard about it, that there has never been the like of it, before or since.

The gig chimed with the times, musically and politically and the memory of Rory Gallagher - who brought his Irish soul to the blues - remains intense with Greek fans to this day.

I doubt it will ever die. Endaxi, Rory.

Acknowledgements

Special thanks to Denise Danks for her patience and wit and to Bernadette Jewell, Teresa Grehan, Emmanuel O'Neill, Elizabeth O'Neill and Martin O'Neill for all the family love and knowledge. Also, big thanks go out to my friends who helped me remember 'the facts' over a few drinks and laughs: Gerry McAvoy, Jim Clarke, Jim Ferguson, Hugh John, John McCullough, Larry Dundass, Geoff Dundass, Phil McDonnell, Tom Driscoll, Daniel Gallagher, Raymond Donnan, Davy Hamilton, Norman O'Neill, Kryssie Jewska, Roy (Suzzie) Patterson, rest in peace, Don Donnaghy, Pete Boardman, Stan Brennan, Terry Holland, James Meredith, Harry Filmer, Trevor Boyce, Mick Carras, Peter Chrisp and Leslie Baer Dinkel for the editing, Peter Guttridge for his insights, and Iosef Avramoglou for his memories of the Greek tour.

Last but not least, thanks to all the musicians and drummers that I have learned from and listened to. Keep drumming, for God's sake.

Discography

Albums

Gerry McAvoy - Bassics

Rory Gallagher - Jinx

Rory Gallagher - Defender

Anthony Thislethwaite - Aesop Wrote A Fable

Rory Gallagher - Fresh Evidence

Rory Gallagher - Etched In Blue

Nine Below Zero - On The Road Again

Ichiro - My Soul

Nine Below Zero - Off The Hook

Nine Below Zero - Hot Music For A Cold Night

Simon Hickling - Straight From The Harp

Nine Below Zero - Ice Station Zebra

Nine Below Zero & Alannah Myles - I Never Loved A Man (The Way I Love You)

Simon Hickling - Blew It

Nine Below Zero - Refrigerator

Nine Below Zero & Bappi Lahiri - One Foot In Heaven, One Foot In Hell

Nine Below Zero - Covers

Nine Below Zero - Chilled

Nine Below Zero - Hats Off

Gwyn Ashton - Fang It!

Nine Below Zero - It's Never Too Late

Gerry McAvoy - You Can't Win Em' All

Glenn Tilbrook & Nine Below Zero - The Cooperative

Michael Mullinger - Rounds (EP)

Geoff Everett - The Quick And The Dead

The Waterboys - Fisherman's Box

Tim Ainsley- Pint Half Full

Sharpeez - Wild One

Slim Chance - New Cross Road

Andy Winfield - Winfield

Geraint Watkins - Rush Of Blood

Rory Gallagher - Kickback City

Rory Gallagher - Blues

Greenslade & Thomas - G & T

DVDS

Rory Gallagher - Live In Cork

Nine Below Zero - On The Road Again

Rory Gallagher - Live At Montreux

Nine Below Zero - Sights And Sounds

Nine Below Zero - Bring It On Home

Rory Gallagher - The Complete Rockpalast

Also by Denise Danks

- The Pizza House Crash
- Better Off Dead
- Frame Grabber
- Wink A Hopeful Eye
- Phreak
- Baby Love
- Torso

1949, on their wedding day LtoR my father, Charlie, and my mother with Father Brendan after whom I am named.

1948, two Belfast girls 1948 L to R my mother, Elizabeth, and her sister in law, Nora

Wee Brendan aged two

With my father in front of our house in Etna Drive, Glennard

Standing by next door's fence in Etna Drive one summer, me and Bernadette.

In my natty new little suit for my first communion, I'm probably smiling because I got a bit of money.

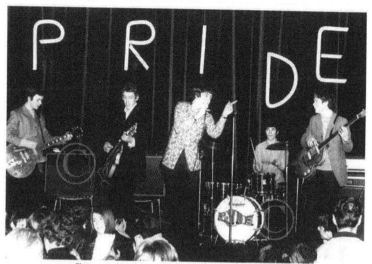

The young lions of Pride at the Inst College, Belfast
L to R Ferg on guitar, Gerry on guitar, lead singer Tom Kidd, me, bass player Don Donaghy.

1969 Gerry photobombing a photo I was taking of Jim and my foot

1968 Brendan The Mod outside my girl Brenda's house Clonlee Drive.

1972 MASH L to R Raymond Donnan, Terry Holland, Terry Fagan, me, Davy Hamilton.

The latest young group to come to Clarkes and one which Cecil sees as having great potential, Deep Joy. They are (left to right) Jim Ferguson, Gerry McEvoy, Adrian Kennedy and Brendan O'Neill.

Our very first press cutting, photo taken outside the car

1969, marketing stickers for Deep Joy and the Marquee Club

1973 Spring L to R Sam Wadell, James Meredith, John McCormack, me, Dusty Hagan and Harry Filmer.

My first born, Gilly, at the Nracknell Jazz Festival

My little boy, Connaire, with my outsize Pro mark promo drumsticks

Me giving it my all for Swift

Swift L to R John Sanderson, Larry Dundass, me, John McCullough and Hugh John

Your man with cigar after recording Bassism with Gerry.

Swift and the van that nearly broke us. On the left, Pete Thomas, who replaced John Sanderson.

1975 Myself with Swift's first manager, Chris Jenkins.

The unlikeliest Casanova, John Sanderson in his Morris Minor

1976 Swift's second manager, Roy Patterson, who ultimately transitioned to be, Suzie, with his then partner, Kryssie Jezeska, our photographer

Rory, Gerry and myself after a days recording the Jinx album

1981 outside Cologne, Germany, promo shots by Brian Cooke for
Jinx

Athens press conference a picture's worth a thousand words

September 1981, the Athens gig

Three sisters L to R Elizabeth, Teresa and Bernadette

Three brothers L to R Emmanuel, me and Martin

Me and my wife Maggie, 1985

My daughters, L to R Katherine and Jennifer. Joshua
Tree 2018

Printed in Great Britain
by Amazon